Sin and the Calvinists

Habent sua fata libelli

Volume XXXII
of
Sixteenth Century Essays & Studies

Charles G. Nauert, Jr., General Editor

Composed by Gwen Blotevogel at Northeast Missouri State University
Kirksville, Missouri 63501
Cover Art and Title Page by Teresa Wheeler, NMSU Designer
Manufactured by Edwards Brothers, Ann Arbor, Michigan
Text is set in Stone Serif 10/13

Sin *and the* **Calvinists**

Morals Control and the Consistory
in the Reformed Tradition

Edited by

Raymond A. Mentzer

Volume XXXII
Sixteenth Century Essays & Studies
1994

This book has been brought to publication with the
generous support of
Northeast Missouri State University

Library of Congress Cataloging-in-Publication Data

Sin and the Calvinists : morals control and the consistory in the Reformed
  tradition / edited by Raymond A. Mentzer
      p.   cm. — (Sixteenth century essays & studies : v. 32)
  Includes bibliographical references and index
  ISBN 0-940474-34-4
      1. Reformed Church—Europe—Discipline. 2. Church Discipline—
  History—16th century. 3. Christian Ethics—Europe—History—16th
  century. I. Mentzer, Raymond A. II. Series.
  BX9425.S56   1994
  284'.2—dc20   94-25541
                                                                  CIP

Contents

Introduction

Raymond A. Mentzer

T he disciplinary dynamics within the Reformed churches of preindustrial Europe have been the focus of considerable recent scholarship. Historians recognize that the Reformation was far more than the transformation of theological tenets or the introduction of new modes of prayer and liturgical practice. It also involved a careful reordering, delimitation, and supervision of the community. Toward this end, Calvinists everywhere set extremely high standards of comportment, which they then compelled through a kind of disciplinary tribunal known variously as the consistory, kirk-session, or presbytery. The pastors and lay persons serving as elders and deacons met weekly to supervise the religious life of the community. They had primary responsibility for ecclesiastical administration, social welfare, and above all, morals control. The elementary role of the consistory, kirk-session, or presbytery has made it the object of intense interest as much for what its workings reveal about Protestant culture as for what it can tell us about early modern society in general. Yet the nature, scope, and effect of the endeavor have not been established in any adequate or precise fashion.

The Calvinist definition and subsequent enforcement of good behavior are clearly areas where comparative analysis seems appropriate and helpful. How do the offenders who appeared before the Genevan consistory compare, for instance, with their fellow delinquents in the German Rhineland, the Netherlands, the French provinces, or Scotland? In what ways does the hierarchy of misdeeds vary from one part of Europe to another? How did the pastors and elders go about punishing offenders and inculcating a sense of moral responsibility? Where did they tend to concentrate their effort? What was the relationship of this undertaking to the interests and authority of the state?

The six essays presented in this collection introduce the rich possibilities for historical research. Their geographic scope generally corresponds to the spread of Calvinism in western Europe, extending from

Geneva to Germany, the Netherlands, France, and Scotland. They examine a variety of subjects and suggest a number of methodological approaches, while maintaining a focus on the Reformed consistory. Several contributions explore the many complex issues surrounding marriage and family life. Robert Kingdon discusses the first Calvinist divorce action, which occurred at Geneva in the mid-1540s. This sensational case suggests the initial framework by which adultery, and later desertion, became grounds for dissolution of the marriage bond with right of remarriage in Calvin's Geneva. Heinz Schilling broadens the discussion of these issues in a sweeping examination of Reformed control over marriage and family life in the neighboring communities of Emden and Groningen from the mid-sixteenth through the early nineteenth centuries. Both German and Dutch Calvinists developed "modern" standards for marriage. Schilling's extensive quantitative analysis, supplemented with narrative materials, makes plain the topography of the presbytery's supervisory endeavor to avert marital strife, discourage separation or divorce, root out concubinage, foster harmonious households, prevent child neglect, and regulate sexuality. Finally, all these actions took place within the context of long-term cultural change.

Philippe Chareyre furnishes a broad portrait of consistorial activity at the southern French town of Nîmes. He focuses on the consistory's efforts to strengthen family cohesiveness, pacify the congregation, and bring an end to profane distractions. The results were mixed, particularly when the pastors and elders challenged popular traditions and time-honored social exchanges. The use of excommunication by the consistories at Nîmes and nine other French towns and villages is the subject of my own contribution. It discusses the reasons behind exclusion from Communion, the rituals for reintegration, and the ways in which people accepted and internalized the structure of discipline.

Drawing on a rich database of nearly forty-six hundred cases from rural as well as urban kirk-sessions, Michael Graham surveys the disciplinary offensive during the first half-century of the Reformation in Scotland. The findings, above all the preponderance of sexual misdeeds, are surprising when set alongside the data from Germany, the Netherlands, and France. Graham views this apparent preoccupation with sex as a sign of the Kirk's early weakness. Only later, when the ministers and elders enjoyed a stronger position, did they gradually turn to the chastisement of Sabbath breach, "superstitious" religious practices, neighborly disputes, and the like.

The concluding essay by Geoffrey Parker is a case study of the kirk session at St. Andrews. He stresses the deliberate yet firm acceptance of church discipline, and the growth of a close beneficial relationship between ecclesiastical and civil authorities. Again, the incidence of sexual wrongdoing dominates the overall pattern. And in what was surely a unique Scottish touch, the ministers and elders sentenced the worst miscreants to the precarious "stool of repentance."

It must also be said that national differences and regional variations, despite their importance, should not obscure the striking commonalities in the Calvinist attempt to discipline the community. The convergencies and affinities affirm the fact that, amid diverse localized circumstances, the Calvinist tradition displayed a remarkable unity of purpose and procedure. The development underscores the strongly international character of Calvinism and the adaptability of its polity and institutions.

Finally, I would like to thank a number of people for their assistance in the planning and preparation of this volume. Geoffrey Parker first suggested the collection, and provided encouragement throughout. Stephen Burnett prepared a fine translation of Heinz Schilling's article. Miral Gamradt and Richard Wojtowicz helped to design and produce the more intricate of the many tables and graphs. Mary Bolhuis clarified many details regarding Reformed belief and practice. The individual contributors, however, deserve the most credit, for in the end this project is theirs.

Chapter 1

The First Calvinist Divorce

Robert M. Kingdon

On December 20, 1543, Pierre Ameaux and his wife Benoite appeared before the Consistory of Geneva, a newly established institution that combined the functions of a court and a compulsory counseling service. Ameaux had married the recently widowed Benoite Jacon three years earlier. He was now asking that this marriage be dissolved and that he be permitted to remarry.[1] He was making a petition that would not even have been considered in Geneva in earlier years; he was initiating a process that would lead to the first Calvinist divorce.

Before the Protestant Reformation, marital problems of the type that concerned Ameaux would have been heard in the court of a bishop. Most of the marital litigation heard by such courts, to be sure, involved breach of promise suits, in which a man or a woman alleged that he or she had entered into a contract of marriage which the other party was trying to evade, and tried to gain the support of the court to force the other party to fulfill the contract. Some of that litigation, however, involved the ending of marriages. Roman Catholic canon law did not permit divorce of the

---

[1] Archives d'Etat de Genève (hereafter A.E.G.), *Registres du Consistoire* (hereafter R.Con-sistoire), t. 1, fols. 149–150.

Earlier and shorter versions of this paper were read: (1) under a different title to a joint meeting of the Sixteenth Century Studies Conference and the Calvin Studies Society, October 29, 1989, and (2) under the same title to the Logos Club of Madison, February 19, 1990. A similar version was published as "How One Genevan Reacted to Calvinist Preaching: The Case of Benoite Ameaux," in Peter De Klerk (ed.), *Calvin and the State* (Grand Rapids: Calvin Studies Society, 1993), 47–55. A considerably expanded version will appear in R. M. Kingdon, *Adultery and Divorce in Calvin's Geneva* (Cambridge: Harvard University Press, forthcoming).

modern sort with permission to remarry. But a bishop's court might issue an annulment, declaring that a true marriage had never taken place, for example in cases of sexual impotency. Or a bishop's court might order a permanent separation, for example in cases where a wife had been so badly beaten that she feared for her life, but without permission for either party to remarry.

With the collapse of bishops' courts and with the abandonment of Catholic canon law in much of Protestant Europe, divorce with permission to remarry at last became legally possible. Pierre Ameaux seems to have been one of the first in Protestant Geneva to have taken advantage of this change. His petition led to a particularly sensational divorce case. It all began at the new Consistory of Geneva, soon after its creation.

This consistory was an institution created at the request of John Calvin in 1541, when he returned to Geneva to take over general supervision of that city's recently reformed church. It was designed to control Christian behavior, as distinct from belief. It was like a court in trying to resolve disputes over marriage and morals and business problems, but it was also like a compulsory counseling service in trying to instruct local residents in the new religious obligations they had incurred as a result of the city government's adoption of Protestantism. It was made up of all the salaried pastors of the city and of twelve elected lay elders. It met once a week to hear cases referred to it by its own individual members or by concerned citizens. When it was at the height of its operations as much as one-fifteenth of the entire population appeared before it in a single year.[2] It was a remarkably hardworking and intrusive institution. And its secretaries kept remarkably detailed registers, most of which survive. They provide an incomparably rich record of how ordinary Genevans behaved during the years marking the beginning of the Protestant Reformation and of how their leaders sought to shape their behavior. These registers have never been studied with the care they deserve.[3]

---

[2]This is the estimate for 1569 of E. William Monter, "The Consistory of Geneva, 1559–1569," *Bibliothèque d'Humanisme et Renaissance*, 38 (1976):484.

[3]Almost all previous studies, most importantly Walter Köhler, *Zürcher Ehegericht und Genfer Konsistorium*, bd. II (X u. XIII in *Quellen und Abhandlungen zur Schweizerischen Reformationsgeschichte* (Leipzig: Heinsius, 1942), 505–652, are based on a set of sample transcriptions from these registers prepared in 1853 by Frédéric-Auguste Cramer. The Cramer transcriptions contain only about 5 percent of the total cases, and are incomplete and often flawed for the cases they do contain.

Throughout his ministerial career Calvin insisted on the importance of the consistory. He refused to come to Geneva in 1541 without a promise that it would be created. He personally drafted the laws that gave it shape, participated actively in its weekly deliberations, and threatened to leave Geneva when its powers were questioned. Disciplinary institutions like the consistory, moreover, were created in most of the many communities that followed Calvin's lead. They were created in the Protestant parts of Calvin's native France, in many Reformed parts of Germany, in the Netherlands, and in Scotland. Strenuous attempts to create them in England led to a measure of success in some of England's North American colonies. Collectively these institutions help to explain in fundamental ways that tightly regulated social system that spread all over Protestant Europe and North America in the late sixteenth and the seventeenth century and that we have come to label "Puritan."

I am now engaged, with the help of several assistants, in an intensive study of the Geneva Consistory during the period of Calvin's ministry.[4] Rather than describe here in any detail that project or our preliminary conclusions, however, this paper concentrates on a single case. It is not a typical case, and thus does not convey very well the normal activities of the consistory. It is rather a sensational case, but for that very reason left a record that is much fuller than usual, and can show us in considerable detail how the consistory operated under pressure. It is a case that combines in an interesting way law, sex, madness, and religion. It is the case of the first Calvinist divorce.

For the people of Geneva, the consistory was the obvious successor to the abolished local bishop's court. So it was the obvious place for an aggrieved party to seek the first divorce.[5] Pierre Ameaux, whose divorce petition began this proceeding, was by profession a maker of playing cards. Some of his cards, I have been told, still survive. He had been active in city politics for some time, and had been a part of the Genevan faction that most strenuously supported the adoption of the Protestant Reforma-

---

[4]Jeffrey and Isabella Watt, Gabriella Cahier, Glenn Sunshine, David Wegener, and Thomas Lambert are together helping me to prepare the first full transcription of the surviving twenty-one volumes of Consistory Registers for the period of Calvin's ministry, from 1542 to 1564.

[5]For a fine recent general study of divorce in Calvin's Geneva, see Cornelia Seeger, *Nullité de mariage, divorce, et séparation de corps à Genève au temps de Calvin*, Troisième série, t. 18, in *Mémoires et documents publiés par la Société d'histoire de la Suisse romande* (Lausanne: Meta-Editions, 1989).

tion in 1536 and the recall to Geneva in 1541 of Calvin to become de facto director of the newly reformed church. Concrete recognition of Ameaux's prominence was provided, during his divorce suit, by his election to the Small Council of twenty-five merchants and professional men that actually ran the city-state of Geneva. He lost that elite position several years later, when he was harshly disciplined for showing disrespect to authority by imprudently criticizing the growing influence in the community of Calvin and other refugees from France. But Ameaux remained a leading citizen of Geneva for many years to come.[6]

The Ameaux divorce case began on December 20, 1543, when Pierre and his wife Benoite appeared together before the Geneva Consistory at one of its weekly meetings. Pierre asked that their marriage be dissolved and that he be permitted to remarry, because Benoite held "an opinion which is against the commandment of God, . . . that she can live with any man and that all men are her husbands."

Benoite was then asked whether she did in fact hold this peculiar opinion. At this point she began a rather odd and rambling answer that raises serious questions about her sanity. That, at least, is my reaction to this text and, as we shall see, was in the end the reaction of many of her contemporaries. In substance, Benoite admitted the accusation. While she complained that her husband contradicted the Word of God and said scandalous things about her, she admitted that she believed in free love. She said she gained this opinion by direct revelation from God himself and had not shared it with anyone else. She said she would be "content to receive a man other than her husband." She claimed that all women who are not married are whores, and could not answer when asked if that included the Virgin Mary. She insisted that sleeping with a Christian brother other than her husband should not be called fornication.

The members of the consistory were shocked by this open defense of adultery. They immediately voted to give Pierre Ameaux his divorce and to refer Benoite to the city council for examination and punishment. But they added an escape clause: if she repented within twenty-four hours, all could be forgiven. She responded in an even less coherent fashion, demonstrating that she certainly did not intend to repent. She insisted that a wife who lives with another man is not necessarily a fornicator, that even

---

[6]For more information on Ameaux, see J. B. G. Galiffe, *Nouvelles pages d'histoire exacte, soit le procès de Pierre Ameaux . . .* , *Mémoires de l'Institut National Genevois*, t. 9 (1863). For the dossier of his trial, see A.E.G., Procès criminels, Deuxième série, no. 684.

Adam could sleep with his daughters, that the Holy Spirit had revealed this to her, and finally that she had learned all this from the preachers.[7] This final admission is particularly suggestive. It raises the very distinct possibility that Benoite had taken a bit too literally some sermons on Christian love. It suggests that the barrage of daily sermons to which all Genevans had been subjected since the beginning of the Reformation was beginning to have some unintended effects. It also reminds us that a preacher, or for that matter any public speaker, can never be sure that his words will have the impact he intends and expects.

A summary of this testimony was prepared by the secretary of the consistory for use by the city council. In the summary the secretary included much of the testimony reported in the consistory registers, but interjected several times that Benoite had uttered many additional outrageous blasphemies that he had not found time to write down. His report concluded that the consistory felt it was absolutely imperative for the government to act in order to reestablish order and administer justice.[8]

The very next day Benoite Ameaux appeared before the city council charged with blasphemy, and was sent to prison pending a full investigation.[9] After two weeks in prison, Benoite quieted considerably. She now denied really believing all these extravagant ideas about free love. She declared that she had fully repented, and agreed to beg public pardon from God, the court, and her husband. The council decided that Pierre Ameaux should be persuaded to take her back and that henceforth they should live together as a proper Christian couple.[10] The case was sent back to the consistory to help in accomplishing this reconciliation. One of the pastors, Aimé Champerault, cross-examined Benoite and reported that he was convinced that her repentance was genuine. The consistory exhorted the couple to return together and live in harmony the way a good wife and husband should. John Calvin concluded the proceedings with edifying admonitions drawn from Holy Scripture.[11]

Pierre Ameaux, however, made it clear that he was not inclined to accept a reconciliation. He presented to the consistory a legal brief in

[7]A.E.G., R.Consistoire, t. 1, fols. 149–150.

[8]This summary is to be found in A.E.G., Procès criminels, Première série, no. 385, a full dossier of two later trials of Benoite Ameaux on charges of adultery. See below for more on these trials.

[9]A.E.G., *Registres du Conseil* (hereafter R.C.), t. 38, fol. 15 (December 21, 1543).

[10]Ibid., t. 38, fol. 24 (January 4, 1544), and 29 (January 11, 1544).

[11]A.E.G., R.Consistoire, t. 1, fols. 157–157v., January 17, 1544.

defense of his claim for a divorce, a brief which was duly copied down in the registers.[12] This brief is one of the more interesting documents to be found in the records of this case. It is an extended translation into French of a highly relevant clause in the Roman civil law on divorce, "De repudiis," specifically from the *Codex Justinianus* in the *Corpus Iuris Civilis*, V.17.8. This clause states that a man is entitled to a divorce if his wife consorts with strange men without his permission and passes nights away from her husband's home. Behavior of this type creates a presumption of adultery. Ameaux's appeal to Roman civil law was very shrewd. It suggests that he had gotten some professional legal help. Before the Reformation, all marital problems should have been resolved by reference to the *Corpus Iuris Canonici*, the canon law of the Roman Catholic Church, which, as we have noted, contains no provision for divorce with permission to remarry. Canon law, however, had been discredited in Reformation Geneva, even more thoroughly than in other Protestant states, because it was a part of a detested system of rule by a prince-bishop whom the Genevans had thrown out when they adopted the Reformation and whose regime they were determined never again to allow within their walls. The abolition of canon law, however, created a considerable vacuum that had to be filled in one way or another. The city of Geneva had not as yet gotten around to drafting its own set of laws governing marriage. (Calvin was ultimately to perform that service for Geneva, but it took some time for him to persuade the city fathers to adopt the sort of marriage code he favored.) Ameaux proposed to resolve his own problem by appealing to the civil law of the Roman Empire. He argued, in effect, that the city courts should replace canon law with civil law for the resolution of marital disputes. In this Ameaux was adopting a tactic followed all over Europe, most obviously in Protestant areas, but also in many Catholic areas. He was arguing for the reception of Roman law. This is a phenomenon well known to all specialists on the legal history of this period.[13] Many have argued that it had profound consequences in supporting the growth of absolute princely power. Most legal historians, however, have concentrated their attention upon adoptions of Roman civil law at princely courts. Here we see an example of it occurring on the grassroots level, in the attempt of a single individual to work out his own personal problems.

[12]Ibid., t. 1, fol. 159v.

[13]For a recent example, see Gerald Strauss, *Law, Resistance, and the State: The Opposition to Roman Law in Reformation Germany* (Princeton: Princeton University Press, 1986).

It would be interesting to discover who had supplied Ameaux with this legal ammunition. There is no evidence that he was highly enough educated in the law to have discovered it himself, and there were not many people in Geneva at that time who were. I think immediately of two who probably knew Ameaux well enough: one was François Bonivard, the former prior of Saint Victor and now official historian of the republic, who had studied Roman law at the university of Freiburg-im-Breisgau; the other was John Calvin, who had studied Roman law at the universities of Bourges and Orleans. To date I have found no evidence, however, that either Bonivard or Calvin, or for that matter anyone else, was acting as Ameaux's lawyer. If I had to guess, I would guess Bonivard. Bonivard was widely known to be a passionate devotee of card-playing, and may thus have been an important customer for Ameaux's cards. Bonivard's card games, in fact, had led to his own appearance before the consistory on the same day Ameaux first filed his divorce petition. Bonivard had been accused of organizing card parties to which ministers had been invited.[14] He had defended himself before the consistory by pointing out that there was as yet no general law against card-playing, only a rule against card-playing by the clergy, and he certainly had never invited Calvin or any other clergymen to his card parties. He added that he needed to play cards. He had reached such a ripe and decrepit old age (actually about fifty) that he was no longer capable of the amusements of younger men. All that was left for him was card-playing, and he did not intend to give it up.[15]

Even though Pierre Ameaux's argument was quite sophisticated legally, it did not work in the short term. The case dragged on for a full year. The authorities kept pressing Ameaux for a reconciliation. Ameaux acquiesced briefly, but soon returned with renewed complaints of his wife's adultery and demands for a divorce. He declared that all his attempts at reconciliation had failed, and soon literally threw his wife out of his house, forcing her to take refuge in the home of her brother. At this point her relatives brought suit against Ameaux, asking that the considerable amount of property from her first marriage that he administered as a dowry be turned over to a guardian to be used to support the children of her earlier marriage.[16] This led to renewed pressure from the city council for reconciliation. Its members were not convinced that Benoite had in

[14]A.E.G., R.Consistoire, t. 1, fol. 146v., December 18, 1543.

[15]Ibid., t. 1, fols. 148–149, December 20, 1543.

[16]A.E.G., R.C., t. 38, fols. 134v. (March 25, 1544) and 138 (March 26, 1544).

fact committed adultery, and seemed to think it was more a case of crazy talk on her part. They also questioned Ameaux's motives in seeking the divorce. They seem to have suspected that what Ameaux was really trying to do in suing for divorce was to win sole control of this dowry property. This reaction makes clear the economic importance of marriage in this period; marriage between two people of substance was a carefully calculated merger of properties, and these properties had to be administered for the joint benefit of a couple or there could be serious trouble. In general, Calvin, the other pastors, and the other members of the consistory were less influenced by these property considerations. They were far more sympathetic than the secular members of the city council to Ameaux in his search for a divorce.

Ameaux, for his part, continued to press his suit. He made more and more specific accusations of adultery, now naming individual men as his wife's partners, identifying specific times and places where the adulterous acts occurred. He argued that this was a pattern that had persisted for years. He claimed that his wife had slept with visitors in their house, including a servant she had seduced, and that she had slept with two men while in jail—one the city's jailor, the other a fellow prisoner who came from a village in neighboring Savoy. He even produced a witness who testified that Benoite had twice offered her body to him. These charges led to two trials.[17] In the first, held in April of 1544, Benoite denied all the accusations and succeeded in persuading the court that there was reasonable doubt of her guilt. She did not persuade everyone, however: Calvin at this point explicitly urged the council to grant Ameaux his divorce.[18] In the second trial, begun in December of 1544, Benoite broke down and admitted everything. She formally acknowledged as true a long series of charges, describing in considerable detail a number of acts of adultery committed over a period of several years. She abjectly admitted that she had sinned and broken the law. She threw herself on the mercy of the court. It is not clear why she broke down so completely during this second trial. One suspects the use of judicial torture to force a confession out of her, a not uncommon procedure at the time. I find no evidence in the trial record, however, that torture was in fact used in this case.

---

[17]For the full dossier of these two trials, see A.E.G., Procès criminels, Première série, no. 385.

[18]A.E.G., R.C., t. 38, fol. 180v., April 29, 1544.

In spite of her confessions, however, Benoite steadfastly refused to admit that the crime she committed could be called fornication. She granted that she had not been faithful to her husband, that she had slept with other men. But she remained true to her initial claim that all Christian men are brothers and that God commands us to love our Christian neighbors. While she may have been guilty of a crime, it was not the crime of fornication.

In the course of the criminal trials of Benoite, three of the city's Reformed pastors became involved. They were Henri de la Mar, pastor in the neighboring village of Jussy, Aimé Champerault, pastor in the city parish of Saint Gervais, and John Calvin himself. De la Mar and Champerault signed lengthy affidavits that appear as parts of the final trial record.

De la Mar reported that he had had several conversations with Pierre and Benoite Ameaux, and that he found her obstinately committed to her crazy opinions. She said repeatedly that she was entitled to have "carnal company" with any Christian man. She even defended incest, claiming that it was all right for a son to live with his mother, and a brother with his sister. Scripture teaches us, she claimed, that the communion of the saints means complete sharing of all our bodies and goods. In fact those who refuse to sleep with others are the real rebels to God, the real fornicators.

Champerault reported on an extended conversation with Benoite in her house in which she went even further. She had repeated her firm belief that she was entitled to sleep with any good Christian, for the communion of the saints enjoined by the confession requires that we share our bodies and our property with all our fellow believers. She went on to confess to a number of specific acts of adultery, including one with a young household servant who had tried to resist but whom she had seduced by promising him good clothes as well as sex. Champerault pointed out during this conversation that her claim to sleep only with good Christians hardly applied to the case of the fellow prisoner with whom she had slept in the jail, because he came from a Catholic village and must therefore have been an abominable papist. She had brushed that argument aside, claiming that according to Saint Paul, when a woman is faithful the man is faithful, and that the children of God never sin. Champerault concluded his report with the horrified remark that Benoite had even expressed a compelling desire to sleep with John Calvin. In my more than thirty years of research on Calvin and Calvinism I had never before heard a suggestion that Calvin might be the object of a woman's mad passion!

That there was something to this report, however, is revealed by a complaint from Calvin himself that Benoite had entered his house and refused to leave.[19] He had her arrested. She was asked in court why she had entered Calvin's house. Her response was that Calvin, after all, was her pastor and that she was in need of pastoral help in dealing with a husband who had seized her dowry property and had just thrown her out of his house. The court seems to have found that response reasonable. It took no further action against her on this charge. There is no further mention of it in the court records.

Given the overwhelming weight of evidence against her, including her own abject confession, the city council, acting as the city's principal criminal court, had to find Benoite Ameaux guilty of adultery. There was then some discussion on the appropriate punishment. Members of the council remembered the Biblical injunction to put anyone convicted of adultery to death. They consulted a lawyer about the appropriate punishment as they usually did in cases that might lead to capital punishment. This lawyer drew up an unsigned brief that remains in the trial dossier. He reported that since Benoite was a convicted and notorious adulteress, who supported her crime with blasphemies, she must be punished. But he reminded the council members that there was no provision in existing city ordinances for capital punishment in such cases. The most severe punishments that could be handed down were public whipping and banishment.

In the final discussion before sentencing, it was observed that Benoite showed clear signs of mental illness, that she was periodically "in a frenzy and weak of spirit."[20] This was clearly a mitigating factor to many on the city council. It was finally decided, therefore, that the appropriate treatment for Benoite would be the one reserved for those with serious mental illness, illness so severe that their families could not cope with it. She was formally sentenced to be chained for life with an iron chain to a pillar in the city dungeon.[21] Only by restraining her permanently in this fashion, the court decided, could she be prevented from continuing to hop from one man's bed to another.

That draconian judgment was modified after only a few months. Members of Benoite's family petitioned for her release to their custody.

---

[19]Ibid., t. 38, fol. 172v., April 24, 1544.

[20]Ibid., t. 39, fol. 109, January 22, 1545.

[21]A.E.G., Procès criminels, Première série, no. 385, final sentence of January 24, 1545.

Their petition was granted, with the stipulation that they must see to it that Benoite remained in her own room within their house, and never again walked the streets.[22] Meanwhile, only a few weeks earlier, Pierre Ameaux had petitioned the city council for permission to marry again. This petition was supported by the consistory. It was granted by the council on the grounds that his wife had committed adultery, held false opinions, and was imprisoned for life.[23] Independent records reveal that Ameaux continued to administer Benoite's dowry property, but for the benefit of her sons from her first marriage.[24] They seem to have eventually inherited this property.[25]

The principle was thus established that in Calvin's Geneva it was possible for the innocent party to gain a full divorce from an adulterous spouse with permission to remarry. In another landmark case, Antoine Calvin, brother of the Reformer, won a similar divorce on grounds of repeated adultery by his wife, Anne LeFert. John Calvin participated actively in the hearings leading up to this judgment, in effect acting as counsel for his brother.[26] In succeeding years this principle was enforced with even greater rigor. Laws were passed permitting the death penalty for notorious adulterers. Several husbands, by complaining of their wives' adultery, provoked trials that found these wives guilty, and ended in the execution by drowning of these unfortunate women.[27] That outcome, quite obviously, left the innocent party free to marry once more. At least once an adulterous husband was similarly put to death, but in this case in spite of his wife's pleas that he be forgiven.[28] The wife may well have

[22]A.E.G., R.C., t. 40, fols. 169v. and 196, July 2 and 27, 1545.

[23]Ibid., t. 40, fol. 133b (verso), June 2, 1545.

[24]In A.E.G., Procès criminels, Deuxième série, 684, the case of slander brought against Ameaux on Calvin's behalf in 1546, on fol. 22, Ameaux petitioned for release from prison in order to take care of the property he was required to administer on behalf of the children of Jehan Mugnier. A.E.G., Notaires, Jean Guillermet, II (1564–1568), fol. 301v, identifies Jehan Mugnier as the first husband of Benoite, widow of Pierre Ameaux.

[25]A.E.G., Notaire Guillaume Messiez, V (1545–1569), fols. 13–14, contract for the sale of a piece of land by Amied, son of Jehan Mugnier, for himself and his brother David, with the consent of their mother, "Hon. Benoyte." This transaction took place in 1562, ten years after the death of Ameaux in 1552 (A.E.G., Morts, I, fol. 64). I assume the piece of land was part of an inheritance because the consent of the vendors' mother was explicitly mentioned.

[26]A.E.G., Procès criminels, Première série, no. 610.

[27]E.g. A.E.G., Procès criminels, Première série, no. 928 (Anne LeMoine); no. 945 (Bernardine Neyrod); no. 1339 (Loise Maistre).

[28]A.E.G., Procès criminels, Première série, no. 944 (Jacques Lenepveux).

feared destitution. The consistory, along with the Company of Pastors, believed in complete equality of treatment for vices of this sort. Both complained several times that the city government was treating male adulterers with too much mildness, at times letting them off with brief prison terms and small fines.[29] A double standard of the traditional sort seems to have existed much of the time in sixteenth-century Geneva, but it was manifest more among the civilian magistrates than among the pastors and their pious lay associates in the Consistory.

Several years later, in the famous case of Marquis Galeazzo Caracciolo, the principle was established that in Geneva divorce could also be granted for desertion. Caracciolo, from a great Neapolitan aristocratic house and a great-nephew of Pope Paul IV, had turned Protestant and fled to Geneva. His wife, a more distant relative of the pope, refused to follow him. Caracciolo asked the leading pastors in Geneva for help. They suggested that his wife should be summoned in writing to join him in Geneva, and that if she continued to refuse he would be eligible for divorce. She had no intention of moving to Geneva and did not even answer the summons. So Caracciolo got his divorce.[30] In the twentieth century one would ask, of course, who was deserting whom in this case. That was not a complication that occurred to Calvin and his associates. Sixteenth-century law almost always required a wife to follow her husband. Neither the Calvinists nor their ideological opponents would have thought of challenging this law. They were so accustomed to a male-dominated society that they assumed that of course only the man should have the right to decide where a couple would live.

The cases of Pierre Ameaux and Galeazzo Caracciolo certainly established the principle of a legal right to divorce in Calvin's Geneva, on grounds of adultery and desertion. That principle was elaborated in a highly erudite and sophisticated way shortly after Calvin's death by his successor, Theodore Beza, also a theologian trained in law. In 1569 Beza first published in Geneva a *Tractatio de repudiis et divortiis* that contained a full Reformed argument for divorce. This treatise was repeatedly reprinted and became a standard manual on the subject. But this entire

---

[29]E.g. *Registres de la Compagnie des Pasteurs de Genève*, ed. Robert M. Kingdon and Jean-François Bergier (Geneva: Librairie Droz, 1962), t. 2, 109.

[30]There are several studies of this case. See the useful summary in the Herzog-Plitt *Real-Encyklopädie für protestantische Theologie und Kirche* (Leipzig: J.C. Hinrichs, 1878), vol. 3, 142–145. See also the celebrated essay by Benedetto Croce, *Il marchese di Vico Galeazzo Caracciolo* in his *Vite di avventure, di fede e di passione* (Bari: G. Laterza, 1936).

development did not in fact make it easy to get a divorce. In case after case the authorities, including those in the city government as much as or more than those in the consistory, regularly delayed requests for divorce. They tended to push hard for reconciliation. They tended to look closely for complications in property distribution that might figure in a marital quarrel and to suspect ulterior motives concerning the control of property as motives for filing divorce petitions. It was not until about two hundred years later that divorce became anything but a very rare exception in the Genevan community. An important first step in that direction, however, had clearly been taken in the case of Pierre and Benoite Ameaux.

Chapter 2

Reform and Supervision of Family Life in Germany and the Netherlands

Heinz Schilling

T his study focuses on two significant aspects of the process that transformed and refashioned the institution of marriage in early modern Europe.[1] The first involves the vow of fidelity that served as the foundation of marriage. This pledge was the enduring basis for married life and the conjugal relationship between husband and wife. Secondly, it examines the mechanisms of self-discipline and external supervision that the Calvinist churches instituted to preserve that vow and to protect both it and the family that it created. Contemporaries considered such measures necessary because of human imperfection, or—to borrow the language of Christian anthropology—human sinfulness. The church assumed a leading role in the definition and supervision of marriage. Church officials cooperated with officers of the early modern cities and territorial states. This rapport reflected the close structural linkage between ecclesiastical and governmental authorities, and their complementary roles in setting

---

[1]See the appendix to this chapter(page 60) for a list of the most important citations.

An earlier, somewhat different version of this article appeared in German as "Frühneuzeitliche Formierung und Disziplinierung von Ehe, Familie und Erziehung im Spiegel calvinistischer Kirchenratsprotokolle," in Paolo Prodi, ed., *Treue und Eid: Treueformel, Glaubensbekenntnisse und Sozialdisziplinierung zwischen Mittelalter und Neuzeit,* Schriften des Historischen Kollegs, 28 (Munich: Oldenbourg Verlag, 1993), 199-235. I wish to thank Ms. Henrike Clotz for her editorial help with the notes.

15

communal norms and socializing their subjects.[2] The institutional remodeling of marriage began in the late Middle Ages and was closely linked to the general societal changes of the early modern period. The transformation of marriage reached its definitive stage in the second half of the sixteenth and early seventeenth centuries, simultaneous to the "fundamental societal process" of confessionalization.[3] The process involved the individual as well as society as a whole, touching all aspects of public and private life. Because religion and politics, church and state, were structurally linked in premodern Europe, the formation of confessional church systems in the wake of the Reformation, the Second Reformation, and the Tridentine "Reformation" was not restricted to religion and ecclesiastical life. Confessionalization affected every aspect of social life, redefining its basis and radically reshaping it. Marriage, family, and child rearing were at the very heart of this process of elementary social change.

THE PROBLEM

Tracing the origins and development of modern marriage largely involves the study of the history of marital theory and practice as taught and enforced by the three dominant confessional churches of the Reformation. The religious dissidents, especially the Anabaptists, also played a significant but more hidden role in the long-term evolution of marriage. A consideration of the relative historical importance of the principal confessional churches, however, must take account of the close connection between them and the early modern state. The social functions performed by both secular and ecclesiastical authorities and their effect upon the modern reshaping of marriage were in principle identical, as were the effects of confessionalization generally. There were practically no differences between the two Protestant confessions in this matter.[4] By contrast, Catholic confessionalization differed to the extent that the sacramental

---

[2]I have explained this social linkage in a number of places, including my *Konfessionskonflikt und Staatsbildung* (Gütersloh: Gert Mohn, 1981), chap. 1, and more recently in "Nationale Identität und Konfession in der europäischen Geschichte der Neuzeit," in *Nationale und kulturelle Identität in der europäischen Neuzeit*, ed. Bernhard Giesen (Frankfurt am Main: Suhrkamp, 1991), 192–253.

[3]For a full explanation of "confessionalization" see Heinz Schilling, "Confessionalization in the Empire," in idem, *Religion, Political Culture and the Emergence of Early Modern Society* (Leiden: Brill, 1992), 205–246, esp. 207 ff.

[4]For a recent case study on the Reformed and Lutheran parts of Hesse, see Uwe Sibeth, *Ehegesetzgebung und Ehegerichtsbarkeit in Hessen (Hessen-Kassel) in der frühen Neuzeit.* Marburg and Darmstadt: Historiale Komminion für Herren, 1994.

character of marriage, as defined by the Council of Trent, precluded a secularization of marriage. The Catholic church continued to bear primary responsibility for marital matters and retain its autonomous jurisdiction independent of the state, a situation which no longer existed in Protestant circles after the Reformers removed marriage from the list of sacraments. In practice, however, the church and religion continued to play an important role in Protestant areas, too. The Protestant churches were unwilling to pursue their desacralized view of marriage and the family to its logical conclusion and renounce all responsibility for them in favor of the state. The northern Netherlands, and for a time England, were exceptions to this trend since a form of civil marriage, free of ecclesiastical influence, was gradually introduced there between the late sixteenth and the mid-seventeenth centuries.[5]

The following study focuses on the contribution of the Reformed or Calvinist church. It will examine two northwestern European congregations, that of the German city of Emden in East Friesland, and that of the Dutch city of Groningen, located only a few kilometers away. The sources for this study are the synodal decisions, church and marriage ordinances, and especially the presbytery records of both communities which have been preserved almost in their entirety. The presbytery, comprising lay elders and preachers, was the German and Dutch equivalent to the Scottish kirk session or Genevan and French *consistoires*.[6] The complete and continuous nature of the presbytery registers makes them valuable for two reasons. They illustrate the Calvinist norms for marriage and supervisory practices and, more importantly, they offer insight into the everyday reality of early modern marital life.

Because of numerous historical similarities, the two sister churches were closely related both structurally and spiritually.[7] Yet their approach to marriage and family matters differed in several important ways, because Dutch marriage law differed from the marital codes of most other Euro-

---

[5]For a more detailed discussion with the relevant bibliography, see Heinz Schilling, "Religion and Society in the Netherlands," in idem, *Religion, Political Culture*, 353–412, esp. 381.

[6]"The first six decades" of these presbytery records have been edited: Heinz Schilling and Klaus-Dieter Schreiber, eds., *Die Kirchenratsprotokolle der reformierten Gemeinde Emden, 1557-1620*, 2 vols. (Cologne: Böhlau, 1989–1992). The introduction provides more details concerning the history and composition of the Emden presbytery.

[7]For the relevant literature on Groningen and Emden see Heinz Schilling, *Civic Calvinism in Northwest Germany and the Netherlands* (Kirksville: Sixteenth Century Journal Publishers, 1991), and idem, et al., introduction to *Kirchenratsprotokolle*, vol. 1.

pean Protestant countries. The first section of this essay describes the characteristic features of the organizational remolding of marriage and the family that occurred in the wake of Reformed confessionalization at the end of the sixteenth century. The second and longer section presents a detailed picture of how the presbyters tried to instill the ideals of early modern Christian marital and family life through day-to-day supervision and the application of discipline.

SOCIAL NORMS IN THE WAKE OF CONFESSIONALIZATION

At Emden, where a Reformed congregation took root at the very latest by the end of the 1540s with the work of John Lasco, marriage and the family were only reordered along Calvinist lines during the mid-1590s. This delay of a full half-century occurred because of external, political reasons. The date also attests to the powerful dynamic that, shortly before, had led to the triumph of Reformed confessionalization at Emden.[8] The magistrates promulgated the marriage ordinance on June 26, 1596, and subsequently revised it in consultation with the presbytery in 1607.[9] Its basis was Roman and canon law as well as the Genevan marriage ordinance composed by Calvin in 1561. Three points of the new ordinance bear particular importance: the procedure for establishing a valid marriage, degrees of consanguinity, and divorce.

The Emden presbytery had repeatedly discussed how marriage ought to be concluded. The members were particularly concerned with the laws and customs that created a marriage, and with the form of the procedure. The presbytery squarely challenged a traditional Frisian process for contracting a valid marriage. The older system had been practiced for generations. The mentality and practices that informed the process were shaped far more by Germanic law than by the religious, moral, and legal standards of medieval canon law. The complaint of Gebbeke Schutemaker against Abel Schipper in September of 1557 illustrates the significance of betrothal (*truwe*) within this process. The case was among the first recorded in the surviving presbytery minutes. Gebbeke testified that she

---

[8]For a more detailed account see Heinz Schilling, "Reformation, Calvinism and Urban Society: The Emden Experience," in idem, *Civic Calvinism* , 11–40.

[9]The ordinance is printed in Emil Sehling, ed., *Die evangelischen Kirchenordnungen des 16. Jahrhunderts*, Bd. 7, zweiter Hälfte, erster Halbband: *Niedersachsen: Die ausserwelfischen Lande* (Tübingen: Mohr Siebeck, 1963), 527–536, together with copious annotations and introductory remarks by Anneliese Sprengler-Ruppenthal.

had become "*truwet*" with Abel. It occurred in her sister and brother-in-law's house.

They came together and slept together. She said that her sister had warned Abel not to betray Gebbeke. He responded indignantly that they should not think of him that way. He would rather die than be unfaithful to her. Then they slept together without another word.[10]

"*Truwe*" was thus a betrothal within the family and without the participation of the church. It was sealed by sexual consummation and was considered a legally binding promise to marry.[11] The presbytery condemned Gebbeke's action on moral and religious grounds. It sternly rebuked her for her sins and loose morals, but never questioned the legal validity of the act. On the contrary, the presbytery exhorted the reluctant bride to marry the man who had become her fiancé in this fashion "and not to do him an injustice, unless she could prove that he had broken his promise of fidelity during the time since their engagement."[12]

The marriage ordinance of 1596/1607 corresponded to the traditional Germanic legal practice of betrothal in that it assigned a decisive role in the marriage arrangements to the families of the couple.[13] Besides kin, "friends" and "neighbors" witnessed the orderly beginning of the engagement.[14] Yet in another no less central respect, the ordinance

[10]Kirchenratsprotokolle Emden 13.9 and 21.12.1557 (hereafter KRP with the date of each meeting, given in the European order: day-month-year; records of meetings until 1620 can be consulted in Heinz Schilling and Klaus-Dieter Schreiber, eds., *Die Kirchenratsprotokolle*).

[11]This German legal custom was also practiced in other countries, particularly in the Netherlands, England, and Scandinavia. See K. Rob and V. Wikman, *Die Einleitung der Ehe: Eine vergleichende ethno-sociologische Untersuchung über die Verstufe der Ehe in den Sitten des schwedischen Volkstums* (Abo, 1937, Acta Academiae Aboensis, Humaniora XI); George Elliot Howard, *A History of Matrimonial Institution, Chiefly in England and the United States*, 3 vols. (Chicago: University of Chicago Press and T. Fisher Unwin, 1904), esp. vol. 1, 308–320; Robert von Friedenburg, "Sozialdisziplinierung in England? Soziale Beziehungen auf dem Lande zwischen Reformation und 'Great Rebellion,' 1550–1642," *Zeitschrift für Historische Forschung* 17 (1990):385–418, esp. 387–388, and 404ff. J. J. Voskuil provides some interesting information from a folkloric perspective in "Van onderpand tot teken. De geschiedenis van de trouwring als voorbeeld van functieverschuiving," *Volkskundige Bulletin* 1 (1975):47–79.

[12]KRP, 13.09.1557.

[13]" . . . niemand unter den jungen Leuten, der noch in der Gewalt seiner Eltern oder Vormünder steht, soll sich ohne deren Vorwissen, Rat und Bewilligung mit Jemandem ehrlich verloben, damit das Recht, welches den Eltern und denjenigen, die ihre Stelle bekleiden, von Gott und der Natur zukommt nicht geschwächt werde." Kirchenordnung Emden, published in Sehling, ed., *Kirchenordnungen* , 527.

attempted to stamp out the older practice of engagement: engaged persons at Emden were henceforth forbidden "to sleep together before their marriage was publicly *confirmed* by the ministers of the church (author's italics)." Those who refused to obey the law were fined the unusually high sum of twenty gulden and were liable to further punishment.[15] At the same time, the engagement period was limited to six weeks,[16] a stipulation that made both supervision and enforcement more feasible. The pastors read these new provisions from the pulpit each year. When engaged couples had their qualifications for marriage reviewed either by civic officials or ministers they were always explicitly enjoined to refrain from "sexual intercourse, which is appropriate only within marriage."[17] The formal publication of banns rounded out the new process.[18]

The Emden ordinance contained detailed rules explaining the degrees of consanguinity that precluded marriage. They largely reflected the provisions of canon law, following the example of the Genevan ordinance.[19] In those instances where the ordinance did not follow the precepts of the medieval church, such as allowing marriage between the children of siblings, i.e. first cousins (a practice permitted by Roman law), couples were required to go through a formal process of examination and approval by the government. The Protestant magistrate insisted upon this procedure, particularly for delicate cases, in order to fend off Catholic charges of irresponsibility. The ordinance did not, however, contain any general provision assigning jurisdiction in contested and exceptional cases. This omission led to heated controversies between the municipal council and the presbytery over jurisdiction, particularly during the first decades. The two powers were sharply divided, above all in instances such as the marriage of a widower or widow to the blood relative of a deceased spouse, a practice that was forbidden by both the Emden marriage ordi-

[14]Ibid., 530, par. 1–3.

[15]Ibid., 532, par. 6.

[16]Ibid., 531, par. 1. This regulation was taken from the Genevan ordinance. See Walter Köhler, *Züricher Ehegericht und Genfer Konsistorium*, 2 vols. (Leipzig: Heinsius, 1932–1942), vol. 2: *Das Ehe- und Sittengericht in den süddeutschen Reichstädten, dem Herzogtum Württemberg und in Genf* (Leipzig: Heinsius, 1942), 642.

[17]See the general overview in J. C. Stracke, "Verlobung und Trauung–Gebräuche und Ordnungen," *Emden Jahrbuch* 58 (1978): 5–21.

[18]*Emden Kirchenordnung*, 531, and also the church ordinance of 1594, ibid., 495–496.

[19]*Emden Kirchenordnung*, 528–529.

nance and canon law. The magistrates tended to make exceptions in such instances, while the presbytery and the ministers insisted upon strict fulfillment of the letter of the law. The marriage of the bookbinder Johann Hindricks with the sister of his deceased wife led to a rupture between church and state. The conflict preoccupied the presbytery for an entire decade and threatened to paralyze the municipal governance of the city-state.[20]

Under the leadership of the first Calvinist minister Menso Alting, who enjoyed an enormous reputation during his final years at Emden, the presbytery declared Hindricks and his spouse guilty of incest and demanded that the magistrate banish them immediately. The majority of city councillors, by contrast, felt that marriage between in-laws was permissible under Protestant marriage law. They based their opinion upon legal practice in the province of Holland. Since neither side was willing to back down, a state of war existed between the consistory and city hall from summer 1608 to December 1610. The leader of the anti-presbytery faction was the city councillor Peter van Eeck, although the syndic Johannes Althusius appears to have been busy behind the scenes, spurring him to action.[21] The constitutional struggle was settled on December 4, 1609, when van Eeck made his peace with the presbytery after long negotiations conducted by a mediator. He stood by his basic contention that the municipal council was competent to decide degrees of consanguinity without consulting the presbytery. The presbytery then finally closed its disciplinary proceedings against the Hindricks. After a decade of maneuvering all that was lacking was a formal reconciliation of the couple with the congregation, a step that Johann Hindricks, who had long before moved to Groningen, flatly refused to consider.[22]

---

[20]There were many discussions of consanguinity recorded during presbytery meetings held between the years 1606 and 1619, particularly from June 1608 to September 1609. See *Emder Protokolle,* ad loc. Sprengler-Ruppenthal mentions a similar case in Sehling, *Kirchenordnungen,* 529 n. 26. There were also conflicts between church and state over the interpretation and use of the marital and wedding ordinance. See Heinz Werner Antholz, *Die Politische Wirksamkeit des Johannes Althusius in Emden* (Leer: Möckel, 1955), 90. Later, the division of responsibility between city council and presbytery seems to have been clarified. The city council alone was responsible for deciding degrees of consanguinity, but its decisions were based on the preachers' recommendations. A series of such recommendations have been preserved in the Emden city archives (Manuskriptabteiling, no. 29), including one discussing the marriage qualifications of a brother-in-law and a sister-in-law during 1713.

[21]See KRP, Emden 23.9.1611, and Antholz, *Wirksamkeit,* 74–75.

The Emden marriage ordinance, unlike its Genevan model, contained no detailed treatment of divorce.[23] In East Friesland, divorce proceedings and other marital disputes were handled by the same secular legal authorities. In contrast to church discipline, it was the state, not the church, which had jurisdiction over divorce. In assuming the legal competence of the medieval episcopal courts and judicial officials, the territorial prince appointed *commissarii in matrimonialibus* as well as regular judges who dealt only with divorce cases, in the latter instance going beyond medieval practice.[24] When Emden became independent in 1595, the existing legal arrangements for secular marriage courts were no longer viable and had to be altered. The *Osterhusischen Akkord* of 1611 completed this reorganization. It provided Emden with its own marital court composed of three representatives of the territorial prince, two Emden city councillors, and one of the city's ministers who was appointed by the city council.[25]

---

[22]KRP, Emden 30.8.1619.

[23]The Genevan marriage ordinance was promulgated with the Ordonnances Ecclesiastiques of 1561; it was reprinted in the *Corpus Reformatorum*, vol. 38, pt. 1 (Braunschweig, 1871), 105ff. The divorce ordinance is on 110ff.

[24]This regulation had already been promulgated in the *Polizeiordnung* of 1545, enacted by Countess Anna; it has been reprinted in Sehling, *Kirchenordunungen*, 198–413, here p. 404. See also the comments of the editor Spengler-Ruppenthal on 348, 355, and 404 n. 75 as well as Joseph König, *Verwaltungsgeschichte Ostfrieslands* (Göttingen: Vandenhoeck, 1955), 275–283, 385, which provides detailed descriptions of the complicated jurisdictional relationships. For a general consideration of divorce, see *Handwörterbuch zur Deutschen Rechtsgeschichte*, s.v. "Ehescheidungsprozess," by A.-P. Hecker, vol. 1, 843–846; Hans Gert Hesse, *Evangelisches Ehescheidungsrecht in Deutschland* (Bonn: H. Bouvier, 1960); A. Stötzel, "Zur Geschichte des Ehescheidungsrechts," *Zeitschrift für Kirchenrecht* 18 (1883): 1–53; Thomas M. Safely, *Let No Man Put Asunder: The Control of Marriage in the German Southwest* (Kirksville: Sixteenth Century Journal Publishers, 1984); Gerhard Dilcher, "Ehescheidung und Säkularisation," in *Cristianesimo Secolarizzazione e Diritto Moderno*, ed. Luigi Lombardi Vallauri and Gerhard Dilcher (Milan: Guiffrè, 1981), 1,021–1,080; Dilcher, "Ehescheidung und Säkularisation," in *Christentum und modernes Recht: Beiträge zum Problem der Säkularisation*, ed. Gerhard Dilcher and Ilse Staff (Frankfurt am Main: Suhrkamp, 1984), 304–359.

[25]The Osterhusischen Accord of 1611 has recently been edited by Harm Wiemann, *Die Grundlagen der landständischen Verfassung Ostfrieslands. Die Verträge von 1595–1611* (Aurich: Verlag Ostfriesische Landschaft, 1974), 212–262, here 243. The treaty text states expressly that marital questions were to be decided by this commission "namens S. G.," i.e., "in the name of the territorial prince." It also clearly spelled out the commission's jurisdiction: "Marital matters include legal questions and the validity or invalidity of betrothals and marriages as well as divorces." After 1643 the consistory of the territorial prince had jurisdiction over all marital and divorce cases from within the territory of East Friesland, apart from the city of Emden and the areas ruled by it.

The Emden presbytery thus had no authority in divorce matters. Analysis of the presbytery registers suggests that the ministers and elders generally accepted this state of affairs. They referred members of the congregation who petitioned them for divorce to the magistrate. This occurred in the case of Martien Jansen, who sought to annul her engagement to a sailor named Jan Mattheysen, because she had not heard from him for three years.[26] Despite the explicit right of the territorial ruler to participate in such decisions, the magistrate appears to have allowed divorces, or at least legal separations (*met de woonige*, i.e. separation of the household), to occur on their own accord.[27] The presbytery was not always willing to recognize such decisions and occasionally initiated disciplinary proceedings against one or both spouses. This course of action, however, lay outside the sphere of secular law. Church discipline was designed to chastise sinners rather than establish jurisdiction over marital matters.

Although founded on the same Reformed understanding of marriage as the Emden presbytery, the activities of the neighboring presbytery of Groningen differed in several notable respects. The differences resulted from the unique ordering of state and church legal affairs in the northern Netherlands. In this region, marriage was considered a matter solely for civil jurisdiction[28] and not a case of *res mixtae*, as it was in Germany where both church and state bore responsibility. The congregations of the Dutch church received rights and legal jurisdiction over marital matters only when these were delegated to them by the civil authorities (the city councils or provincial estates). In Groningen, this occurred on September 16, 1594, when the magistrate passed a civic marriage ordinance.[29] The most important provision in the ordinance was state recognition of the practice of marriage among the Calvinists as a privileged "public church," without conceding a social monopoly over the institution of marriage. The ordi-

---

[26]KRP, Emden 10.12.1696/5.

[27]KRP, Emden 13.02.1699.

[28]Schilling, "Religion," 381ff., gives the older literature. For more recent discussions see Donald Haks, *Huwelijk en gezin in Holland in de 17e en 18e Eeuw* (Assen: Van Gorcum, 1982), and Herman Roodenburg, *Onder censuur* (Hilversum: Verloren, 1990), 90–95.

[29]The Groningen church ordinance is reprinted in H. H. Brucherus, *Geschiedenis van de opkomst der Kerkhervorming in Groningen* (Groningen: Veenkamp en Zoon, 1821), 425–470. For the historical background, see C. H. van Rhijn, *Templa Groninga . . . en het beheer van de Nederduitsch Hervormde Gemeente te Groningen* (Groningen: Wolters, 1910), 127ff.; Wiebe J. Formsma, et al., eds. *Historie van Groningen, Stad en Land* (Groningen: Wolters-Noordhoff, 1976), 207ff.

nance also acknowledged the role of the church in fulfilling several related public functions for the city as a whole. They included maintaining a marriage register and announcing publicly from the pulpit on three successive Sundays the names of couples who were to be married without regard to their religious affiliation.[30]

The presbytery of Groningen had little problem with this new arrangement. It did not tenaciously insist that marriage should be a *res mixta*, as did the church at Emden and in Germany generally. Instead, the Groningen Calvinists consistently treated marriage as a "political matter."[31] They left regulation, surveillance, and sanctions completely in the hands of the magistrates. Where the church acted to serve society as a whole—by maintaining the marriage register and announcing upcoming weddings—it did so clearly at the behest of secular authorities. These actions represented a form of derived secular authority over marriage rather than an original, theologically based one. Because of this clear distinction in the jurisdiction of church and state, there were few conflicts between the two, such as occurred in Emden over degrees of consanguinity. The government also had complete jurisdiction over divorce cases.[32]

In summary, the Calvinist reordering of early modern marriage in northwestern Europe rested upon three pillars. The first was the couple's betrothal vows, which were similar in character to an oath. Couples exchanged their engagement vows within the circle of family and friends as they did in traditional medieval practice. Moreover, the Emden Synod of 1571 declared that it was "also necessary that one of the deacons or elders of the church be present."[33] This provision applied only to members of refugee churches and "churches under the cross," those subject to

---

[30]Groningen church ordinance in Brucherus, *Geschiedenis*, par. 59–62, 461–468. Paragraph 62 makes extensive references to the marital decisions of the great Dutch ecclesiastical synods of Dordrecht, Middelburg, and The Hague as well as to Theodore Beza's, *De Divortiis* whose stipulations were also considered valid for Groningen. The Dutch synodal proceedings were edited by C. Hooijer, *Oude kerkordeningen der Nederlandsche Hervormde Gemeenten, 1563-1638* (Zaltbommel, 1865); for the decisions mentioned here see 157, 207, 277, 457.

[31]This is illustrated by the following case: before a man with a fatal illness was allowed to be married by a preacher, he had to receive permission from the burgomaster, because the presbytery itself had ruled that it was a political matter. KRP, Groningen 24.08.1597.

[32]See Hooijer, *Kerkordeningen*, 157, and the canons of the synod of Dordrecht in 1578, par. 90–91.

[33]J. F. Gerhard Goeters, ed., *Die Akten der Synode der Niederländischen Kirchen zu Emden vom 4. bis 13. Oktober 1571*, Beiträge zur Geschichte und Lehre der Reformierten Kirche, Bd. 34 (Neukirchen/Vluyn: Neukirchener Verlag, 1971), 29.

a hostile magistrate. Where an official Calvinist congregation existed, as in Emden, representatives of the church no longer participated in the official engagement. Yet in any case—and this is the second pillar—the parents or extended family had to give consent. Without it, the validity of a marriage could be questioned, in sharp contrast to the position of Tridentine Catholicism.[34] Of course, the parents and guardians, for their part, were bound by the standards of Christian responsibility when making their decision.[35]

Divorce was theoretically possible, reflecting the Calvinist nonsacramental understanding of marriage. In practice, the Calvinist church leadership erected formidable barriers and hindered the dissolution of a marriage, as can be inferred from synodal decisions and presbytery minutes. In principle, divorce with the right to remarry was only granted if one of the spouses had committed adultery, and this had to be proven in a regular trial "before the authorities."[36] In other aggravated circumstances, such as when a couple lived in continual strife, only a "separation of bed and board" was allowed, i.e., the dissolution of the household and common life without the right to remarry. Occasionally, the presbytery refused to recognize a civil divorce and imposed church discipline upon both parties. This restrictive stance was one consequence of the oathlike promise of fidelity that formed the basis for the Christian conjugal relationship between a man and woman. According to Calvinist marriage law, even an engagement was binding and "could not be broken without the consent of both parties."[37] The promise of fidelity, which had a binding character similar to an oath, replaced the "eternal" bond of sacramental marriage. Doubtless this can be considered a form of desacralization. However, since the promise of fidelity was tied to the Christian virtues of faithfulness and responsibility for other people, which together constituted the guiding principles of Calvinist church discipline,[38] the secular

[34]Calvin thought that one of the most harmful consequences of the Catholic doctrine of the sacrament of marriage was the recognition of the validity of a young couple's marriage when contracted without parental consent. *Institutio Christianae Religionis*, IV.19.37.

[35]This was expressly stated in the Emden church ordinance. See Sehling, *Kirchenordnungen*, 528, par. 3.

[36]Canons of the Dutch national synod of Middelburg, 1581, par. 57, published in Hooijer, *Kerkordeningen*, 207.

[37]Goeters, *Akten*, Generalia, 29, par. 23.

[38]For detailed discussions, see Heinz Schilling, "Calvinism and the Making of the Modern Mind," in idem, *Civic Calvinism*, 41–68, and idem, "Reformierte Kirchenzucht als Sozialdisziplinierung?—Die Tätigkeit des Emder Presbyteriums in den Jahren 1527–1562 (Mit vergleichenden Betrachtungen über Kirchenräte in Groningen und Leiden sowie mit einem

oath of faithfulness was no less stable a foundation for marriage than the sacramental marital bond of Tridentine Catholicism.[39] A comparison of the divorce practices in episcopal marriage courts and the Roman Rota with the stance of the Calvinist synods and presbyteries might even reveal that in reality the Protestant secular promise was more stable than the Catholic sacramental basis for marriage. In the Catholic world, a later inquiry could declare the conditions for a valid marriage to be unfulfilled and thus the marriage itself invalid, allowing de facto divorce.[40]

The third pillar, which is the most important characteristic of modern marriage, was the public announcement and the public documentation of marriage in a marriage register. This publicity occurred in the church, and at Emden marriages were entered in the church register. At Groningen, only members of the Calvinist "public church" solemnized their marriages in the church; all others did so in the city hall. Another essential feature of the new procedure for concluding a marriage was continence prior to marriage, and a stigmatization of the traditional practice of sexual consummation immediately after betrothal. This prohibition was further support for the publicity principle rather than a fourth essential element, since neither obeying it nor disobeying it affected the validity of a marriage. At any rate, the rule that engaged couples abstain from sexual relations, which had initially been enacted for practical reasons, was increasingly understood in a moral and ethical sense by the eighteenth century. Ultimately, it assumed a central role in the routine "marital and family policy" of the presbyteries, although this development occurred over many generations.[41]

Ausblick ins 17. Jahrhundert)," in *Niederlände und Nordwestdeutschland*, ed. Wilfried Ehbrecht and Heinz Schilling (Cologne and Vienna: Böhlau, 1983), 261–327.

[39]The binding character of the Protestant marriage vows had a strong continuing influence on burgher society during the nineteenth century. Ibsen's tragedy *The Woman from the Sea* shows the psychological trauma that could result, especially for women, from the decision of one partner to break this promise of fidelity.

[40]A. Lottin provides a quantitative and qualitative evaluation of diocesan records in "Vie et mort du couple: Difficultés conjugales et divorces dans le Nord de la France au 17e et 18e siècles," *17e siècle*, 102–103 (1974):59–78, and in A. Lottin, J. R. Machnelle et al., *La désunion du couple sous l'Ancien Régime: L'exemple du Nord* (Paris: Editions Universitaires, 1975).

[41]Concerning the Emden presbytery's intensified efforts to stamp out the practice of sealing betrothals with sexual intercourse, see Schilling, "Calvinism and the Making," 64ff. It appears that there was a corresponding campaign against "sexual anticipation" in the territory of East Friesland already at the end of the seventeenth century. At any rate, there were complaints by the territorial estates against various practices by the territorial commissioners, such as "summoning married women who had given birth to children within eight months

THE EVERYDAY "MARRIAGE POLICY" OF THE PRESBYTERIES, ESPECIALLY IN THE REALM OF CHURCH DISCIPLINE

Supervision of Marriage Apart from Church Discipline
The records of both congregations indicate that, over the centuries, the presbyteries sought to mold the daily married life of parishioners to fit the behavioral norms that had been established through the process of confessionalization. The formalized church wedding ceremony, Christian counsel and care provided by the elders and preachers, and above all, the pervasive presbyterial supervision and the sanctions of church discipline served to enforce these standards. This study analyzes the activities of the Groningen and Emden presbyteries relating to "marriage, the family, and child rearing" for an extended period—from the mid-sixteenth through the first third of the nineteenth century. Seven sample sets, each consisting of the records from five consecutive years for each half-century, have been selected. Each set was analyzed, and the various activities of the presbyteries, including church discipline, church administration, and governance, pastoral care, and theological or dogmatic discussions have been noted.[42] With regard to the formation of modern marriage, the qualitative and statistical material suggests that the process of molding parishioners to the norms of the modern confessional churches took centuries. Not until the end of the eighteenth century does it seem that the congregation accepted the new standards as normative for Christian conjugal and family life,[43] even though they did not actually live up to them on every point. Only then could the nineteenth century concept of family develop upon this basis.

---

of marriage, and couples who had been married ten years or more for reason of sexual activity before marriage." König, *Verwaltungsgeschichte,* 279. In other parts of Europe both ecclesiastical and secular courts appear to have moved energetically to punish "sexual anticipation" even by the end of the sixteenth century, possibly in response to the demographic crisis. Cf. von Friedeburg, "Soziale Beziehungen," 387–388, 404, 406.

[42]For a detailed discussion of the theoretical and methodological basis as well as the mechanics of the inquiries themselves, see my articles listed in note 38 as well as "'History of Crime' or 'History of Sin'?" in *Politics and Society in Reformation Europe,* ed. E. J. Kouri and Tom Scott (London: Macmillan, 1987), 289–310; a German version of this article appeared in *Annali dell'Instituto storico italo germanico in Trento* 12 (1986):169–192.

[43]The tenacity of popular opposition to the new marriage standards is reflected in the widespread popular ignorance of the reasons behind the ecclesiastical prohibition against "sexual anticipation," even as late as the mid-eighteenth century. Cf. Schilling, "Calvinism and the Making," 65.

The Emden documents show, in particular, that the elders and preachers took seriously the rights and obligations that the marriage ordinances of 1596 and 1607 gave them. They energetically sought to Christianize marriage and family life in the Calvinist city-state according to modern Reformed standards. They tried primarily to eradicate practices such as marriage without parental consent or public announcement. They also fought against "clandestine marriage," i.e., secret or foreign marriage. Similarly, they tried to ensure that couples observed their marriage vows and that marriages actually took place after a formal betrothal.[44] If necessary, they could always appeal to the secular arm for support.

The Groningen presbytery dealt with marital matters far less frequently than did the Emden presbytery, and ceased such involvement altogether in the eighteenth century according to the sample years analyzed for that period.[45] There were several cases dealing with the question of the purely ecclesiastical wedding ceremony.[46] Sometimes there were specific inquiries from the congregation about degrees of consanguinity, questions regarding divorce, or requests for exclusively spiritual or religious counsel. The presbytery answered these queries with a strict eye to the competence of civil authority.[47] Most of the problems concerned prior announcement

---

[44]KRP, Emden 24.08.1699/6; 06.11.1699/1.

[45]Of course it is possible that marital matters were mentioned during years that were not included within the sample.

[46]They were not considered church discipline, but were placed under the category of Aktionfeld 2 "Calvinistische Gemeinde und Kirchenverband," under heading 2.02.14: "wedding ceremony" (*Traugottesdienst*).

[47]The Dutch synods recognized, even during the sixteenth century, that the secular magistrate was responsible for deciding all divorce cases and determining degrees of consanguinity. Thus they were able, if the occasion arose, to differ with the dictates of both canon law and the emperor. The Groningen presbytery only concerned itself with such questions in exceptional cases. Once it did so at the request of burgomaster Gruy, who was privately asking for advice on behalf of the city council (KRP, Groningen 06.01.1602/2). Another time the presbytery discussed the proposed marriage between Jan Hendrix and his paternal uncle's widow, which it decided was a clear case of prohibitive degree of consanguinity, following canon law (KRP, Groningen 01.01.1648/6). The latter case was similar to the marriage of the bookbinder Hendriks with his sister-in-law, which led to a severe constitutional crisis in Emden. The Groningen case never provoked such an outcome; the magistrate alone was responsible for making such determinations. The Groningen presbytery only discussed a divorce case once during the first sample year: a man requested confirmation of his divorce from a woman who had already been married once. It was promptly given by a deacon who was probably a Catholic. The presbytery disapproved of the deacon's decision, but also declared itself to be incompetent to decide the case. They would make a recommendation only after the city council had taken the matter under advisement and made a formal request for the opinion of the presbytery. KRP, Groningen, 12. and 27.07.1603.

of weddings, and these only occasionally broached fundamental matters of procedure, such as extending to members of the military the obligation to publish marriage announcements.[48] This step was almost certainly taken with the prior approval of the civil magistrate. Most cases were individual petitions, such as an appeal to shorten the public announcement from three to two weeks because the bridegroom expected to be transferred by the West India Company,[49] or requests to cease or (in instances of objections to the scheduled marriage) to continue the public announcements. Appeals to suspend the publication of banns suggest a wide variety of arguments—e.g. because the bride was an executioner's daughter and had been married previously; because the partners were not of the same social standing; because the bridegroom was little more than a child and had been dishonestly "enticed"; because the marriage banns were announced without the consent of the bridegroom, and so forth. These objections were raised by parents, friends, and relatives.[50] The presbytery sometimes stopped the proclamation immediately, sometimes it initiated an investigation,[51] occasionally it even referred the matter to the city magistrates.[52]

General Marital Discipline

From the outset, the Emden presbytery energetically practiced marital discipline in a stricter sense, imposing ecclesiastical discipline in individual cases involving marriage. By contrast, the Groningen Consistory only began to concern itself with such proceedings after the mid-seventeenth century, and did so with far less frequency than the presbytery of Emden.

The differing activities of these two presbyteries reflected dissimilarities in the legal relationship between church and state in Germany and the Netherlands. At Emden, the Calvinist presbytery and the city council were jointly responsible for marital questions, an arrangement that no one questioned despite the tensions between the two sides as described in the first section of the present essay. Responsibility was not restricted to members of the official Calvinist church but extended to Lutheran, Anabaptist, and Catholic inhabitants of the city. By contrast, the Groningen presbytery imposed marital discipline only upon its own Calvinist parishioners.

---

[48]Ibid., 15.04.1646/5.
[49]Ibid., 29.09.1647/2.
[50]Ibid., 27.05.1646; 14.04.1647/7; 15.10.1645.
[51]Ibid., 22.08.1649/4; 15.10.1645; 27.05.1646/4; 28.07.1647.
[52]Ibid., 10.06.1643/3; 14.04.1647.

Sin and the Calvinists

Table 1: Offenses Subject to Church Discipline (Emden)

4.00 Categories of Proscribed Activities: Individual Church Discipline	1558–62 n	%	1596–1600 n	%	1645–49 n	%	1695–99 n	%	1741–45 n	%	1791–95 n	%	Average for the Early Modern Era n	%	1821–25 n	%
4.01 Offenses against Religion and Divine Worship	179	27.6	16	14.0	46	11.0	70	8.3	8	6.0	—	—	319	14.3	2	0.9
4.02 Apostasy	34	5.2	3	2.6	3	0.7	5	0.6	—	—	—	—	45	2.0	—	—
Subtotal for 4.01 and 4.02	213	32.8	19	16.6	49	11.8	75	8.9	8	6.0	0	0	364	16.3	2	0.9
4.03 Marriage, Family, Childrearing	48	7.4	14	12.3	73	17.5	263	31.3	27	20.1	7	8.9	432	19.4	4	1.8
4.04 Sexuality	52	8.0	10	8.8	45	10.8	160	19.1	50	37.3	—	—	317	14.2	3	1.3
4.05 Social Conduct	174	26.9	59	51.8	156	37.4	219	26.1	24	17.9	3	3.8	635	28.5	—	—
4.06 Work and Economic Activity	80	12.3	6	5.3	34	8.2	63	7.5	5	3.7	11	13.9	199	8.9	3	1.3
4.07 Political Conduct	—	—	—	—	—	—	—	—	—	—	—	—	—	—	—	—
4.08 Capital Crimes	8	1.2	2	1.8	4	1.0	12	1.4	2	1.5	—	—	28	1.3	—	—
4.09 Other Moral Offenses	—	—	—	—	—	—	—	—	—	—	—	—	—	—	—	—
Subtotal for 4.03 to 4.09	362	55.9	91	80.0	312	74.8	717	85.5	108	80.6	21	26.6	1161	72.2	10	4.4
4.10 Character References and General Oversight	15	2.3	—	—	10	2.4	25	3.0	6	4.5	58	73.4	114	5.1	215	91.3
4.11 Oversight within the Presbytery (*Censura Morum*)	22	3.4	—	—	7	1.7	15	1.8	11	8.2	—	—	55	2.5	—	—
4.00 Other Unspecified Offenses	36	5.6	4	3.5	39	9.4	7	0.8	1	0.7	—	—	87	3.9	1	0.4
Total Cases	648	100	114	100	417	100	839	100	134	100	79	100	2231	100	228	100
Valid Cases	407		83		298		609		115		78		1590		227	

Table 2: Offenses Subject to Church Discipline (Groningen)

4.00 Categories of Proscribed Activities: Individual Church Discipline	1594–1600 n	%	1601–1605 n	%	1645–49 n	%	1695–99 n	%	1741–45 n	%	1791–95 n	%	Average for the Early Modern Era n	%	1821–25 n	%
4.01 Offenses against Religion and Divine Worship	1	5.4	7	25.4	5	3.5	9	5.5	5	7.5	—	—	27	5.0	—	—
4.02 Apostasy	1	5.9	—	—	3	2.1	6	3.7	4	6.0	—	—	14	2.6	—	—
Subtotal for 4.01 and 4.02	2	11.8	7	25.9	8	5.6	15	9.1	9	13.4	—	—	41	7.6	—	—
4.03 Marriage, Family, Child rearing	1	5.9	2	7.4	36	25.4	10	6.1	3	4.5	6	5.0	58	10.5	—	—
4.04 Sexuality	2	11.8	1	3.7	18	12.7	72	43.9	6	9.0	17	14.3	116	21.6	16	94.1
4.05 Social Conduct	6	35.0	13	48.1	21	14.8	12	7.3	5	7.5	1	0.8	58	10.8	—	—
4.06 Work and Economic Activity	4	23.5	2	7.4	6	4.2	8	4.9	—	—	5	4.2	25	4.7	—	—
4.07 Political Conduct	—	—	—	—	—	—	—	—	—	—	1	0	1	0.2	—	—
4.08 Capital Crimes	—	—	—	—	—	—	1	0.6	1	1.5	1	—	2	0.4	—	—
4.09 Other Moral Offenses	—	—	—	—	—	—	—	—	—	—	—	—	—	—	—	—
Subtotal for 4.03 to 4.09	13	76.5	18	66.7	81	57.0	103	62.8	15	22.4	30	25.1	260	48.5	16	94.1
4.10 Character References and General Oversight	1	5.9	2	7.4	10	7.0	5	3.0	6	9.0	67	56.3	91	17.0	—	—
4.11 Oversight within the Presbytery (*Censura morum*)	1	5.9	—	—	43	30.3	41	25.0	37	55.2	22	18.5	144	26.9	1	5.9
4.00 Other Unspecified Offenses	—	—	—	—	—	—	—	—	—	—	—	—	—	—	—	—
Total Cases	17	100	28	100	142	100	164	100	67	100	119	100	536	100	17	100
Valid Cases	8		19		122		129		60		105		443		17	
Missing Cases	131		86		301		229		229		389		1364		101	

Table 3: Specific Categories within the Category of "Sexual Discipline" (Emden)

4.04 Sexuality	1558-62 n	%	1596-1600 n	%	1645-49 n	%	1695-99 n	%	1741-45 n	%	1791-95 n	%	Average for the Early Modern Era n	%	1821-25 n	%
11 Adultery	15	28.8	2	20.0	11	24.4	10	6.3	1	2.0	—	—	39	12.3	—	—
12 Adultery with Members of the Household	6	11.5	—	—	3	6.7	1	0.6	—	—	—	—	10	3.2	1	33.3
13 Coitus anticipatus	—	—	—	—	3	6.7	4	2.5	35	70.0	—	—	42	13.2	—	—
21 Fornication; Prostitution	22	42.3	5	50.0	16	35.6	91	56.9	4	8.0	—	—	138	43.5	—	—
22 Pandering; Brothel Operation	—	—	—	—	1	2.2	15	9.4	1	2.0	—	—	17	5.4	—	—
23 Homosexuality, Sodomy	2	3.8	—	—	1	0.6	—	—	—	—	—	—	3	0.9	—	—
24 Contraception	1	1.9	—	—	—	—	—	—	—	—	—	—	1	0.3	—	—
32 Abortion	—	—	1	10.0	—	—	—	—	—	—	—	—	1	0.3	—	—
33 Illegitimate child	3	5.8	1	10.0	8	17.8	28	7.5	6	12.0	—	—	46	14.5	2	66.7
41 Other	1	1.9	1	10.0	2	4.4	6	3.8	—	—	—	—	10	3.2	—	—
42 Undetermined	2	3.8	—	—	—	—	1	0.6	3	6.0	—	—	6	1.9	—	—
Other Unspecified Offenses					1	2.2	3	1.9					4	1.3		
Total Cases	52	100	10	100	45	100	160	100	50	100	0		317	100	3	100
Valid Cases	43		10		39		139		47		0		277		3	
Missing Cases	863		189		555		1154		358		472		3592		2162	

This amounted to internal ecclesiastical punishment of sin and had little influence upon society as a whole. Marital discipline at Emden was far more comprehensive and better defined than at Groningen, although both presbyteries had substantially the same understanding of marriage. Consequently, concentrating on Emden provides a more detailed account of marital discipline.

The importance that the Emden presbytery attached to marriage and the family can be inferred from the proportion of the church discipline proceedings that involved marital matters. Roughly 19 percent of all disciplinary proceedings concerned infractions against Christian standards of marriage and family life, when all the figures from the six sample sets of the early modern period (sixteenth to eighteenth centuries) are averaged (Table 1, 4.03, penultimate column). If the statistics for the sexual discipline of married couples (which were entered under a separate category— see Table 3, above all 4.04.11–13) are added to these figures, sexual and family matters dominated the disciplinary priorities of the Emden presbytery. Only infractions against "social coexistence" (*Gesellschaftliches Zusammenleben*) were more common.[53] While sexual discipline was apparently less rigorously enforced from the sixteenth through the mid-seventeenth century, this situation changed by the end of the seventeenth century. In 1695–1699, disciplinary matters involving "marriage and the family" amounted to 31 percent of the total, while "social coexistence" cases accounted for only 27 percent. This was the age of Pietism, a theological movement that paid particular attention to marital standards. Though church discipline proceedings became less common by the mid-eighteenth century,[54] offenses against the established conventions of marriage and family life continued to be examined. There were 27 references to such matters during this five-year period, comprising 20 percent of disciplinary cases. The presbytery charged men with breaches of marital and family conduct far more frequently than women, except for the five-year sample taken from the end of the eighteenth century (and these figures

---

[53]The figures for 4.03 (19.4 percent) from Table 1 should be added to the figures for 4.04.11–13 from Table 3 (that is, 28.7 percent of the 14.2 percent listed separately in Table 1 under sexual discipline, i. e., around 4 percent). Thus if the figure for marital matters is 19.4 percent plus 4 percent for sexual discipline then the total is about 23 percent for marital and family discipline, which is a substantial figure when compared with the proportion of all cases that concerned "social coexistence" (4.05 in Table 1), which amounted to roughly 28 percent.

[54]Schilling, "Sündenzucht," 276.

Table 4: Infractions within the Category of Marital Discipline—Gender Specific (Emden)

4.03 Marriage, Family, Child Rearing (Gender Specific)	1558–62 m (n)	1558–62 m (%)	1558–62 w (n)	1558–62 w (%)	1596–1600 m (n)	1596–1600 m (%)	1596–1600 w (n)	1596–1600 w (%)	1645–49 m (n)	1645–49 m (%)	1645–49 w (n)	1645–49 w (%)	1695–99 m (n)	1695–99 m (%)	1695–99 w (n)	1695–99 w (%)
11 Marital Strife	6	18.2	—	—	4	33.3	—	—	19	48.7	16	47.1	52	36.9	30	24.8
12 Bigamy or Suspicion of Bigamy	2	6.1	—	—	2	16.7	1	50.0	1	2.6	—	—	6	4.3	4	3.3
13 Marital Separation or Abandonment	11	33.3	2	13.3	—	—	—	—	2	5.1	7	20.6	16	11.3	16	13.2
14 Divorce	—	—	1	6.7	—	—	—	—	1	2.6	5	14.7	13	9.2	7	5.8
15 Broken Engagement Vows	—	—	—	—	1	8.3	—	—	5	12.8	1	2.9	8	5.7	4	3.3
16 Secret Marriage	—	—	—	—	—	—	—	—	—	—	—	—	4	2.8	4	3.3
21 Concubinage	1	3.0	1	6.7	2	16.7	—	—	3	7.7	3	8.8	10	7.1	8	6.6
22 Confessionally Mixed Marriage	1	3.0	2	13.3	—	—	—	—	—	—	1	2.9	1	0.7	3	2.5
31 Other Marital Offenses	5	15.2	5	33.3	—	—	—	—	3	7.7	—	—	6	4.3	11	9.1
Subtotal for 4.03.11 to 4.03.31	26	78.8	11	73.3	9	75.0	1	50.0	34	87.2	33	97.1	116	82.3	87	71.9
41 Disorderly Household	1	3.0	1	6.7	3	25.0	1	50.0	4	10.3	—	—	5	3.5	10	8.3
42 Child Neglect	1	3.0	1	6.7	—	—	—	—	—	—	—	—	4	2.8	6	5.0
43 Disobedience to Parents/Guardians	—	—	—	—	—	—	—	—	—	—	1	2.9	5	3.5	1	0.8
44 Offenses against Relatives (Refusal to Provide Help, Etc.)	1	3.0	—	—	—	—	—	—	—	—	—	—	1	0.7	10	8.3
45 Other Familial Infractions	3	9.1	—	—	—	—	—	—	—	—	—	—	7	5.0	5	4.1
Subtotal for 4.03.41 to 4.03.45	6	18.1	2	13.4	3	25.0	1	50.0	4	10.3	1	2.9	22	15.6	32	26.5
	1	3.0	2	13.3	—	—	—	—	1	2.6	—	—	1	2.1	2	1.7
Total Cases	33	100	15	100	12	100	2	100	39	100	34	100	141	100	121	100
Valid Cases	32		13		11		2		36		33		120		99	
Missing Cases	451		98		115		9		216		98		432		218	

Table 4: Infractions within the Category of Marital Discipline—Gender Specific (Emden—continued)

4.03 Marriage, Family, Childrearing (Gender Specific)	1741–45				1791–95				Average for Early Modern Era				1821–25			
	m		w		m		w		m		w		m		w	
	n	%	n	%	n	%	n	%	n	%	n	%	n	%	n	%
11 Marital Strife	11	73.3	9	81.8	—	—	—	—	92	37.9	55	29.4	—	—	—	—
12 Bigamy or Suspicion of Bigamy	—	—	1	9.1	—	—	—	—	11	4.5	6	3.2	—	—	—	—
13 Marital Separation or Abandonment	0	0	0	0	2	66.7	3	75.0	31	17.8	28	15.0	—	—	—	—
14 Divorce	—	—	—	—	1	33.3	1	25.0	15	6.2	14	7.5	—	—	—	—
15 Broken Engagement Vows	1	6.7	—	—	—	—	—	—	15	6.2	5	2.7	—	—	—	—
16 Secret Marriage	—	—	—	—	—	—	—	—	4	1.6	4	2.1	—	—	—	—
21 Concubinage	—	—	—	—	—	—	—	—	16	6.6	12	6.4	1	100	3	100
22 Confessionally Mixed Marriage	—	—	—	—	—	—	—	—	2	0.8	6	3.2	—	—	—	—
31 Other Marital Offenses	1	6.7	—	—	—	—	—	—	15	6.2	16	8.6	—	—	—	—
Subtotal for 4.03.11 to 4.03.31	13	86.7	10	90.9	3	100	4	100	201	86.7	146	78.1	—	—	—	—
41 Disorderly Household	—	—	—	—	—	—	—	—	13	5.3	12	6.4	—	—	—	—
42 Child Neglect	—	—	—	—	—	—	—	—	5	2.1	7	3.7	—	—	—	—
43 Disobedience to Parents/Guardians	—	—	—	—	—	—	—	—	5	2.1	2	1.1	—	—	—	—
44 Offenses against Relatives (Refusal to Provide Help, Etc.)	—	—	—	—	—	—	—	—	2	0.8	10	5.3	—	—	—	—
45 Other Familial Infractions	2	13.3	1	9.1	—	—	—	—	12	5.0	6	3.2	—	—	—	—
Subtotal for 4.03.41 to 4.03.45	2	13.3	1	9.1	—	—	—	—	37	15.3	37	19.7	—	—	—	—
	—	—	—	—	—	—	—	—	5	2.1	4	2.1	—	—	—	—
Total Cases	15	100	11	100	3	100	4	100	243	100	187	100	1	100	3	100
Valid Cases	16		12		3		3		216		162		1		3	
Missing Cases	108		59		51		23		1527		505		151		70	

Table 5: Infractions within the Category of Marital Discipline (Emden)

4.03 Marriage, Family, Child Rearing	1558–62		1596–1600		1645–49		1695–99		1741–45		1791–95		Average for the Early Modern Era		1821–25	
	n	%	n	%	n	%	n	%	n	%	n	%	n	%	n	%
11 Marital Strife	6	12.5	4	28.6	35	47.9	82	31.2	21	77.8	—	—	140	34.3	—	—
12 Bigamy or Suspicion of Bigamy	2	4.2	3	21.4	1	1.4	10	3.0	1	3.7	—	—	17	3.9	—	—
13 Marital Separation or Abandonment	13	27.1	0	—	9	12.3	32	12.2	0	—	5	71.4	59	13.7	—	—
14 Divorce	1	2.1	—	—	6	8.2	21	8.0	—	—	2	28.6	30	6.9	—	—
15 Broken Engagement Vows	—	—	1	7.1	6	8.2	12	5.3	1	3.7	—	—	20	4.6	—	—
16 Secret Marriage	—	—	—	—	—	—	8	3.0	—	—	—	—	8	1.9	—	—
21 Concubinage	2	4.2	2	14.3	6	8.2	18	6.8	—	—	—	—	28	6.5	4	100
22 Confessionally Mixed Marriage	3	6.3	—	—	1	1.4	4	1.5	—	—	—	—	8	1.9	—	—
31 Other Marital Offenses	10	20.8	—	—	3	4.1	17	6.5	1	3.7	—	—	31	7.2	—	—
Subtotal for 4.03.11 to 4.03.31	37	77.1	10	71.4	67	91.8	204	78.3	24	88.9	7	100	349	80.8	4	100
41 Disorderly Household	2	4.2	4	28.6	4	5.5	15	5.7	—	—	—	—	25	5.8	—	—
42 Child Neglect	2	4.2	—	—	—	—	10	3.8	—	—	—	—	12	2.8	—	—
43 Disobedience to Parents/Guardians	—	—	—	—	1	1.4	6	2.3	—	—	—	—	7	1.6	—	—
44 Offenses against Relatives (Refusal to Provide Help, Etc.)	1	2.1	—	—	—	—	11	4.2	—	—	—	—	12	2.8	—	—
45 Other Familial Infractions	3	6.3	—	—	—	—	12	4.6	3	11.1	—	—	18	4.2	—	—
Subtotal for 4.03.41 to 4.03.45	8	16.7	4	28.6	5	6.8	54	20.6	3	11.1	—	—	74	17.1	—	—
	3	6.3	—	—	1	1.4	5	1.9	—	—	—	—	9	2.1	—	—
Total Cases	48	100	34	100	73	100	263	100	27	100	7	100	432	100	4	100
Valid Cases	45		13		69		220		29		6		382		4	

are statistically insignificant). Altogether, 216 men were accused of such offenses as opposed to 162 accusations against women during all sample years of the early modern period. This pattern was especially evident during the sixteenth century with accusations against 32 men and 13 women (respectively only 11 versus 2 in the 1590s; see Table 4: valid cases).

The greatest number of cases centered on domestic quarrels and violence—148 complaints, or about 34 percent (Table 5: 4.03.11). This feature of married life conformed closely to a portrait of society in which arguments, verbal provocation, and physical violence were daily occurrences.[55] In about 14 percent of cases (59 times), one spouse abandoned the other (4.03.13). Only occasionally were other infractions discussed, either because they seldom occurred or because the presbytery did not pursue them. These included 8 cases each of "interconfessional marriage" and "secret marriage" (1.9 percent), and 28 instances of "concubinage" (6.5 percent). These figures suggest that the new criteria for contracting a valid marriage with the cooperation of church and family, relatives, and friends worked reasonably well in early modern Emden. There were only 29 cases (6.2 percent) where "divorces" were the subject of disciplinary proceedings because, as previously noted, secular authorities had jurisdiction over divorce. In any event, requests for divorces were extremely rare given the social expectations and attitudes of ancien régime Europe.

The gender specific results (Table 4) show a surprisingly balanced proportion between men and women for many categories of misbehavior. In cases of abandonment 31 men and 28 women were cited; for divorce: 15 men and 14 women; for clandestine marriage 4 men and 4 women, and for concubinage 16 men and 12 women. These figures reflect the practice whereby the Emden presbytery summoned both partners when considering marital cases—as opposed to issues of sexual discipline—even if only one of them was apparently at fault.[56] Men and women were unevenly represented in other kinds of proceedings, such as domestic quarrels (92 men and 55 women), bigamy (11 and 6), and broken betrothal promises (15 and 5). Bigamy and breach of betrothal promises were unquestionably masculine failings. In instances of marital discord, it was women who often sought help from the presbytery, particularly when the disagreement involved alcohol. Overall, 10 percent of these cases were initiated at

---

[55]Ibid., 285–286, 288–289.

[56]When pursuing disciplinary cases against unwed mothers, the presbytery seldom summoned the male offenders to answer for their deeds. Ibid., 298ff.

the request of one of the spouses (16 of 156 cases) rather than the presbytery. Only in the case of interconfessional marriage was the proportion of women higher than men (6 women and 2 men), perhaps the result of a surplus of women within the Reformed congregation.

Altogether, there were 74 instances of offenses against Christian principles of family life and child rearing (4.03.41–45). They constituted about 17 percent of all discipline cases. There were 12 cases of child neglect, and 7 others where children were disobedient to parents or guardians. There were 12 instances of a lack of solidarity among relatives and, the most common of these sorts of offenses, 25 cases of "disorderly situations" within the household and the family. A further 18 cases cannot be classified. The small number of disciplinary proceedings directed against family offenders probably reflects the desire of immediate and extended kin to resolve these problems within the household, and among relatives and children. Family members tended to seek outside arbitration only in extreme cases.

The gender specific findings for family disputes are even more remarkable, since they divide evenly, with 37 for men and 37 for women. Yet when the higher rate of male delinquency in specifically marital matters is taken into account, it appeared that women were more often the offenders in the area of "family and child rearing" (19.7 percent versus 15.3 percent), while men dominated infractions against "marriage" (82.7 percent versus 78.1 percent). The distribution of specific violations according to gender within the category of marriage and family deserves comment: the presbyters charged both women and men with "running a disorderly household" (13 times versus 12), and with child neglect (5 times versus 7). By contrast, women had more frequent problems with relatives (10 times versus 2), although this may simply indicate that complaints against women came before the presbytery more often than those against men.

The sample years (1695–1699) from the presbytery's operation during the age of Pietism were markedly different from the overall pattern. There were 54 cases involving "family and child rearing matters," roughly 21 percent of cases during this period. The proportion was higher than ever before or afterward (see the subtotals 4.03.41–4.03.45). There were 15 cases of disorderly households, 10 of child neglect, 6 of disobedience to parents, and 11 of discord with relatives. The Pietistic ideal that every sphere of life should be subject to Christian values refocused church discipline on problems associated with the household and the immediate and extended family. This change lacked enduring impact, however, as the reduction in these types of cases during later sample years attests.

Marital Strife

The cases of marital strife offer special insight into a pattern of everyday life that was determined by the close linkage between professional and family life in the premodern "household." In a small town like Emden with twenty thousand inhabitants at the peak of its sixteenth-century expansion and less than ten thousand after the Dutch refugees returned to the newly established Republic of the Netherlands, this association affected the lives of almost the entire population until well into the nineteenth century. The internal dynamics of marriage often reflected the general readiness of Emden's inhabitants to engage in verbal disputes or physical violence. Even women resorted to violence, although coercive male behavior was far more frequent and usually more brutal. Men tended to regard their wives as part of the economic and occupational fabric, or members of the neighborhood rather than as partners in a close, intimate family relationship. In any event, marital conflict quickly became public knowledge, and this fact made it easier for the presbytery to take action.

Two examples from the sixteenth century suggest the often volatile nature of the relationship between spouses. Hans van Emecke already had a reputation for violence against both neighbors and animals. He threw— probably in a smithy—a pair of tongs at his wife's head "so that she fell to the floor as if dead."[57] Uffo, a resident of the hamlet of Borsum and clearly a well-to-do farmer, caused his wife's death in childbirth by refusing to allow the family servant women to put her to bed "in her desperate need." He claimed that she did not require special treatment.[58]

Most frequently the presbytery summoned craftsmen and day laborers, including soldiers and their wives,[59] for reason of conflict and strife, even though members of all other social strata were sometimes obliged to appear. Unsettled social circumstances often aggravated this discord and violence.

In the mid-sixteenth century, the Emden presbytery repeatedly summoned Quirinus, a day laborer from the nearby hamlet of Faldern.[60] The circumstances of his troubled marriage concerned Quirinus's financial difficulties. Since the quarrel between Quirinus and his spouse had been

[57]KRP, Emden 17.01.1558.

[58]Ibid., 03.04.1559.

[59]Ibid., 28.07 and 04.08.1647; 29.12.1645.

[60]There are repeated references to this case in ibid., including 27.06, 25.07, 27.07, 22.08, and 10.10.1558; 06.02, and 24.04.1559; 12.02, 05.03, 11.03, and 04.06.1565.

public, the presbytery determined the accuracy and truthfulness of conflicting accusations through the interrogation of witnesses. These witnesses revealed that the accusations, vicious complaints, and physical beatings in which both partners pulled each other's hair and tore each other's clothing occurred regularly. The particulars behind this behavior were that Quirinus, whose name suggests that he had received an academic education, lacked regular employment and refused to provide for his wife and children through temporary labor, or as he put it, refused "to work my fingers to the bone" (*die Glieder abzuarbeiten*). During one of these regular quarrels—which so enraged him (according to his wife's statement) that he "could not cool down unless he was on top of her"—he sarcastically offered to "open a brothel with her" since she was a whore anyway. Quirinus ignored the presbytery's admonition that he should work during the current harvest season;[61] laborers were in demand and he should learn how to earn his keep. Since his wife constantly picked at her husband's open wounds, the witnesses agreed that "he is guilty, but she is not without fault." Thus the presbytery punished the wife "because she was neither patient nor obedient as she ought to be, but instead provoked his naturally hot temper." The presbyters also "punished the husband, condemning him for his intemperate anger, which could not be tolerated either in a servant or in a member of the congregation." In addition, they admonished him for being "unfit to serve either as a schoolmaster or minister of the church. Therefore, he should learn a craft." Both husband and wife accepted the rebuke, promised to improve, and reconciled. They declared their willingness to be reconciled with "all the other people who knew of their situation." Their conjugal relationship, however, remained static. Quirinus returned briefly to the Netherlands where he converted to Catholicism. He later reappeared at Emden where he repented and was eventually accepted back into the Calvinist congregation.

The disciplinary action against Daniel Hodo or Haudeau and his wife at the end of the seventeenth century suggested that unhappy marital situations affected all social strata.[62] This family numbered among the most

---

[61]Ibid., 27.06.1558, 4.06.1565, 5.02.1567.

[62]References to status and profession were especially common in discussions of marriage offenses. The following references have been preserved under the heading "marital strife" (4.03.11): barber, metal worker, optician (*Brillenmacher*), captain, corporal, schoolmaster, midshipman, inn keeper, wood cutter, copper worker (twice), lieutenant, lower court judge (Hodo), potter, lawyer, cobbler, ship's carpenter, tailor, clerk, ropemaker (*Touwslager*), sergeant, drummer, carpenter.

prominent members of the leading French congregation and belonged to the political elite of Emden. Lack of love and respect, not the imponderables of material life, resulted in deep divisions and a grotesque conjugal relationship.[63] The wife tore her husband's wig to pieces, and he cursed her, asking that God let the devil take her. Even in the consistory chambers, the two attacked each other like furies. The single specific charge by the husband against his wife, which emerged from the stormy proceedings, was that she loved her mother more than him, and that she could no longer stand him or his daughter (clearly from an earlier marriage). The presbytery considered this outlandish case with considerable sincerity and patience (twenty-four meetings between October 1697 and March 1699), a measure of its concern for the couple's high social standing. At first, the presbytery chose not to summon both spouses, deciding instead to appoint a committee composed of the moderator and two socially prominent elders to examine the matter. When this action proved fruitless, the presbytery convoked the parties and excluded them from the Communion service. The presbyters, unwilling to accede to the wife's demand for a divorce, insisted instead upon a confession of sin and repentance, especially from the husband. They also demanded that both parties undertake to lead a Christian marital and family life. When, after a long struggle, Daniel finally showed signs of humility, the presbytery slowly removed all ecclesiastical sanctions, deciding to "wait in love for the best" and keep an eye on the couple.

In another case, the presbyters initiated disciplinary proceedings against the Aaldricks after they had separated of their own accord.[64] Their situation offers an especially graphic illustration of how many cases of marital discord resulted from the inability of individuals to master the circumstances of their lives, which were often only too desperate. The beginning of the affair was an abusive quarrel between husband and wife. At one point in the argument, the husband called his pregnant wife a whore and implied that she was bearing another man's child. He threatened to "cut off her mouth," by which he may have meant a violent abortion (*der Muttermund*, literally the "mother's mouth," means the mouth of the womb, i.e. the cervix). The husband may also have been threatening to reveal the identity of the child's true father. The wife responded by label-

---

[63]There are numerous references to this case in KRP Emden between October 1697 and March 1699; the most important entries are 18.08 and 21.11.1698; 12.03.1699.

[64]Ibid., 24.01, 04.03, and 31.03.1698.

ing her husband a criminal and a thief. Then—as Aaldricks later testified—
she abruptly gathered her property from the wardrobe and left the house
with it, so that (it can be assumed) she could start a new household for
herself and her child, living apart from her husband.

In the cases described above, as in others, the presbytery diligently
tried to discover the reasons for marital discord, often through the interrogation of husband and wife as well as neighbors, friends, and other witnesses. The presbyters sought repentance by the guilty party and a
willingness to be reconciled with his or her partner, and sometimes "with
the congregation" as well. To this end, ecclesiastical discipline and supervision served to steady the newly reconciled couple and make the solution
work until the marriage was back on the right track.[65] As a rule, the presbytery excluded both husband and wife from participation in the Lord's
Supper,[66] and readmitted them only after a probationary period designed
to ensure their reconciliation. This practice was informed by the belief
that participation in the Lord's Supper by two unreconciled members of
the congregation would defile the communicant community, and that the
duty of Christian love and willingness to make peace was doubly important for married couples. Thus Herman Holtsager committed an especially
heinous sin because he struck his wife during the preparation time—the
period between the announcement of the upcoming Communion service
and the service itself. He subsequently aggravated his misdeed by going
forward with other members of the congregation to the Lord's Table.[67]

The presbytery rarely regarded the separation or divorce of a married
couple as a viable option. Situations where one spouse wanted to separate,
or actually did so—as occurred in the cases of Daniel Hodo and the Aaldricks[68]—were exceptional. Frau Aaldricks left her husband, for example,
because he was a threat to life and limb. Yet even here the presbytery took
an inflexible position and punished both parties because they had will-
fully separated. Early modern Europeans, in contrast to a modern understanding, did not consider strife and violent behavior damaging to the
essence of marriage. People understood these disorders as the wages of
sin—something that infected human life on earth and which both partners had to confront, countering the difficulty through vigilance and a

---

[65]See, for example, ibid., 29.11.1557; 03.01, 27.06, and 25.07.1558.

[66]Ibid., 19.09.1698, etc.

[67]Ibid., 24.01.1648.

[68]Cf. the description of the cases above.

readiness to forgive. The presbyters themselves did not think that such conduct affected the fundamental basis of the marriage covenant.

Most married couples appear to have understood the matter in similar fashion. Frau Ter Brake, for instance, complained that her husband had beaten her; she explained that she could not take such treatment because she was pregnant. At the same time, she assured the presbytery that she did not consider physical abuse sufficient grounds for a dissolution of the marriage. She was willing to be reconciled with her husband, even though he showed no signs of remorse. Instead, he sarcastically remarked that he could not understand how his wife got a black eye. The presbytery accepted the reconciliation and did not seek further clarification toward establishing the guilt of one or another of the spouses.[69]

This religiously based attitude affirmed by the presbytery and many members of the Reformed congregation also assumed a secular veneer that could be turned against presbyterial, theologically based discipline of marriage. Consider the case of the Mensenborgs. The Pietistic presbytery heard their problems at fourteen different meetings. The case was just as lengthy and even more grotesque than the Hodo affair.[70] An intense violence permeated the relationship. In addition, the Mensenborg union was a "mixed marriage" between a Reformed man and a Mennonite woman. The couple's combativeness spread beyond the usual domestic quarrels; the pair was also involved in a civil trial before the magistrate. Finally, affairs reached the point that the wife "slashed her husband's hand with a knife and threatened to stab him through the heart." Nevertheless, they stayed together. The husband refused to have their child baptized out of respect for the religious feelings of his Mennonite wife. Despite his wife's knife attack, he contended that their married life was not unusual, although they occasionally spoke harshly with each other when provoked. When finally both parties agreed to appear before the presbytery, the wife was asked, "What is wrong between you and your husband?" She replied that she was not "obliged . . . to reveal the secrets of their household," and abruptly left the consistory chamber. The presbytery saw the matter differently. Marital strife was a public scandal that threatened the sanctity of the congregation and the common weal of civil society. Therefore, the Mensenborgs were placed under strict presbyterial supervision. There is

[69]KRP, Emden 27.03 and 08.05.1699.

[70]Ibid., fourteen meetings between 10.02.1696 and 04.12.1699. The following description has been taken from 29.06, 06.07, and 03.08.1696; 08.11.1698, 16.01, and 23.01, 04.12.1699.

some evidence that this burdensome surveillance triggered a major change in the couple's attitude toward marital discord, since Frau Mensenborg filed a formal, albeit unsuccessful, divorce petition with the city council less than a year later. Instead of instituting divorce proceedings, a committee composed of a municipal officer and an ecclesiastical elder attempted to mediate the dispute and reconcile the couple.

The matter was complex and even contradictory. The presbytery endeavored to instill greater civility in married life, without fully accepting the fact that divorce might be the logical solution for some shattered unions. Yet, many couples evidently felt no need to change comportment. The mentality of naive acceptance of verbal mistreatment and physical violence only changed over a long period, and there was a substantial transitional phase in which old and new expectations and standards of behavior coexisted.

Separation and Divorce

Separation (4.03.13) and divorce (4.03.14), which were sometimes indistinguishable, were not in and of themselves reason for disciplinary action. Yet the Reformed concept of marriage made correction a likely occurrence for couples whose divorce had been formally pronounced by the magistrate.[71] The Emden presbytery usually initiated an inquiry when it learned that a couple was considering a divorce or living apart. A desire to prevent frivolous divorce lay behind these actions. The presbytery excluded Hans Hindriks and his wife, who had privately agreed to separate, from the sacrament because "so presumptuous a divorce was inappropriate for Christians."[72] It sharply rebuked Margaret, the wife of Sergeant Jacob, because, by separating from her husband, she had "badly neglected her obligation to show him the gentleness and marital devotion that befitted a Christian wife."[73] In the case of the Uden family, the presbytery determined that the wife had refused for half a year to meet her "marital obligations." She wanted to force her husband, who had gotten into business problems, to agree to a divorce. The presbytery rebuked the wife and made it clear to her that even after she left her husband it was her duty to care for him.[74]

---

[71]The recommendation mentioned above, that the wife of an alcoholic should "stay away from that man," is clearly a special case. Furthermore it is unclear whether they were a married couple.

[72]KRP, Emden 15.07 and 22.07.1695.

[73]Ibid., 28.10.1695.

[74]Ibid., 18.12.1699/4.

The desire for a divorce often led to disciplinary sanctions, even when the couple was only betrothed.[75] Wyert Folckerts acknowledged that a disorderly household and his wife's refusal to cook for him lacked sufficient grounds for divorce.[76] In an analogous case, the presbyterial officers reproached Henrik Classen for his irresponsible, "almost Jewish view" of divorce. A request for divorce presupposed adultery or malicious desertion.[77] Trespass against marital fidelity, the basis of Christian married life, provided the only justification for divorce. Even when the magistrate permitted a divorce, the action did not necessarily protect them from ecclesiastical sanctions. This happened, for example, when the municipal council allowed Daniel Hodo "to live apart from his wife," after its long inquiry revealed the miserable state of their marriage. When Hodo sought ecclesiastical recognition of his legal separation, however, the presbytery declared that the request was "extravagant" and demanded a public confession of sin.[78]

The concerned parties often informed the presbytery of proposed or actual divorces. During the 1640s in particular, an appeal to the presbytery apparently served as a last resort for those whose marriages and families fell victim to the seemingly endless Thirty Years' War. Two women came forward to complain about their husbands' unfaithfulness and to accuse them of infecting them with a "dreadful disease," which these men had contracted through sexual contact with unclean women. The wives demanded divorces to protect themselves from the grim consequences. When one of the two accused men contested his wife's claim that he was ill and offered to let the presbytery "inspect" him, the members of presbytery referred him to a physician. They further ordered that he refrain from sexual relations with his wife until the conclusion of the inquiry. Ultimately, they rejected his wife's petition for divorce, since she was unable to prove that her husband had committed adultery.[79] A son of the Garbrandet family from Norden told the presbytery, in a tone both outraged and worried, that his father had left his mother without just cause; she too had left and did not return home for weeks. Honke Claesen spoke on behalf of his daughter, accusing her husband of abandoning her just

---

[75]Ibid., 06.09.1697/5.

[76]Ibid., 15.03.1697/2.

[77]Ibid., 31.07.1699/3.

[78]The presbytery allowed Hodo "te scheiden met de wooning." Ibid., 13.02.1699.

[79]Ibid., 10.03.1645 (Sara Kistenmaker), 16.11.1646 (Clara Heenks).

after she had given birth.[80] The marriages of soldiers were in special peril during this period. The soldier Johann Geerdes asked for a declaration from the presbytery affirming that his wife had abandoned him without cause. He needed the statement for submission to the secular marriage court.[81] Not long afterward, Colonel Schwarzenberg requested that the marriage of one of his soldiers be "dissolved," since the man's wife had become pregnant by his lieutenant. In most of these instances, the presbytery did not limit itself to disciplinary measures but sought to help the couples, often in cooperation with the magistrate.[82]

Separation and divorce were the only marital offenses that the presbytery continued to investigate during the final five-year sample from the ancien régime (i.e. 1791–1795). The sole case involved Captain Haike Hindriks Schmid and his wife, who had separated. The presbytery assembled a committee to determine the reasons and try to reunite them. When the committee failed, the presbytery declared itself satisfied and did not institute disciplinary proceedings in the strict sense of the term.[83] In the sample years from the 1820s, there were no instances of marital discipline.

Bigamy, Concubinage, Clandestine Marriage, and Breach of Betrothal
Bigamy and concubinage during the first five-year sample from the mid-sixteenth century resulted mostly from flight and exile brought on by the harsh Counter-Reformation measures of the Spanish. Husbands and wives became separated during these odysseys, or subsequently parted and went their own ways. Many persons lived together without formal marriage. Johann, who first lived in Aachen and then joined the exile congregation at Emden, returned to Kampen in the Netherlands and "became a papist." His pregnant wife Tyeske stayed at Emden and requested help from the presbytery. A year later, she received a written request (from the burgomaster of Kampen) that she rejoin her husband there. The Emden presbytery demanded written assurances that Tyeske would be well received and would not be forced to become a "papist." A year later, Johann was back in Emden. The presbytery accused him of behaving faithlessly toward his

---

[80]Ibid., 28.04.1645 and 02.12.1649.

[81]Ibid., 08.03.1646.

[82]A wife's refusal to meet marital obligations was occasionally the grounds for disciplinary inquiries. The presbytery usually exhorted the wife to do her duty, but there was also an unmistakable effort to help reestablish social harmony within the marriage itself. See, for example, ibid., 06.10.1645.

[83]Ibid., 13.11 and 09.12.1791, 06.01.1792.

wife and the congregation; he was placed under church discipline. Shortly thereafter, he again left Emden and the congregation once more had to support Tyeske.[84]

In 1558, the mason Fedde was placed under church discipline, because he had abandoned his wife Hille, alleging that her first husband was still alive. He then remarried. The presbytery ruled that Hille and Fedde were still man and wife until he proved that her first husband was, in fact, alive. Fedde had to obtain an official declaration that the first husband was alive from a judge of the area where the man allegedly now lived.[85]

The presbytery continually pursued time-consuming and wide-ranging investigations and inquiries in an effort to restore marriages and families shattered by flight from war and other dangers. The presbyters believed in the ideal of an unblemished community of communicants that, in their view, presupposed a well-defined partnership within the Christian bonds of marriage. For this reason, they aimed at the timely reestablishment of orderly married life.[86] They had but limited success, however, and in their new marriage ordinance of 1580, the estates of Holland acknowledged the widespread irregularities within the family situations of many Dutch persons, the result of incessant warfare and the attendant flight of refugees.[87]

Even after this age of refugees ended, some individuals found it possible to exploit gaps in the marriage registers or the difficulties in the exchange of information between cities and states in order to contract bigamous marriages. In such cases, the presbytery made use of the communication network among the Calvinist congregations. This web of exchanges spanned many regions in the interest of providing information and maintaining social order.

During the 1590s, the Emden presbytery opened disciplinary proceedings against Levin Jansen Koppenholl, a linen weaver who had immigrated to Emden from Leiden. The presbyters had learned that he had a wife in Leiden besides his family in Emden. At first, ecclesiastical officials kept the matter secret, perhaps in an attempt to leave room for a quiet

---

[84]Ibid., 26.08.1560, 23.06.1561, 01.06, and 24.08.1562, 16.04.1565.

[85]Ibid., 18.04 and 25.04, 13. 06 and 24.06, 25.07.1558.

[86]For more detailed discussion, see Schilling, "Kirchenzucht," and "Sündenzucht."

[87]*Kerkelyk Plakaat Boek, Behelzende de Plakaaten, Ordonnantien, Ende Resolutien, Over de Kerkelyke Zaken*, compiled by N. Wiltens, 4 vols. (The Hague, 1722–1798), here vol. 1, 804. Cf. also Schilling, "Religion," 382ff.

solution to this difficult situation. The presbyters publicly acknowledged the case only after the couple fled the city.[88] A century later, the presbytery asked an unmarried man and woman who were expecting a child to justify their behavior, especially since they lacked proof that the woman's first husband had died. During the same five-year sample period, the pastors and elders accused a sailor of multiple marriages. His wife and his mother-in-law in Emden presented proof that he had married a second time in Groningen, a third time in Danzig, and had fathered a child in Amsterdam.[89] The final investigation of suspected bigamy from the sample occurred in 1743. A woman married a much younger man without first substantiating the death of her previous spouse. The presbytery referred the affair to the magistrate.[90]

There were only occasional disciplinary inquiries into cases of concubinage, and the church pursued them without particular urgency. In 1645, for example, when a couple who lived together "day and night, eating and drinking together, engaging in the most intimate behavior, and forming a household," appeared before the presbytery, it admonished the pair to marry and warned of the dangers to the soul.[91] The Pietistic presbytery of the 1690s appeared exceptional in its desire to enforce systematic sexual discipline.[92] It focused on the lives and household circumstances of groups that were "at risk" for sexual misbehavior, by which the presbyters usually meant younger people, but sometimes included widows and widowers.

A young man, for instance, was reported to have lived with his niece for three years. The two conducted themselves as husband and wife, with the knowledge of her father. The presbytery cited the couple when it discovered that witnesses had seen the pair in the same bed. The presbytery demanded that they live apart, although the accused argued convincingly that the young man had been in bed because he had fainted after drinking and smoking to excess. Nothing "unclean" had taken place.[93] Another investigation concerned an old man and his son who lived with young girls. The defendants admitted this fact to the presbytery but denied

---

[88]KRP, Emden 31.10.1597, with the text of the public pronouncement from the chancel in 14.11.1597.

[89]Ibid., 29.07.1697.

[90]Ibid., 05.08.1743/3.

[91]Ibid., 12.11 and 24.11.1645.

[92]Schilling, "Sündenzucht," 290–302.

[93]KRP, Emden 19.04 and 26.04.1697.

engaging in immodest behavior or prostitution.[94] Similarly, the elders cited the widow Hasekam and the soldier Jan Brands because they had had banns of marriage published three times but had not yet wed. The woman resisted the final step and refused to be married because, as she indicated, they could not support themselves. The presbytery, for its part, thought that the couple should "enter the estate of marriage" through a "solemn proclamation."[95]

By the eighteenth century, the presbytery, if judged by the ten years represented in our sample, no longer worried about these sorts of relationships. This lack of concern made it all the more remarkable when individual instances of concubinage arose again during the early nineteenth century. In the case of Banke Theetje Bort, a woman who lived with a Lutheran for many years, the presbytery even notified the territorial consistory of East Friesland.[96]

The only instances of church discipline for clandestine marriage occurred during the sample from the 1690s. Heilke Hiskes left the city and secretly married the Mennonite brewer Jan Hindricks. The presbytery placed them under church discipline because they had married against the will of their guardians and in defiance of municipal prohibitions.[97] Yet, no one questioned the validity of the marriage. There were some instances of parents and guardians' requests for a disciplinary hearing to forestall a marriage, if it became known that the child was intent upon marrying against their wishes.[98] Church officials expected that even people who had long been independent of their parents and enjoyed high social prestige would seek parental consent before getting married. After Dr. Mejer married without his father's express permission, the presbytery immediately barred him from Communion. Only when he showed himself ready to seek reconciliation with his father was he able to request readmission to communicant status.[99]

Illicit marriage, consequently, comprised a serious offense, punishable by the gravest of ecclesiastical penalties. This assessment went beyond the view of the presbytery, and was deeply rooted in the society.

---

[94]Ibid., 07.02 and 14.02.1698.
[95]Ibid., 14.08 and 28.08.1699.
[96]Ibid., 03.10.1823.
[97]Ibid., 22.07 and 05.08.1695/2.
[98]Ibid., 23.05.1698/4.
[99]Ibid., 05.12.1598/7 and 09.01.1699/1. A similar case is recorded in 29.09.1696/2.

When, in the course of a doctrinal inquiry concerning a private conventicle, the presbytery questioned Lysabeth of Friesland about her bad reputation, she explained her position as an outsider by revealing that years ago, against the will of his mother, she had married her husband, who had since died.[100]

Disciplinary proceedings against persons for breach of promise to marry appeared in the registers either as instances of sexual discipline or as inquiries made pursuant to the injured party's notification of the presbytery. While these cases were fairly common, they were especially prevalent during the 1640s. Perhaps the Thirty Years' War led to a shortage of men, resulting in a surplus of marriageable women, thereby making it easier for men to make fraudulent promises of marriage.[101] Disciplinary hearings involving widows and soldiers occurred with remarkable regularity.[102] In only one instance did a man accuse a woman of not keeping her promise to wed.[103] The records suggest that the presbytery treated refusal to honor the promise to marry as a legal rather than a moral offense. This attitude might be connected to the traditional understanding of betrothal, the *truwe* described at the beginning of the essay. This view, which assumed consummation following mutual agreement to marry, survived until well into the eighteenth century. The presbytery repeatedly scolded the magistrate and demanded that he enforce the marriage ordinance in order to eradicate these fraudulent practices.[104] Ecclesiastical disciplinary sanctions appeared mild by contrast. Excommunication on these grounds occurred infrequently. In one instance, the presbytery excommunicated a widow because her whirlwind courtship with a soldier caused a public scandal.[105] For these cases of breach of promise, the presbytery generally applied church discipline because of people's "irresponsible" attitude toward marriage, rather than for breaking an engagement promise or for premarital sex.[106]

---

[100]Ibid., 28.09.1696/2.

[101]Ibid., 17.03.1645; 25.03 and 05.09.1646; 15.02.1647; 24.01.1648.

[102]Ibid., 03.06.1599; 17.03.1645; 19.08.1695; 10.12.1696; 04.04.1698.

[103]Ibid., 04.04 and 18.04.1698: the soldier Matthias Everhard against the servant girl of Dr. Stael.

[104]Ibid., 17.03.1645; 25.03.1646.

[105]Ibid., 03.06.1597.

[106]Ibid., 05.09.1646; 07.04 and 11.05.1696; 15.03.1697.

Disorderly Households and Neglect of Children and Relatives
Maintaining a disorderly household was rarely the reason for disciplinary inquiry. The greatest number occurred during the Pietist period, with fifteen cases. Two-thirds were directed against wives. The pattern parallels the tendency of the Pietistic presbytery to prosecute breaches of sexual discipline energetically, a policy that primarily affected women.[107]

A wife bore the responsibility for maintaining the household, but she lacked authority over its finances. The disciplinary hearing against the Claassens illustrates the situation. Frau Claassen's husband accused her of having squandered his resources as well as two hundred gulden that belonged to her father. She admitted making financial misjudgments, but argued that bad economic times had complicated the running of their household. The presbytery sided with the husband: when a woman spent money without telling her husband it was theft.[108] The presbyters came to a similar conclusion in the case of the Ter Braak family. The complaint contended that Frau Ter Braak strove to "play the master" in household matters and to draw up papers such as contracts on her own authority.[109]

There were two cases of child neglect during the earliest set of sample years from the mid-sixteenth century. In each instance, the parents or guardians were accused of refusing to provide their children with an education (the opportunity "to learn a trade").[110] These trials manifested the "educational revolution," which church and state, Reformed as well as Lutheran, supported. The educational changes evidently influenced the ruling circles of individual congregations by the mid-sixteenth century. At the same time, the statistics revealed that these endeavors had minimal impact, at least not at Emden, where only three of the 650 cases from the sample years mentioned education. These figures also suggested that the educational revolution sparked little enduring, vital interest in the status of children within the family. None of the samples from the 1590s, or the 1640s, or even those of the eighteenth and nineteenth centuries, contained cases regarding the care of children. Only the Pietistic presbytery concerned itself with the issue, but it did so with a different emphasis from the cases of the 1550s. It paid less attention to a child's

---

[107]Schilling, "Sündenzucht," 293.
[108]KRP, Emden 31.07.1699.
[109]Ibid., 08.05.1699.
[110]". . . ein Amt zu erlernen." Ibid., 17.01. and 24.01.1558; 22.11.1557/4.

opportunity for attending school or learning a trade than to the religious and moral training of Emden's youth.

Sometimes, the presbytery performed much the same function as present-day social welfare agencies that intervene when there is evidence of child neglect. The presbytery summoned Antje Vroumerus, because her daughter Mette became pregnant out of wedlock. It called another woman to appear because she had neglected to teach her daughter the fundamentals of the Christian religion, apart from the Lord's Prayer.[111] Church officials rebuked Frau Folckers, whom they had earlier admonished for refusal to prepare her husband's meals, for not taking a greater interest in her children's prayers.[112] Other cases involved the neglect of the material needs of children due to alcoholism or general indifference.[113]

Presbyterial proceedings focusing on disobedience to parents or guardians (4.03.43) and offenses against relatives mostly reflected general structural problems of the early modern family and extended family relationships. Examples of children who were punished include Abel Schipper's daughter. She spoke ill of her would-be stepmother so often that the latter dropped her plans for the marriage. The daughter of a pastor's widow rudely insisted that she have all the latest in fashionable dress. These demands left her mother impoverished and threatened by lawsuits.[114] The continued dependence of even grown children upon parental approval for their marriages repeatedly led to intolerable situations in the family. The presbytery required the baker Willem Christoffer, his mother, and a young woman to answer for their behavior when Willem visited the girl against his mother's express wishes. He remained unmoved when forbidden to take Communion since, he claimed, the problem could easily be resolved if his mother allowed him to marry the girl.[115]

Often these problems were an outgrowth of conflicts between several generations living under the same roof. This fact prompts revision of modern romanticizing about early modern circumstances. The presbyters disciplined two mothers-in-law because they constantly provoked their married children to quarrel, and then complained about the situation.[116] One man sided with his mother against his wife, "eagerly looking for

---

[111]Ibid., 21.10.1695; 29.06.1696/2.
[112]Ibid., 29.06.1696 or 15.03.1697/2.
[113]Ibid., 16.01 and 20.02, 04.12.1699 or 13.01.1696.
[114]Ibid., 21.12.1597 or 02.12.1695/6.
[115]Ibid., 24.10 and 31.10.1698.
[116]Ibid., 02.09.1695.

faults" as the records dramatically expressed it.[117] An old man complained of his treatment at the hands of his son and daughter-in-law; they no longer even greeted him.[118] Many husbands quarreled constantly with their in-laws.[119] One woman struck her aged mother, who lived in the same house. Such instances of beatings between siblings and in-laws occurred regularly.[120]

Again, it was primarily women whom the presbytery summoned to face charges involving conflicts with relatives. During the 1690s, the ratio was ten to one. These statistics reflect less presbyterial bias in the prosecution of women than the fact that women were more immediately involved with household and family conflicts. Men often evaded these clashes by devoting themselves to their trades. Besides assigning punishment, the presbyteries worked to move both parties toward unity and reconciliation to establish long-term harmony within the household. The Pietistic presbyters especially emphasized this ideal, but their successors during the eighteenth and nineteenth centuries no longer concerned themselves with "filial obedience" and "respect for relatives."

Marriage and Sexual Discipline
A brief examination of complaints against married persons involving sexual discipline completes discussion of the regulation of marriage and family at Emden. These cases have not been included in the statistics for "Marriage, Family, and Child rearing," but have been listed separately under sexual discipline.[121] The documents leave no doubt that, for the presbytery, marriage and sexuality were indissolubly linked. Consequently, any action contrary to this fundamental principle was sinful and subject to sanction. A quantitative and qualitative analysis of sexual discipline at Emden reveals that, although the restriction of sexuality to marriage did not result in a different attitude toward the sexual sins of married and unmarried persons, it did lead to different treatment for them.

Sexual discipline of unmarried persons became increasingly punitive in character; the goal was deterrence. This harshness occurred especially in cases involving unmarried mothers during the sample years of the

---

[117]Ibid., 17.06.1695/6.

[118]Ibid., 15.08.1698/5.

[119]Ibid., 13.01.1696 or 10.08.1696, or 30.08.1698/7.

[120]Ibid., 14.03.1698, 08.04.1561, 10.06.1695, or 06.07.1696.

[121]This category of discipline is discussed in great detail in Schilling, "Sündenzucht," where the supporting evidence for the following is summarized.

Pietistic presbytery. If the ecclesiastical discipline practiced by the Emden presbytery was ever in danger of degenerating into the simple prosecution and punishment of criminal offenders, then it was at this point. By contrast, members of the presbytery treated adultery, the sexual sin of married persons, much differently. They doubtless considered it a grave offense and a serious sin. As a rule, they forbade adulterers from participating in the Lord's Supper. Still, proceedings against adulterers were not simply a matter of punishment and deterrence. The presbyters made a concerted effort to impress the guilty parties with the gravity of their sin and to move them to reconciliation with their spouses. They hoped to restore and strengthen the marriage vow of mutual respect and responsibility among fellow Christians. Taking this principle into account, it becomes easier to understand the surprising fact that although the Emden presbytery prohibited engaged couples from consummating their marriage before the ecclesiastical ceremony, it took no decisive steps against the practice. If an engaged couple began their married life immediately after the betrothal according to traditional German custom, they followed a customary usage that violated the Reformed norms for concluding a valid early modern marriage, a public procedure overseen by church and state. Yet because the *consummatio carnalis* led to marriage, the couple did not violate the Christian virtues of faithfulness and responsibility. This concept was decisive for the Calvinist presbyters. A complete accommodation between ecclesiastical disciplinary policy and the standards for a valid marriage, which were important for state interests, was only reached in the eighteenth century. The reactions of couples whom the presbytery censured for premarital sexual activity suggest that it took several decades before this shift in mentality occurred among members of the congregation. It was a long way from the early modern formulation of rules and practices for contracting marriage—indeed for the institution of marriage itself as shaped by the process of confessionalization—to the marital and sexual code of the nineteenth and early twentieth centuries, which stigmatized a pregnant bride and shamed her parents and other relatives.

TOWARD BOURGEOIS INTIMACY WITHIN MARRIAGE AND THE FAMILY?

The important historical question of how the activities of the presbytery affected the long-term social development of marriage evokes only qualified response. Both the nature of the sources and methodological questions of how best to analyze and interpret the data are complicated. Nevertheless, it is obvious that the development of modern marriage was neither a swift nor a linear process. The process involved long transitional phases where old and new values and practices coexisted. The discussions of both traditional German betrothal customs and the statistics on "marital strife" (Table 5, 4.03.11) attest to the transition. Although the presbytery energetically prosecuted "marital strife" from the outset, the effort failed to achieve the desired result. Instead, the number of cases rose dramatically from less than ten a year to thirty-five and even eighty-two during the last sample year from the seventeenth century. The wording in the presbytery registers gave no hint that anything had changed in these strife-torn marriages. The elders recorded complaints, horrible insults, and violence, even against pregnant women. Modern emotional restraint was rare, even by the end of the seventeenth century. The evidence suggests several possibilities. Was the civilizing process delayed at Emden? Did the city's populace become more savage between the sixteenth and eighteenth centuries? Or can the rising number of disciplinary hearings be interpreted as an indicator of an increasing sensitivity to marital strife, at least among the presbyters? Analysis of all the records pertinent to the category of "Marriage and the Family"—not just cases involving marital discord—indicates that the presbytery became more decisively involved, thereby supporting the second interpretation. The change in attitude on "marriage and the family," at least within the religious and political elite, preceded real social change. This understanding accords with the notion of a civilizing process in which the views of the cultural and political elites typically changed first. Other social groups followed. Only a general shift in mentality effected a genuine change in behavior. The sources, unfortunately, do not indicate precisely when this behavioral change occurred at Emden.

An analysis of the presbytery's disciplinary activity regarding children and other members of the household has yielded similar conclusions. Hearings for persons accused of maintaining a disorderly household (Table 5, 4. 03. 41) served without doubt to emphasize and spread modern rational and disciplined living habits, particularly among the middle and lower strata of the population. Still, the presbyters tended to focus upon a small number of extreme problems, mostly involving the families of alcoholics. Consequently, in this field church discipline was hardly a pervasive instrument for supervision and education, or for the creation of orderly and temperate standards of behavior and work. These particular cases illustrate the "Calvinist spirit" of the presbyters themselves; yet they can hardly be said to prove the genuine and extensive influence of this spirit upon the congregation, much less upon the populace as a whole.

The same can be said for disciplinary hearings concerning child neglect (Table 5, 4.03.42). They are sparsely represented in terms of both the number and quality of cases. Children had virtually no legal protection within early modern society. The results garnered from studying the Emden documents indicate that the confessional churches energetically strove to educate children through various decrees, catechism lessons, and pastoral as well as pedagogical writings. Yet they were unable to make up for the structural and legal deficiency of children's position within early modern society. Even Calvinist church discipline, among the most intensive and thoroughgoing instruments for changing popular mentalities, respected the autonomy of the family to a greater extent than might be expected.

The church records on sexual discipline similarly offer little direct evidence for a collective change in behavior. Yet they reveal a great deal about the spirit and guiding principles of Calvinist influence upon sexual behavior. Sexual activity ought to occur only within the confines of marriage. Furthermore, sexuality must be ordered according to fundamental precepts of Christian social ethics, which the presbyters also attempted to apply to other areas of life. The honored values included sincerity, faithfulness, and responsibility toward others. All Christians needed to maintain these virtues and adjust or restrain their passions accordingly, especially in their sexual and marital lives. The sexual ethic of Calvinism obviously made no further demands—for magical or sacral reasons—of its adherents, either with respect to procreation or limitations upon marital conduct during particular days of the week or year.

By restricting sexual activity to married couples, church discipline at Emden based itself upon accepted social foundations by which family and clan bound a man and woman. At the same time, these actions contributed to the civilizing process that reshaped early modern society. According to Calvinist standards, it was not primarily the natural constraints of traditional life and economics that played the significant role in binding individuals to marriage and the family; rather, it was a personal sense of Christian responsibility for the neighbors whom God had entrusted to them. This conviction lay firmly anchored in the conscience and soul. From this perspective, sexual discipline contributed to the internalization of Christian values. The age of Pietism doubtless marked the high point of presbyterial concern for marriage and the family. Pietism strove to internalize godliness and to create a sensitivity for the common problems of husbands, wives, and children.

This high point for church discipline also marked a decisive turning point. Admittedly, the presbytery investigated a large number of cases of marital strife during the 1740s (Table 5, 4.03.11).[122] But the phraseology of the records themselves demonstrates that there was markedly less concern for individual situations than in previous years, since they speak only in general terms of "disorderly life" or "strife."[123] The registers do not contain any cases of marital strife in the sample years after the 1740s. Nor were there any inquiries concerning household management, children, or problems with relatives during the samples from the eighteenth century (Table 5, 4.04.41–44). Even the way that a case of divorce was examined during the 1790s[124] illustrates that the presbyters had lost considerable interest in applying religious sanctions for failures in the area of marriage and family life. Thus, it appears that the intensification of marital discipline during the Pietist era may have had mixed results. It could have resulted in a tension between the high esteem for the traditional institution of marriage and the new stress upon individuality as well as the demand for individual expression within marriage. This dialectical tension may have generated a new perspective during the eighteenth century, in which marriage and the family constituted a private sphere of life, and the church and state ought to play only an indirect role within it. All of this was preceded by the Pietist subjectivism that left religion and piety as well as moral supervision to individuals and their consciences. These factors support the statistically demonstrable shift away from the presbyterial surveillance that was standard for marriage and family discipline during the sixteenth and seventeenth centuries.

Over the course of the eighteenth century, the Enlightenment[125] became a powerful force in East Friesland, particularly within the leadership of the Emden church. It played an important role in altering the perspective of presbyters and parishioners. There had always been a residue of eschatological and prophetic thought in early modern marital disci-

---

[122]Table 5 shows twenty-one instances of marital strife for the years 1741–45. They constitute 78 percent of all cases concerning "Marriage, Family, Child rearing" and amount to almost one-fifth of the 115 disciplinary cases from this five-year period (Table 1, columns 1741–55 valid cases).

[123]For example, KRP, Emden 11.03 and 11.11.1743.

[124]Cf. above, p. 46.

[125]Menno Smid, *Ostfriesische Kirchengeschichte* (Leer: Risius, 1974), 402ff.

pline and in moral discipline generally. Sin and conflict were not simply private and personal failings; they affected the entire congregation. Above all, these failings were a public scandal that promised to incur the wrath of God against both city and state if they were not energetically prosecuted and expiated. This dire expectation applied particularly to sins and discord within marriage and the family, the very foundation of Christian society. Marriage had been instituted by God and strengthened through a religiously sanctioned oath of fidelity. A new understanding emerged from Pietism and became widely accepted during the Enlightenment. This new perception distinguished between peace and order in state and society, which was no longer understood to be an expression of sacred history (*Heilsgeschichte*), and peaceful, morally responsible family life. From a Christian perspective, faults that led to the failure of marriage were still considered sinful, even after this shift had taken place. With the end of presbyterial church discipline, however, it was solely the responsibility of the individual to come to terms with his or her sin. Even repentance became an internal matter, expressed in private rather than public fashion. Divorces were still considered "scandalous," but they were secular scandals within burgher society, not an affront to both religion and society as they had been in the early modern Calvinist city-state.

It is hardly the historian's task to pass moral judgment, much less to condemn. Yet in bringing their findings regarding past societies to the present discussion of contemporary political, moral, and ethical culture, historians can make two major contributions. They can describe historical developments and they can point out alternatives, both in the forms of socialization and the opportunities available for individuals to order their lives and pursue their happiness. Both of these contributions relativize the present and thus make change possible. Our specific field of inquiry, "marriage and the family," is an impressive example of this process. Several "liberating" insights can be derived from the results of this historical study. They elucidate the "hereditary" dimension of current problems in relationships between men and women, and also relativize them through comparison with historical alternatives. This kind of analysis is impossible within the scope of the present essay. Yet in conclusion, it is worth remembering that every form of sexual and marital relationship has its costs and benefits, both socially and, even more, in personal and subjective terms. This insight is important for the sake of historical fairness, and because a degree of modesty is appropriate when discussing the fundamental questions of how human life and society are shaped. The costs of early modern marital discipline are only too apparent. They can be found in historians' discussions, and even more so in the amorphous notions of "repression and coercion," which purportedly characterized the marriages of even our parents' generation. By contrast, the costs of the newer pattern of relationships between men and women have only begun to emerge. The renunciation of clear norms and models for relationships between men and women has unquestionably had results that are not uniformly positive. Psychoanalysts such as Wolfgang Schmidbauer offer the strongest evidence. In his recent book *Du verstehst mich nicht* (*You Don't Understand Me*), which stood atop the German best-seller list for several weeks in 1991, Schmidbauer writes:

> We are not only dealing with individual failures, but also with historical changes. Today love has become, as it were, the central illusion. The flexibility that people in modern industrial society enjoy in shaping their lives has broadened enormously. Couples today have to determine how they wish to structure their relationships, and although they have more choices than before, they also are under more pressure to decide. When they have problems with their partners, they often feel that they have been left completely alone. I think that, at this point, psychology has sometimes assumed the function of a substitute religion.[126]

---

[126]Wolfgang Schmidbauer, *Du verstehst mich nicht* (Reinbek: Rowohlt, 1991); quotation from "Illusion der Gleichheit," an interview with Schmidbauer in *Der Spiegel*, 18 (April 29, 1991), 231.

Appendix

Literature on Marriage in Early Modern Europe

Aries, Philippe. "Liebe in der Ehe," in idem et al., *Die Masken des Begehrens und die Metamorphosen der Sinnlichkeit*, 165–175. Frankfurt am Main: Suhrkamp, 1986.

Bernsdorff, Wilhelm, ed. *Wörterbuch der Soziologie*, 2d edition, 1969, s.v. "Ehe und Ehescheidung," by René König, 197–207.

Buchholz, Stephan. *Recht, Religion und Ehe: Orientierungswandel und gelehrte Kontroversen im Übergang vom 17. zum 18. Jahrhundert*. Frankfurt am Main: Suhrkamp, 1988.

Bulst, Neithard, Joseph Goy, and Jochen Hoock, eds. *Familie zwischen Tradition und Moderne: Studien zur Geschichte der Familie in Deutschland und Frankreich vom 16. bis zum 20. Jahrhundert*, Kritische Studien zur Geschichtswissenschaft, no. 48. Göttingen: Vandenhoeck, 1981.

Conrad, Hermann. "Das Tridentinische Konzil und die Entwicklung des kirchlichen und weltlichen Rechtes," in *Das Weltkonzil von Trient: Sein Werden und Wirken*, edited by Georg Schreiber, vol. 1, 257–324. Freiburg: Herder, 1951.

Conze, Werner, ed. *Sozialgeschichte der Familie in der Neuzeit*, Industrielle Welt, no. 21. Stuttgart: Klett, 1976.

Crouzel, Henri (Alte Kirche), Leendert Brink (Mittelalter), and Maurice E. Schild (Reformation). "Ehe," "Eherecht," and "Ehescheidung" in the *Theologische Realenzyklopädie*, 308–362. Berlin: Walter de Gruyter, 1982.

Dieterich, Hartwig. *Das protestantische Eherecht in Deutschland bis zur Mitte des 17. Jahrhunderts*, Jus ecclesiasticum, no. 10. Munich: Beck, 1970.

Erle, Manfred. *Die Ehe im Naturrecht des 17. Jahrhunderts. Ein Beitrag zu den geistesgeschichtlichen Grundlagen des modernen Eherechts*. Göttingen: Vandenhoeck, 1952.

Flandrin, Jean-Louis. *Familles: Parenté, maison, sexualité dans l'ancienne société*. Paris: Hachette, 1976.

Köhler, Walter. "Die Anfänge des protestantischen Eherechts," *Zeitschrift der Savigny-Stiftung für Rechtsgeschichte, kanonische Abteilung* 30 (1941): 271–310 (abbreviated ZSRG [KA]).

Luhmann, Niklas. *Liebe als Passion: Zur Codierung von Intimität,* 4th edition. Frankfurt am Main: Suhrkamp, 1984.

Lüthi, Kurt. "Das Eheverständnis des Protestantismus," *Theologisch-praktische Quartalschrift* 127 (1979): 33–44, 833–836.

Métral, Marie-Odile. *Die Ehe.* Frankfurt am Main: Suhrkamp, 1981.

Mikat, P. "Ehe" in *Handwörterbuch zur Deutschen Rechtsgechichte,* vol. 1, 809–833. 1981.

Mitterauer, Michel. *Zur Geschichte Illegitimes Geburten in Europa.* Munich: Beck, 1983.

Reif, Heinz, ed. *Die Familie in der Geschichte.* Göttingen: Vandenhoeck, 1982.

Roper, Lyndal. *The Holy Household: Women and Morals in Reformation Augsburg.* Oxford: Clarendon Press, 1989.

Schröter, Michael. "Wo zwei zusammenkommen in rechter Ehe . . ." *Sozio- und psychogenetisch Studien über Eheschliessungsvorgänge vom 12. bis 15. Jahrhundert.* Frankfurt am Main: Suhrkamp, 1985. Should be read with the review by Johannes Fried in *Historische Zeitschrift,* 242 (1986): 681–84.

Schwab, Dieter. *Grundlagen und Gestalt der staatlichen Ehegesetzgebung in der Neuzeit bis zu Beginn des 19. Jahrhunderts,* Schriften zum deutschen und europäischen Zivil-, Handels-, und Prozessrecht, no. 45. Bielefeld: E. und W. Giesking Verlag, 1967. See also his two encyclopedia articles: *Geschichtliche Grundbegriffe,* s.v., "Familie," vol. 2, 253, and *Handwörterbuch zur Deutschen Rechtsgeschichte,* s.v. "Familie," vol. 1, 1067–1071.

Shorter, Edward. *The Making of the Modern Family.* New York: Basic Books, 1975.

Sprengler-Ruppenthal, Anneliese. "Zur Rezeption des Römischen Rechts im Eherecht der Reformatoren," *ZSRG (KA)* 99 (1982): 363–418.

Stone, Lawrence. *The Family, Sex and Marriage in England 1500–1800.* London: Weidenfeld and Nicolson, 1979.

Stutz, Ulrich. "Zu den ersten Anfängen des evangelischen Eherechts," *ZSRG (KA)* 22 (1983): 288–331.

Wendel, François. *Le mariage à Strasbourg à l'époque de la Réforme, 1520–1692.* Strasbourg: Imprimerie Alsacienne, 1928.

Chapter 3

"The Great Difficulties One Must Bear to Follow Jesus Christ": Morality at Sixteenth-Century Nîmes

Philippe Chareyre

S ituated at the southern extremity of the Rhône valley between the Cévennes mountains and the Mediterranean coast, Nîmes was an energetic crossroads of people, goods, and ideas. News of the religious changes unfolding at Geneva and elsewhere arrived early, and enjoyed a welcome reception. Notions of reform quickly took root in the city and, over time, profoundly marked the history of the region. Even today Nîmes remains among the most important Protestant cities of France.

Although the first preachers and martyrs appeared in the early 1530s, the Reformation only gathered force at the end of the decade when Claude Baduel, who had spent time at Strasbourg with Calvin, assumed direction of the royal *collège des arts* established by Francis I in 1539. Genevan missionary efforts began later, in the mid–1550s,[1] and culminated with the arrival of Pastor Guillaume Mauget and the establishment of a church in 1559. The consistory met for the first time on March 24, 1561,

---

[1]R. M. Kingdon, *Registres de la Compagnie des pasteurs de Genève au temps de Calvin*, vol. 2 *(1553-1564)* (Geneva: Droz, 1962).

The author thanks Professor R. A. Mentzer, who shares a deep interest in sixteenth-century Languedoc, for his translation of the text.

Abbreviations: AD., Gard Archives départementales du Gard, Nîmes.
  BN Bibliothèque Nationale, Paris.

and continued without interruption until 1685. A nearly complete set of the proceedings—only the 1563–1577 volume is missing—bear witness to its tireless activity. Protestantism triumphed in the town, the surrounding countryside, and the nearby Cévennes. The Calvinists comprised the majority and this fact spared the region many horrors, including the Saint Bartholomew's Day massacre. Still, the Reformed consistory of Nîmes faced an enormous challenge in its reformation of religion and society.

The task of reforming morals within the community accounts for more than two-thirds of consistorial activity between 1561 and 1684. In the course of their deliberations, the pastors and elders dealt with 8,648 cases of moral delinquency (see Table 1).[2] Altogether the pattern is consistent with that of other consistories throughout the Midi.[3] In addition, the period between 1578 and 1614 deserves special attention. These years represent about one-third of the time during which the consistory operated, yet they contain some two-thirds of all offenses. It was a golden age of

Table 1: The Reformation at Nîmes: Matters Handled by the Consistory

Period	Moral Reform	Religious Reform[a]	Religious Practices[b]	Others	Total
1561–1563	286	41	140	9	476
1578–1584	1,206	187	340	13	1,746
1585–1594	1,751	268	370	38	2,427
1595–1604	1,662	341	278	48	2,329
1605–1614	1,079	420	215	60	1,774
1615–1654	1,761	764	374	108	3,007
1655–1684	903	106	102	48	1,159
TOTAL	8,648	2,127	1,819	324	12,918

[a]Efforts against pagan practices, magic, and Catholic usages.
[b]Infractions concerning matters of worship, the sacraments, and doctrine.

[2]P. Chareyre, *Le consistoire de Nîmes de 1561 à 1685*, 4 vols. (Thèse de Doctorat d'Etat en Histoire: Université Paul-Valéry-Montpellier III, 1987).

[3]B. Vogler and J. Estèbe, "La genèse d'une société protestante: Etude comparée de quelques registres consistoriaux languedociens et palatins vers 1600," *Annales: Economies, Sociétés, Civilisations* 31 (1976):362–388.

censure among southern French Protestants. The motto of the Nîmes consistory as displayed on the first page of its sixth register was wholly appropriate: *Disciplina nervus ecclesiae* (Discipline is the sinews of the church).[4]

Although the pastors presided over the meeting of the consistory, their principal duty was to preach the word of God. Consequently, it fell to the elders to direct the church and advance substantively the reform of morals and religion. These elders formed two distinct groups at Nîmes. Nine were elders in the strict sense of the term. They functioned within the context of eight districts or *surveillances*; the ninth elder had charge over the suburbs, the area outside the walls.

There were also four deacons, one for every two districts. As a practical matter, deacons drawn from the higher social ranks such as the nobility or legal profession rapidly acquired preeminence over their colleagues who were merchants or members of the bourgeoisie. As a result, they tended to coordinate and reinforce the activity of the two elders for the districts that they served. This double structure assured the efficacy of the consistory, and more so because these officials were chosen from among the most exemplary and respectable men of the city. They exercised a moral ascendancy over their fellow citizens. Moreover, the annual rotation of ecclesiastical officers fostered close supervision of the community. In effect, each new member of the consistory made it a point of duty to regulate matters within his family, his street, and his neighborhood.

The consistory's efforts occurred then within a grid system far finer and more precise than traditional municipal districts or quarters. The elders apportioned the streets and watched everywhere for misbehavior. They noted each suspicious move, relying upon informing neighbors or the trained eye of the preceding elder. They relayed the details to the consistory and discussed these matters with their colleagues. The consistory often directed the elders to resolve minor infractions, either by themselves or with the assistance of a pastor. Nothing escaped their attention; nothing was long hidden from them. The sheer volume of the consistory registers attests to the fact.[5]

In addition to the moral influence exercised by elders and pastors, the consistory possessed a wide range of techniques to deal with wrongdo-

[4]R. A. Mentzer, "*Disciplina nervus ecclesiae*: The Calvinist Reform of Morals at Nîmes," *Sixteenth Century Journal* 18 (1987):89–115.

[5]Chareyre, *Le consistoire de Nîmes*, 337–392. See also J. Boulenger, *Les Protestants à Nîmes au temps de l'Edit de Nantes* (Paris: Fischbacher, 1903).

ers once the matter proceeded beyond the investigatory phase. For lesser offenses, it applied censures or issued exhortations to improve. Far more serious was suspension from the Lord's Supper. Depending upon the gravity of the offense, the suspension could be public or private, as could the subsequent repentance ceremony. Suspension from the sacrament was especially dreaded and dissuasive because it entailed a demonstration of humility which, when performed publicly, touched the extremely sensitive nerve of individual honor. Moreover, for a society founded upon religion, being barred from the sacrament amounted to banishment from the community of the faithful.

Public authority at Nîmes was firmly Protestant. The consulate was entirely in the hands of the Reformers until the suppression of Rohan's revolt in 1629. Most judges on the royal presidial court were likewise Protestant. The town was, according to one historian, a model Protestant Republic.[6] Over the course of this Reformed supremacy, any and every measure was invoked to instill respect for church discipline. The temporal and ecclesiastical powers worked to the same effect.

Requests for banishment, formulated by the consistory and presented to the civic authorities, amounted to an extension of consistorial jurisdiction, power, and effectiveness. Those banished included the heresiarch Olaxe, various persons who adamantly refused to submit to the decisions of the consistory, the utterly depraved, and even some Catholics. The last group included a priest, who, in 1594, railed against the king, and a Catholic man who forced his Protestant wife to attend Mass.[7] While very few Catholics were touched so spectacularly, everyone felt the effect of routine patrols, the closing of shops during religious services, and the elimination of gambling and prostitution. Carnival masks were seized and burned; violins used at dances were confiscated and broken; one of the city consuls personally forbade the charivari.[8] For better protection against the external dangers and vices that threatened the town, the consistory recommended closing the gates during services, and as late as 1600, despite the calm of peacetime, raising the drawbridge each evening.[9] The gatekeepers had their orders; only those who passed inspection could

---

[6]R. Sauzet, "Religion et pouvoir municipal: Le consulat de Nîmes aux XVI et XVIIème siècles," *Ethno-psychologie* (1977), 2/3:277–285.

[7]AD, Gard 42 J 30, 28/04/1593, 11/08/1593, 16/03/1594.

[8]BN, MS Fr. 8667, 12/01/1583. AD, Gard 42 J 28, 06/02/1585.

[9]AD, Gard 42 J 31, 13/09/1600.

enter. Thomas Platter, a Swiss medical student, could not have visited the Roman ruins at Nîmes had he not clearly specified with whom he was staying and the purpose of his trip.[10] A Protestant moral order held sway over the entire town. Finally, beginning in 1562, the consistory issued certificates that verified membership in the true faith and, in the case of travelers, attested to their good behavior. This device allayed suspicion in the host community and sometimes even helped in finding employment.

Proper conduct was as much a private as public matter. Nothing escaped moral definition. Respect for the family, the pacification of society, and the struggle against worldly dissoluteness were matters that engaged the Nîmes Protestants along the path toward societal reform and, by extension, modernity itself.

Table 2: The Creation of a New Social and Moral Order

	1561–1562 1578–1584	1585–1594	1595–1604	1605–1614	TOTAL
A Moral Society	376	556	431	391	1,754
A Pacified Society	538	730	552	301	2,121
A Solemn Society	578	465	679	387	2,109
Total	1,492	1,751	1,662	1,079	5,984

A MORAL SOCIETY: THE REINFORCEMENT OF THE FAMILY CELL

The consistory focused enormous energies on the family, the basic unit of modern society. The number of cases touching upon it and related issues suggests the constant care that the consistory took to curb transgressions and stabilize the institution. From 1561 to 1614, 1,754 cases centered on the struggle against fornication and adultery, the resolution of family disputes, and the development of respect for the institution of marriage (see Table 3). Greater direction over betrothals and the strict regulation of sexuality, both marital and premarital, also affected the nuclear family.

[10]*Félix et Thomas Platter à Montpellier* (Montpellier: Coulet, 1892), 230.

Table 3: A Moral Society

	1561–1562 1578–1584	1585–1594	1595–1604	1605–1614	TOTAL
Fornication	120	267	214	196	797
Respect for marriage	147	157	98	90	492
Family Disputes	109	132	119	105	465
TOTAL	376	556	431	391	1,754

Respect for the Institution of Marriage
The consistory sought to instill respect for the institution of marriage, and the process served to pacify and modernize society. According to the *Discipline of the Reformed Churches of France*, the ultimate purpose of marriage was procreation as well as the avoidance of adultery and fornication.[11] Restoring the honor of marriage meant, above all, insisting upon the indissolubility of the bonds and steadfastly opposing those who might question the matter and seek to break them. Nonetheless, marriage was neither a sacrament nor an ecclesiastical institution. The consistory, when acting in this realm, often pushed the limits of its powers. Enhancing the value of marriage began with establishing respect for the acts that created marriage. It meant emphasizing the engagement between the two parties even more than the legal contract that they drew up with the assistance of the notary.

The betrothal ceremony, while it had no particular religious significance, was marked by the gift that the bridegroom bore: often a purse or silk belt. For its part, the consistory insisted upon a ring as the only valid gift.[12] The ceremony, in certain instances, concluded when the couple drank from a common cup. These practices, as P. Bels has shown, confirm the continuation at Nîmes of betrothal by the "words of the present tense." The "words" constituted an irrevocable promise to marry so long as there was sufficient proof of the act and the couple had followed the proper forms.[13] A simple verbal promise made in a private conversation

[11] Isaac d'Huisseau, *La Discipline des Eglises Réformées de France ou l'ordre par lequel elles sont conduites et gouvernées* (Geneva, 1656), chap. 13, art. 14. See also J. Aymon, *Tous les Synodes Nationaux des Eglises Réformées de France*, 2 vols. (The Hague: Charles Delo, 1710).

[12] AD, Gard 42 J 29, 22/02/1589, fol. 117; Gard 42 J 30, 22/03/1595, fols. 336–337.

[13] P. Bels, *Le mariage des protestants français jusqu'en 1685: Fondements doctrinaux et pratique juridique* (Paris: Pichon et Durand-Auzias, 1968), 129–131. A. Burguière, "Le rituel du mariage en France, XVI–XVIIIème siècles," *Annales: Economies, Sociétés, Civilisations* 33 (1978): 637–649.

did not suffice, nor did prolonged negotiations among kin, unless both parties clearly and knowingly pronounced the vows. If the attending witnesses swore to the proper procedure, there could be no subsequent authorization to dissolve the promises and, despite whatever difference might later arise, the banns of matrimony were published and the marriage proceeded.[14]

A valid betrothal, in conformity with the civil law of the kingdom, also required parental consent. Philippe, a young journeyman originally from Normandy, had to furnish authorization from his "old and papist" father before he could marry. The consistory insisted upon parental consent from the beginning: it regularly asked the elders to verify whether engagement promises had been exchanged in the presence of parents, the notary, or other witnesses.[15] The national synod, meeting at Paris in 1559, forbade clandestine marriages.[16] The rigor evident at Nîmes was, of course, shared by the Protestant churches throughout the province of Languedoc.[17]

In some cases, the consistory's decisions closely followed those of the secular magistrate. It recommended that Gaspare Surre, whose fiancée was already married to another man, seek remedy in the courts before returning to the consistory. The judge's decision was, in the end, determinative. Eight years after the disappearance of her husband, Catherine Martelle wished to remarry. The marriage contract had been signed, the banns were published, and she was already pregnant. Yet the consistory demanded that she appear before the secular judge and secure the right to proceed with the ceremony. Even so, when she reappeared before the consistory and presented the judicial act recognizing the death of her spouse, the pastors and elders made additional demands: proof that she had diligently searched for her husband, that he had never before been absent for so long, that they were not on bad terms when he disappeared, and that she gave him no special reason to abandon her.[18]

[14]AD, Gard 42 J 30, 22/03/1595.

[15]BN, MS Fr. 8666, 11/03/1562; MS Fr. 8667, 14/05/1578, 21/05/1578.

[16]Bels, *Le mariage*, 169.

[17]R. A. Mentzer, "Ecclesiastical Discipline and Communal Reorganization among the Protestants of Southern France," *European History Quarterly* 21 (1991): 163–183.

[18]BN, MS Fr. 8667, 13/06/1582. AD, Gard 42 J 29, 03/02/1591, fol. 590 (conforming with Huisseau, *La Discipline*, chap. 13, art. 31), 42 J 29, 13/02/1591, fol. 595, and 20/02/1591, fol. 598.

Assuming the agreement between the parties was mutual and correct, the next stage was publication of the banns from the pulpit. It occurred on three successive Sundays in the resident church of the engaged couple. The consistory insisted upon the rules as stated in the *Discipline*, even in cases of marriage to someone of "contrary" religion.[19] The elders also made some preliminary checks before announcing the banns, to avoid the scandal of public objections. The regulations of 1562 envisaged a system of verification whereby the clerk of the consistory and the elders signed the announcement or *"cartel,"* which the pastor then read from the pulpit. Once the required conditions had been met, the consistory urged the parties to wed without delay. It demanded that Jean Carrière, who delayed his marriage for a year because of financial troubles, proceed immediately on pain of excommunication and expulsion from the city.[20]

In cases of disagreement among the parties, the consistory attempted to reconcile them through admonitions and arbitration. Thus the agreement between the silk worker, Joseph Simon, and Françoise Faget, by its very precision and open expression of grievances, suggests that it was a question of achieving not so much a reconciliation of principles as a workable and lasting solution.[21]

The civil betrothal was called the "marriage," while the religious blessing was known as the "espousals" or the "celebration." The distinction points up the unequivocal assimilation of the Protestant theory of marriage by "words of the present tense." This system remained in force until 1612 when the national synod meeting at Privas abandoned it in order to conform with royal law. This latter procedure, inspired by the decisions of the Council of Trent, had been established in 1579 by the ordinance of Blois.[22] This change accounts for the near disappearance of censure for delay of marriage after 1615. In effect, the *Discipline* created a system in which no more than six weeks would elapse between betrothal and celebration.[23]

---

[19]Huisseau, *La Discipline*, chap. 13, art. 16, 17, 20. P. Chareyre, "Les conversions au Protestantisme à Nîmes de 1561 à 1683," *Cahiers de Généalogie Protestante* (September 1990), 115–132. AD, Gard 42 J 30, 16/02/1595, fol. 329.

[20]BN, MS Fr. 8666 11/03/1562; MS Fr. 8667 14/05/1578. AD, Gard 42 J 29, 10/05/1589, p. 177; 42 J 31, 03/05/1600, fol. 346.

[21]BN, MS Fr. 8667, 02/12/1579.

[22]Bels, *Le mariage*, 125–126.

[23]Huisseau, *La Discipline*, chap. 13, art. 26.

The consistory remained inflexible regarding requests for the celebration of marriage in the villages surrounding Nîmes. Such petitions aroused immediate suspicion. The elders saw no good reason to marry in a church other than that in which one regularly worshiped. The only possible motivations were frivolous worldly considerations, an uneasy conscience, or fear of opposition to the marriage. Ministers who, for reasons of kinship or friendship, consented to these arrangements were rebuked. Some persons, to escape censure, celebrated their marriages on the farm or estate of Catholic friends.[24] Marriages outside Nîmes seem nonetheless to have increased during the early years of the seventeenth century, despite the many consistorial admonitions.[25] Finally, the marriage of persons from another Reformed church was forbidden unless they presented an attestation of good standing from that church.

Beyond the strict application of the procedures required by the *Discipline*, the consistory sought to guarantee the proper functioning of marriage. It played the role of repairer to the unexpected tears in the marital fabric. The reconciliation of feuding couples and condemnation of adultery proved an endless task.

In order for the consistory to intervene successfully, both spouses had to acknowledge the authority of the church. In 1563, a woman left her husband and then refused to appear when summoned by the consistory. The case was subsequently transferred to the civil magistrate. The consistory also intervened whenever and wherever possible to check violence. It admonished Jacques Bois not to beat his wife, but to bring her to reason peacefully and through instruction in the Divine Word. One of the most difficult cases was that of Jacques Guiraud, a cobbler who returned his wife to her family when her dowry went unpaid. He refused to take her back and threatened to go live in Rome rather than be forced to accept her. Threatened with expulsion from Nîmes, he finally agreed to conciliation.[26] Other less serious cases, occupying no more than a few lines in the consistory registers, involved simple and brief reconciliations. These actions were discreet and effective. They very often put an end to nasty quarrels that might otherwise have had far graver consequences.

---

[24]AD, Gard 42 J 34, 03/05/1609, fols. 87–88.

[25]AD, Gard 42 J 31, 05/09/1609; 42 J 32, 24/03/1604. P. Falgairolle, "Mariages des pasteurs célébrés ou publiés à Nîmes de 1623 à 1685," *Bulletin de la Société de l'Histoire du Protestantisme Français* 55 (1906):33–39, 116–118.

[26]BN, MS Fr. 8666, 09/08/1561, 20/01/1563. AD, Gard 42 J 29, 26/07/1589, p. 224; 13/09/1589, p. 272.

The Struggle against Extramarital Misconduct
Imparting respect for the institution of marriage meant the condemnation of irregularities such as concubinage and sexual relations prior to the celebration of marriage.[27] In 1562, Vidal Du Vray converted; several weeks later, the consistory insisted that he marry the servant woman with whom he had lived for some ten years and by whom he had several children. Nor did the elders and pastors appreciate the attitude of Pilot, who lived in notorious concubinage without any intention of marrying; they denounced him to the civil magistrate. The most common cases involved couples who began living together immediately after their betrothal. The consistory censured Monsieur Percet, whose son was born six months after the celebration of his marriage, for having trespassed upon "civil propriety."[28]

Far more serious was suspicion of bigamy. The accusation weighed especially on newcomers whose background was obscure or ambiguous. This sort of offense was nonetheless rare. Jean Hattemate, a hatter from Paris also known as Jean de La Roche, was suspected in 1581 of having one wife at Paris, a second at Bordeaux, and preparing to marry a third at Nîmes.[29]

Adultery also had severe consequences and was grounds for possible divorce. Witness the request of Ouillier, who wanted a copy of his wife's confession to adultery for use in his scheme for divorce and remarriage.[30] Still, few cases of adultery ended in such extreme fashion. Instead, they were the occasion for biting accusations and angry squabbles. In 1561, a man handed his wife over to the consistory for having had an affair with a priest. Naturally, both men and women were guilty of such failings. Laurent Bastié had a painful surprise in 1589. In the assembled presence of the elders, he learned that his wife was cheating on him. According to neighbors, while he slept soundly, she called to her lover, a servant in their employ: "Etienne, the ass is asleep!" Loneliness also created problems, especially for the wives of merchants who were gone for months on end. Louise Favier consoled herself with the servant of Sen Chicard. Millet had the discomfort of discovering an additional child in his house upon

---

[27]Huisseau, *La Discipline*, chap. 13, art. 25.
[28]BN, MS Fr. 8666, 18/11/1562. AD, Gard 42 J 28, 25/09/1585; 42 J 37, 15/05/1624, fol. 50.
[29]BN, MS Fr. 8667, 27/09/1581.
[30]AD, Gard 42 J 30, 15/05/1592, fol. 68.

returning from a three-year absence. The birth of a child as the result of these illicit love affairs only aggravated the situation, and more so as the guilty party was responsible for the child's support. Robert, a doctor of laws, discovered an infant left at his door with a note attached, indicating that the child was his.[31]

The arrival of an extra child was hardly to the tastes of most wives. Gally's wife beat and chased their servant woman, protesting that her husband had made her "wear the banes." In other words, she had been shamed, deceived, and "cuckolded." The wife of Petit didn't mince words in threatening to poison his soup or wine if he brought his bastard son to live with them. To keep peace, he entrusted the child's care to a certain Laurent Brun whom he then paid through the intermediary of his cousin, de Poussac. Zaccharie de Saintes assumed responsibility for the infant whom he had by his servant woman, deeming it "reasonable" to do so. Yet he must have acted reluctantly, for two years later, the child was reported to have died the "cruel death of starvation."[32]

Creating respect for the institution of marriage included removing all temptations that might provoke its dissolution, particularly since one purpose of marriage as endorsed by the *Discipline* was the elimination of sexual misconduct. In this sphere, the consistory had a great deal to do. The condemnation of illicit love accounted for an enormous part of its endeavors.[33] A proverb reported by Anne Rulman, the celebrated humanist of Nîmes, takes full measure of this affliction: "The most prudent lose their pants."[34] Temptation increased with the arrival of a servant in the household. Some women, as previously noted, had intimate relations with their own or a neighbor's servant. Female servants were the object of amorous advances by the family's sons, if not the master himself. Along these lines, the consistory condemned a farce performed at the wedding celebration of the royal criminal judge. The theme was "an old man enamored

---

[31]BN, MS Fr. 8666, 22/11/1561, 27/12/1561. AD, Gard 42 J 28, 29/01/1586; 42 J 29, 19/05/1589, fols. 189, 190; 06/08/1589, p. 230.

[32]AD, Gard 42 J 28, 25/11/1587; 42 J 29, 03/07/1590, p. 445; 18/07/1590, p. 445; 42 J 31, 11/03/1597, fol. 170; 05/05/1599, fol. 280.

[33]Between 1578 and 1594, 40 percent of the instances of adultery and fornication (*paillardise*) involved servant women. It was 31 percent between 1595 and 1614.

[34]"As pus sages las brailles ly tombon." A. Rulman, *Les proverbes du Languedoc*, ed. Dr. Mazel (Montpellier, 1880), 11. On the subject of Rulman's life, see: A. de Rulman, *Chronique secrète de Nîmes et du Languedoc au XVIIème siècle*, ed. P. Chareyre (Nîmes: Lacour, 1990).

of his servant girl."[35] The favorite haunts for these assignations were lofts and barns, stables and sheds, and wholly typical of Nîmes, the "crypts" or vaulted passageways of the ancient Roman arena.

The consistory condemned this debauchery from the outset. In 1562, it decided that before the converted canon Brignon could participate in the Lord's Supper, he must end his affair with his servant woman. The elders also checked on a supposed secret door connecting his house to the servant's adjoining residence. The device would have concealed any illicit liaison.[36] The persons most affected by such behavior were migrant women from the rural Cévennes. Descending from their mountain valleys, they sought employment as domestics and "hired girls" in the city. Few among them could or would, or even knew how to, resist a hasty promise of marriage, the threat of dismissal, or a flattering gift. Even fewer took legal action. Only the most capable were able to recover their lost honor in accord with the variations of the popular Occitan "love square."[37] The forms of redemption were many. The master might offer the woman a meager dowry and marry her to a male servant, who may or may not have been responsible for her pregnancy;[38] or he might compensate her materially and promise to support the infant, who was often placed with a wet nurse in the surrounding suburbs or a nearby village. The consistory, given its task, encroached upon the double domain of privacy and honor and frequently encountered the most obstinate denials, even in the face of witnesses. People did not so much fear the knowledge of their error as they did its public disclosure. Consistorial deliberations make clear that very often the matter was a common secret that had not escaped the neighbors' shrewd attention. Instead, they resented the open acknowledgment and admission of guilt. Yet the consistory left no stone unturned in conducting its investigations. The lengthy interrogations and many witnesses associated with these cases have left a wealth of documentation replete with detailed and powerful descriptions.

The consistory endeavored, with the assistance of municipal consuls and judicial magistrates, to eradicate prostitution, a form of licentiousness even more scandalous because it was public. Inculcating a sense of guilt on this subject proved a formidable task. Pierre Teissier, called

---

[35]AD, Gard 42 J 32, 29/02/1601, fol. 395.

[36]BN, MS Fr. 8666, 02/10/1562 and 12/10/1562.

[37]E. Le Roy Ladurie, *L'amour, l'argent et la mort en pays d'Oc* (Paris: Seuil, 1980).

[38]AD, Gard 42 J 31, 14/02/1601, fol. 393.

Looset, admitted having "enjoyed a woman" at Trinquetaille for two and a half sous. He testified before the entire consistory "that it was a popular pastime and that it meant nothing."[39] The consistory's power of course did not extend over a large geographic area, and its efforts centered on "purifying" the space within the walls and the adjoining suburbs. The elders compiled lists of "whores and debauchees" and sent them to the councillors and judicial officers. In 1601, the *viguier*, a municipal judicial officer, notified the consistory that, in making his nightly rounds, he discovered and imprisoned two prostitutes. During this same time, the elders kept a careful eye on the taverns in the suburbs; some apparently housed women of unsavory reputation. Meanwhile, the pastors thundered from the pulpit against "debauchery and whoring." The faithful, notably the women of the congregation, took the message to heart. A group of them gathered before Vidal Raymond's house, beating on the door in pursuit of a prostitute who had hidden herself within, beneath a pile of straw.[40]

The consistory also battled a more discreet sort of prostitution, attacking those who conducted such activities in their houses. In 1589, the royal prosecutor requested that the consistory give him the "list of bawds." Five years later, it gave the city consuls a list of women who, according to the elders, were kept in great numbers in private residences.[41] Action quickly followed recognition of the facts and suggested the fundamental agreement between civil and religious authorities in this realm. The consistory certainly prodded and pushed the councillors and judges to greater diligence and effectiveness.

The case of a woman named Fromentine is among the best examples of people's imperviousness to the *Discipline*. She drew attention initially when she betrothed a Catholic and then refused to marry him. Suspected of opening her door too easily to a priest and of having permitted games and gambling in her home, she exacerbated matters by visiting gypsy fortune tellers, and then participating in the Lord's Supper at a neighboring village when she could not do so at Nîmes because of the charges against her. She answered to the consistory in May 1585 for dancing and was

---

[39]BN, MS Fr. 8667, 14/05/1578.

[40]AD, Gard 42 J 29, 22/07/1588, fol. 32, 05/07/1589, p. 217; 42 J 31, 11/03/1597, 13/01/1599, 18/04/1601, 26/12/1601; 42 J 32, 18/09/1602, 05/02/1603, fol. 148. BN, MS Fr. 8667, 08/06/1583.

[41]AD, Gard 42 J 29, 28/06/1589, p. 216; 42 J 30, 03/08/1594, fol. 287.

recalled for sexual misconduct the following month. Her name regularly appears in the consistory deliberations for 1589. It became a test of wills that ultimately worked against her. Summoned for prostitution, she denied the accusation, though the elders maintained that it was common knowledge. When the consistory suspended her from the Communion service, Fromentine defiantly retorted that she was ready, as before, to do anything necessary to appeal the decision to the regional colloquy. The testimony was both overwhelming and damning, and considering the amplitude of her misdeeds, the consistory extended her suspension from the sacrament into September. Again, she appealed. The colloquy, which met several months later at Aigues-Mortes, simply confirmed the consistory's judgment. Turning a deaf ear, Fromentine next appealed to the provincial synod. Her obstinacy led in the end to banishment. In March 1590, she was summarily expelled from Nîmes.[42]

Such consistorial ferocity is representative of its operation in the domain of extramarital relations during the last quarter of the sixteenth century and the first third of the following. To achieve its ends, the consistory had two means of action at its disposal. The first was exclusion from the sacraments, an especially humiliating ecclesiastical weapon when accompanied by public repentance. Secondly, the consistory had recourse to the secular arm, which possessed the power to constrain by force or to banish.

These examples suggest that the "order" contemplated by the Reformers could not have spread throughout Nîmes but for the participation of the political and judicial powers, who were temporarily enlisted in this common enterprise for the reformation of society. The Protestant moral order brought these powers together in the interests of creating a well-policed community. The municipal consuls established public order in the streets. The judges efficiently enforced royal legislation. Together, in the absence of any true police machinery, they benefited from the inquisitorial structure of the consistory.

---

[42]BN, MS Fr. 8667, 26/02/1582. AD, Gard 42 J 28, 15/08/1583, 01/10/1583, 28/03/1584, 11/04/1584, 21/05/1585, 19/06/1585; 42 J 29, 15/03/1589, 22/03/1589, 31/03/1589, 05/04/1589, 18/05/1589, 09/08/1589, 16/08/1589, 30/08/1589, 31/08/1589, 15/11/1589, 21/03/1590, 24/03/1590.

Familial peace

Taming the family and harmonizing domestic relationships did not stop with the resolution of problems surrounding married couples. The issues encompassed all the familial ties (see Table 4). While the elders occasionally remarked upon the mistreatment of children, the problem failed to capture their full attention. Following Roman tradition and respecting a father's authority, they did not forbid Sire Rousset from chastising his children; they simply recommended that he do so with "discretion and moderation." The honor due parents and grandparents received greater consideration, perhaps because the members of the consistory were themselves men of a respectable age. Indeed, this concern over the proper behavior of the young toward their elders can be found among the consistories throughout Languedoc, and elsewhere in western Europe.[43]

Table 4: The Nature of Family Quarrels

	1578–1584	1585–1594	1595–1604	1605–1614
Parents/children	34	34	20	11
In-laws	25	57	60	51
Brothers/sisters	29	34	34	32
Others	5	7	5	11

Jean Marot, who did not get on well with his Catholic father, admonished the older man for his blasphemy. Yet, despite the son's good intentions, the consistory urged Marot to treat his father better and to be obedient "even if he was a papist."[44] Often, a disagreement with a child broadened into a quarrel with a son-in-law or daughter-in-law, and these were more difficult to resolve because they came to involve questions of material possessions or a dowry.

Violence and maltreatment were a recurrent problem. Jacques Rémond's daughter, for example, sent him to the floor with a punch to the stomach when he surprised her in the act of robbing him; his son-in-law repeatedly threatened him with a knife.[45] The consistory condemned the

[43]AD, Gard 42 J 31, 21/05/1597, fol. 179. Vogler and Estèbe, "La genèse d'une société protestante," 377.

[44]BN, MS Fr. 8666, 07/10/1562.

[45]AD, Gard 42 J 36, 09/02/1622, fol. 157.

shame which some children felt over their parents' poverty, to the point that the very sight of their parents was unbearable. Thus Hercule Julien, a master tailor, would not eat at the same table with his father and gave him no more than a threadbare old shirt to wear. The son was sure that his father had only come into town to disgrace him. The consistory sided with the father and loaned him the money to take his son to court and thereby obtain decent support.[46]

A PACIFIED SOCIETY

The pacifying activity of the consistory was not limited to the family, but extended to the whole of society. The respect for familial order was part of a general respect for public order; both were considered essential for the advance of the divine kingdom. The love of fellow human beings was inseparable from the love of God. The inscription on the Reformed Church at the nearby village of Calvisson expressed the notion forcefully: "Love God and your neighbor as yourself."[47]

The consistory devoted a sizable portion of its activity to settling disputes and legal suits between the faithful, and to condemning duels, intrigues, usury—anything that might corrupt or disturb society. When honor was at stake, the elders had to find a way out of the conflict, not through force but through arbitration or legal redress. The consistory's power lay principally in the recognition of its moral authority and integrity. Hearing the complaints of one of the parties or forestalling problems by summoning the antagonists, the consistory became a veritable surgeon in the remedy of wounded honor. It was a moral instrument capable of reestablishing everyone in the image of her or his dignity. The task of sorting out property matters and making good for bodily injury fell, on the other hand, to civil justice. Consistories everywhere in France played a similar infrajudicial role,[48] one that was doubtless facilitated by the unfailing presence of lawyers serving as elders.

A final observation before proceeding to an examination of the specific categories of disputes focuses on the predominance of men among

---

[46]Ibid., 42 J 30, 18/08/1592, fol. 93.

[47]"Aime ton Dieu et ton prochain come toy meme. 1597 de may." M. Aliger, *La Réforme en Vaunage* (Nîmes: Bene, 1986).

[48]A. Soman and E. Labrousse, "Le registre consistorial de Coutras, 1582–1584," *Bulletin de la Société de l'Histoire du Protestantisme Français* 126 (1980): 193–227.

the quarrelsome and combative individuals called before the consistory. Disputes between men were by far the most common; those between women were roughly one-third fewer; and differences between men and women two-thirds fewer (see Table 5).

Table 5: A Pacified Society

Nature of the disputes	1561–1562 1578–1584	1585–1594	1595–1604	1605–1614	TOTAL
Between men	261	362	249	140	1,012
Men/women	81	109	102	47	339
Between women	136	210	161	103	610
Various	60	49	40	11	160
TOTAL	538	730	552	301	2,121

Quarrels

Quarrels and legal suits had a good measure of their origins in the exaggerated words and gestures that oscillated between fear and bravado. The cycle of violence reveals two distinct patterns. One was the "hypersensitivity of temperaments,"[49] and the other was the disconcerting ease with which disputes ended up before the consistory. The accounts of these quarrels were invariably inflated, pompous, and as a result, banal. Many of these actions, despite their brutality, did not constitute a well of lasting dissension. They bear witness to the integration of a certain amount of habitual aggressiveness in sixteenth-century relationships. The same can be found at Aimargues, a short distance from Nîmes, and among other rural churches of the region.[50]

Anger proved an enemy that deceived a person's judgment and put friends and neighbors at odds. Impulsive, sudden and brief rage led to the most regrettable acts. Once these were past, remorse set in and presaged reconciliation. Because of the futility of such conduct, it was critical to fight these spontaneous, undisciplined human reactions in the expecta-

---

[49]R. Mandrou, *Introduction à la France Moderne, 1500–1640* (Paris: Albin Michel, 1961).

[50]P. Chareyre, *Extension et limites du dimorphisme social et religieux en Bas-Languedoc: Aimargues, 1584–1635* (Mémoire de Maîtrise d'histoire: Université Paul-Valéry-Montpellier III, 1978). R. A. Mentzer, "Le consistoire et la pacification du monde rural," *Bulletin de la Société de l'Histoire du Protestantisme Français* 125 (1989): 373–389.

tion of a peaceful society, one governed by "civil propriety." The struggle was nonetheless difficult in a crowded city plagued by a shortage of housing. In addition, the constant danger which Protestant towns faced during the second half of the sixteenth century simply exacerbated the rigors of daily existence.

When Vidal Du Vray beat the son of Done Loyse, she responded by yanking his beard. In the case of Captain Allier and Vidal Aulbert, bloodshed was not the source of inextinguishable conflict. Following a conversation that had degenerated to physical blows, Allier injured his adversary by a blow to the head with a scabbard. Following the episode, Aulbert took to carrying a pistol under his coat and seemed determined to empty it into the captain if he came near him. Admonished to "get along with one another," they made up on condition of reimbursement for the care necessitated by the injury.[51]

The origin of a quarrel was often a peccadillo that the parties quickly regretted. Percet was extremely sorry to have uttered an unfortunate word to his friend Blaise Baudan. It led to insults and blows.[52]

The consistory also sought to play a preventive role by attempting to eliminate that which might be a cause of disagreement. It fought against defamatory placards and libels. Mésieu, surprised in the act of recopying a song written about the daughter of Sire Aymon, was suspended from the Lord's Supper. Jacques Corrazie received the same punishment for a placard posted on Madeleine Blanche's door. Its contents as reported in the consistory minutes attest to the flimsiness and vulgarity of these libels. Exceeding its role in 1594, for this task fell properly to the city councillors, the consistory drew up a list of eight retailers who used false weights and scales.[53] It also condemned usury, but the number of cases was minimal; there were only three. The elders urged masters to be kindly toward their servants, not to mistreat them, and to pay them all they were due when discharged. The consistory, in its own way, attempted to instill honesty in working conditions.

---

[51]AD, Gard 42 J 31, 21/08/1596. BN, MS Fr. 8667, 25/01/1581.

[52]AD, Gard 42 J 28, 29/02/1584, fol. 86.

[53]Ibid., 42 J 30, 2,16 and 23/02/1594; 42 J 31, 12/04/1596, fol. 56; 42 J 31, 23/05/1597, fol. 180.

Duels

The insult became the popular retort at Nîmes by the seventeenth century. It usurped the place of knives, swords, sticks, and other weapons. The phenomenon undoubtedly revealed consistorial success in the pacification of society, and the resolution of neighborhood quarrels became easier. Thus, duels account for only a small part of the consistory's conciliatory activity (53 cases, of 1,012 disputes among men). On the other hand, these armed clashes are particularly helpful in understanding the conditions of violence. The religious wars were responsible for overarming the urban population. Everyone owned a sword or halberd, if not a pistol or musket. Much later, the arms seizures at Nîmes preceding the revocation of the Edict of Nantes were impressive—thirteen cartloads.[54] The example of Jean Carbonnel, awakened by noise which afterward proved to be a charivari, was instructive. He rushed into the street with sword in hand. The populace was in a state of permanent alert, living in constant fear of a Catholic surprise attack on the city.[55] Generally, only persons having some experience with weaponry responded to a challenge. To do otherwise was dangerous, and this reality likely had a dampening effect on the number of duels. The late sixteenth century at Nîmes saw more dueling, above all in the years after 1584 when the Protestant armies began to demobilize. The phenomenon also occurred in other regions; the area around Bordeaux was a good example.[56] Duels then diminished in the seventeenth century; they became exceptional and increased in frequency only during the troubled period of the Fronde. The entire spectrum of the urban populace—artisans, students, lawyers—participated. By the same token, two groups dominated: nobles and members of the civic guard (captains, sergeants, and gatekeepers) who were by definition armed.[57] The consistory's deliberations over these disputes were generally brief. It usually appointed one or two members to seek out the parties and resolve the matter. Opposition to dueling was not based on a theological vision of "divine constraint," but the wholly terrestrial worry that it could lead to murder. The consistory acted as soon as it learned of possible resort to arms. In 1585, it

---

[54]L. Ménard, *Histoire civile, ecclésiastique et littéraire de la ville de Nîmes* (Paris: Chaubert et Hérissant, 1750–58; reprint, Nîmes: Clavel et Ballivet, 1875), vol. 6, bk. 24, chap. 36 (3/11/1683).

[55]Gard 42 J 28, 06/02/1585.

[56]G. Hanlon, "Les rituels de l'agression en Aquitaine au XVIIème siècle," *Annales: Economies, Sociétés, Civilisations* 40 (1985): 244–268.

[57]For a list of duels: Chareyre, *Le consistoire de Nîmes*, 3:132.

attempted to reconcile Captain Fauquier and Sire Duprix, who were "in great danger" of fighting.[58] On an ecclesiastical level, circumstance of time and place worsened the offense. The day for celebration of the Lord's Supper, the public market, a main square, or the highway leading to Montpellier drew extra attention.

The agreement to meet in combat, whether direct or through intermediaries, followed soon after the quarrel. Thus Captain Robert said to Jacques Blanc: "It's settled Blanc, tomorrow we cut each other's throat." Captain Robert and a group of witnesses went the next day to fetch the protagonist from his shop. The conversation heated up along the way to the site selected for combat and the angry captain, unable to control himself, wounded the then unarmed Blanc on the shoulder.[59] Still, most duels mentioned in the consistory registers possessed more swashbucklery and bluster than real peril; not a single death from dueling was recorded during the sixteenth century. It may be that the civil courts rather than the consistory resolved extreme cases.

Not everyone viewed these armed clashes positively, and the publicity accorded them is by no means an indication that they ran their full course. Rather, duels provided the means to demonstrate publicly that you had the power to answer an affront in dignified fashion, all the while counting upon the rapid intervention of those present to prevent serious harm. Thus Captain Robert and Jacques made as though to fight, but the spectators immediately put a stop to their stylized circling.[60] The duel became symbolic because, as a result of the publicity surrounding it, the fight would be stopped at the first blows of the swords; Rulman in his *Chronique secrète* offers a model in his description of the duel between La Cassagne and de La Ferrassière.[61] This attitude, ever more frequent, pointed up the social neutralization of the duel and its imminent decline. Royal edicts beginning in 1602, as well as the enforcement of the canons of the Council of Trent within the Catholic community, soon reinforced consistorial action in this area.[62]

---

[58]AD, Gard 42 J 28, 12/02/1585.

[59]BN, MS Fr. 8667, 26/02/1582, fol. 291.

[60]Hanlon, "Les rituels de l'agression," *Annales: Economies, Sociétés, Civilisations* 40 (1985): 255. BN, MS Fr. 8667, 26/02/1582.

[61]Rulman, *Chronique secrète*, 229.

[62]F. Billacois, *Le duel dans la société française (XVI-XVIIe siècle): Essai de psychosociologie historique* (Paris: Ecole des Hautes Etudes en Sciences Sociales, 1986). A. Jouanna, *Ordre social, mythes et hiérarchies dans la France du XVIème siècle* (Paris: Hachette, 1977).

Reconciliation

The large number of quarrels did not always allow for their resolution during the consistory meetings proper. Upon learning of a dispute, the consistory often appointed an elder assisted by a deacon or pastor to resolve it. Only the more delicate matters or those that could not be resolved by this initial expedient were handled during the regular sessions. Still, the proportion of reconciliations undertaken during the consistorial sessions was substantial—yet another indication of its astonishing capacity (see Table 6).

Table 6: The Task of Reconciliation

	1578–1584	1585–1594	1595–1604	1605–1614
Reconciliations outside session	201	263	137	146
Reconciliations during session	138	233	186	137
Total	339	496	323	283

Reconciliation followed one of several patterns. The most common was a mutual renunciation of animosity, together with a handshake or kissing of hands, and a reciprocal declaration to respect one another as honorable and trustworthy. The language which sometimes accompanied these gestures was designed to signal an aggressor's remorse and atone for the offense given to the aggrieved's honor. One antagonist, in a rash excess of zeal, even offered to be strung up if he repeated his transgression.[63] The consistory's deliberations revealed a spectrum of words and expressions. Most of these utterances were highly formal. Yet other statements, which may have touched the scribe by their sincerity, were recorded in vivid fashion and seem to have been faithful to reality. In exceptional instances, the reconcilement could be signed or worked out and written into the consistory register, thereby taking the form of an actual pledge. The most striking is that of Jean Carbonnel and Jacques Gerbal who, declaring their hearts cleansed of bitterness and rancor, ended with "May God be glorified by our actions, the church edified, and each of us consoled unto the Lord."[64]

---

[63]AD, Gard 42 J 30, 30/10/1591, fol. 12. BN, MS Fr. 8666, 25/11/1562.
[64]AD, Gard 42 J 35, 26/11/1614, fol. 136.

Whenever property was at stake, the consistory invited the parties to conclude an agreement. In a case from 1579, three elders acted as arbiters; and the disputants bound themselves to their finding on pain of paying six écus to the poor.[65] This measure was wholly exceptional. Later, arbiters were chosen outside the membership of the consistory and with the consent of the aggrieved parties. Article five of the local *Discipline of the Church of Nîmes* precluded consistorial arbitration of civil differences without the consent of the parties, suggesting a strong sense of prudence.[66] The consistory occasionally acted as a justice of the peace for minor conflicts, but did not claim to interfere in the magistrate's sphere. The boundaries of the two powers in these affairs were quickly defined.[67] In effect, the consistory made a clean distinction between the reconciliation of persons, which belonged to its jurisdiction, and property settlements, which were the proper domain of the courts. Still, it was not inappropriate for the consistory to orchestrate an agreement and simultaneously permit a settlement through the judicial process. The situation of Percet and Agulhonnet is a good example. Following mutual insults and batterings, they reconciled before the consistory and promised to pursue litigation with "complete cordiality." The prestige of the consistory was so strong in matters of reconciliation that some persons presented themselves voluntarily. Madières, for instance, requested that the elders bring an end to the animosity in which his neighbor Antoine Crozat had inexplicably held him for over a year. The consistory's good reputation in this area even extended to Catholics such as Monsieur Castel's widow, who asked the consistory to settle a disagreement between her and her sister. The consistory agreed; both women appeared and were reconciled. Apothecaries, surgeons, consuls, and judges had equal recourse to the consistory. The chief magistrate of the presidial court even did so when in conflict with an associate judge in 1588.[68]

The consistory spent much of its time pacifying society, eradicating the sources of quarrels, settling nascent differences, and making certain that conflicts did not take root and fester. Eliminating bitterness and anger

[65]BN, MS Fr. 8667, 28/01/1579.

[66]AD, Gard 42 J 28. Chareyre, *Le consistoire de Nîmes*, 3: 38.

[67]AD, Gard 42 J 32, 05/04/1602.

[68]A. H. Guggenheim, "The Calvinist Notables of Nîmes during the Era of the Religious Wars," *Sixteenth Century Journal* 3 (1972):80–96. BN, MS Fr. 8667, 27/09/1581, fol. 242v. AD, Gard 42 J 28, 14/01/1588; 42 J 32, 04/04/1602.

in social relations became a well-appreciated objective. Impartial arbitration had to be substituted for heated outbursts. Subsequently, parties sought, with as little animosity as possible, the settlement of property disputes in the civil court. Altogether, the consistory had its liveliest success in the difficult chore of reconciliation and bringing the guilty to a recognition of error. In this instance, the authority of the consistory, in Languedoc as elsewhere, was least contested.[69] On the other hand, in those matters considered the most futile, it encountered the greatest resistance.

THE STRUGGLE AGAINST WORLDLY DISSOLUTENESS

Reforming the family and society through the pacification of the relationships among individuals appealed to a personal and mutual effort at understanding. The enterprise extended to the reform of behavior and presupposed the disappearance of many practices capable of threatening the entire edifice. The censure of public morality also allowed each person to gather strength along the arduous path of salvation.

Table 7: A Sober Society: The Struggle against Worldly Dissolutions

Nature of the infractions	1561–1562 1578–1584	1585–1594	1595–1604	1605–1614	TOTAL
Comportment	113	76	24	25	238
Dancing	244	132	405	304	1,085
Games	113	140	87	26	366
Comedies and plays	0	28	48	9	85
Carnival/charivari	169	89	115	23	396
Total	639	465	679	387	2,170

Infractions of Appearance and Comportment

The individual in general and certain types of behavior in particular had to be corrected, or reformed. The consistory severely condemned sloth, gluttony, and drunkenness, and more so because they usually occurred in taverns and cabarets, places given over to lechery, debauchery, and gaming. In 1561, Champignon was censured for "dissipation." He promised to live soberly and to avoid games and other "delights." The following year,

[69]Vogler and Estèbe, "La genèse d'une société protestante," 386.

the consistory gave Mathieu Biscornet to understand that belonging to the Reformed Church did not mean casting out his Catholic mother-in-law. Instead, he should take her back, and quit gambling and drinking. Yet drunkenness and gluttony were not prominent vices at Nîmes. The number of censures for these faults was only 128 cases between 1578 and 1685. It was the same for obscene language and gestures. Pierre Bravard who, at the conclusion of supper with friends, exhibited "his private parts" was thoroughly exceptional.[70]

Excessive attention to dress and appearance was, on the other hand, the distinctive defect of the Nîmois, particularly during the last twenty years of the sixteenth century when about 80 percent of such cases occurred. The years 1581–82 and 1590 were especially noteworthy. The provincial synod, which met at Montauban in June 1581, condemned indecent dress and plunging necklines and, in the process, nudged the Nîmes consistory to greater diligence. The following year, a letter from the church of Orange complained of the bad example set by the women of Nîmes.[71] Whatever the action taken, it was hardly effective, for in 1590 the regional colloquy expressed disapproval of scandalous dress and makeup. The elders and pastors of Nîmes, during a special consistory session, concluded that their church was unusual and had fallen behind the churches of Castres and Montauban where one "sees a great reformation."[72] Ultimately, the consistory's actions in these matters were firm if sporadic.

Vanity in appearance had three aspects: makeup, "twisted" or elaborate hairstyles, and "dissolute" clothes. Cosmetics, a particular problem during the 1590s, were purchased from apothecaries. In 1589, the consistory forbade them from selling these items, but probably without much success.[73] In 1592 and 1598, it again admonished apothecaries for peddling *rouget d'Espagne*.[74] One among them, who sold *arcanettes*, or rouge, became openly hostile toward this restriction on his business.[75] The elders also took offense when women fashioned their hair into "horns" around a metal frame. More than the form, which might have masked some satanic symbol, it was the artifice that the consistory condemned. By the

[70]BN, MS Fr. 8666, 29/05/1561, 22/05/1562; MS Fr. 8667, 30/03/1580.

[71]BN, MS Fr. 8667, 21/06/1561 (see the condemnation in the *Discipline*, chap. 14, art. 25); MS Fr. 8667, 07/11/1582.

[72]AD, Gard 42 J 29, 11/04/1590, p. 384; 42 J 30, 03/12/1592, fol. 127.

[73]Ibid., 42 J 29, 11/01/1589, p. 96.

[74]Ibid., 42 J 30, 29/01/1592, 13/09/1595; 42 J 31, 18/10/1595.

[75]Ibid., 42 J 31, 20/09/1595, fol. 1. *Arcanette* was red ocher and by extension makeup.

same token, male students who wore "cables," that is to say long hair, were admonished to cut it. Fashion and the disregard of authority were such that in 1598 the consistory remarked that even the wives of the pastors had their hair done up in elaborate "horns."[76]

Immodest dress designed to draw attention and incite sexual excess was closely watched. Usually it was a matter of low-cut necklines or "exposed bosoms," even when covered by some gauzy veil while in public. The elders censured Mademoiselle de Gatuzières for daring to enter church wearing this sort of garb;[77] she could not have been the only offender, for the consistory decided to "decry" such behavior from the pulpit.

The elders also condemned artifices in dress, things such as *cachebâtards* and *hausseculs* or farthingales, elaborate hoops that flared the skirt at the hips. As early as 1562, they cautioned the tailor Pierre Saillet to quit making them. In 1589, and again in 1592 and 1600, the consistory railed against the number of offenders and drafted a list of these women with the intention of scolding them individually.[78] The regular recurrence of these admonitions probably indicated that the warnings had but a temporary effect, and that these "lewd" clothes and other vanities came back out of the wardrobe once the storm passed.

Still, consistorial censure over these questions rarely applied to the entire population, but usually to the elite. The consistory targeted its directives against noblewomen, the wives of judges, and bourgeois women. Only women of this status could afford corsets and farthingales, and had the time to prepare their hair carefully. The censures meted out in these instances may well have been a form of social retaliation against the luxury of the urban elite, and an appeal to modesty and propriety. The elite's haughty attitude caused resentment. Take the caricature offered by Guillaume Reboul who, in a 1599 pamphlet, stigmatized the grotesque and arrogant faces of the elders. Cast as artisans, these elders sat while the more prominent members of the town stood and explained themselves or were made to kneel and bare their head in repentance.[79]

---

[76]AD, Gard 42 J 28, 24/12/1586; 42 J 30, 25/05/1594, fol. 277; 42 J 31, 25/11/1598, fol. 248.

[77]Ibid., 42 J 32, 09/06/1604, fol. 236.

[78]BN, MS Fr. 8666, 18/03/1562. AD, Gard 42 J 29, 31/08/1589, p. 258; 04/10/1589, p. 280; 42 J 30, 25/12/1592, fol. 134; 42 J 31, 31/05/1600, fol. 352.

[79]P. Labbé, *"La cabale des Réformez" attribuée à G. Reboul*, annotated with commentary (Master's Thesis: Université de Clermont-Ferrand II, 1981).

Discipline and Sociability: Dancing and Games
The struggle against dancing fully mobilized the consistory. There were
1,085 cases between 1561 and 1614. Dancing was the second most common
of all infractions; only quarrels and disputes were more frequent. After
1594 and into the first two decades of the seventeenth century, for
instance, the correction of dancing surpassed faults of comportment
(thirty-seven cases in 1603 and fifty-two in 1610). Not surprisingly, the
Counter-Reformation made its first inroads at Nîmes during this period.[80]
The Catholic bishop, who reestablished residence, organized a ball in
1606; many Catholics, now protected by the Edict of Nantes, returned permanently and often entertained themselves by dancing.

The *Discipline of the Reformed Churches of France* stipulated that persons who danced or were present at a dance were, if they persisted, to be
excommunicated.[81] "Dancing is the devil's pimp; he has the honor of
having invented it," according to Anne Rulman, who served as elder in
1609 and 1610; it was time to "sound the alarm" against this dissolute
excess of the flesh.[82] Dancing led to profanation of the Sabbath, threatened marital fidelity, and distracted the faithful from the path of salvation. Consistorial intransigence over this root of all evil was matched only
by the stubbornness of those who insisted upon doing it. In 1578, Done
Anne told her guests, "Ha, what shall we do? We shall dance!" and then
took them by the hand to dance a round.[83] Dancing was a favorite social
pastime and there were many different forms in which people took an
honest pleasure. The round, rhythmically measured by the dancers' sing-
ing, gave the least offense. The participants did not consider it a true
dance and even the consistory was inclined to go easy, qualifying it as
"banter."[84] The *branle, volte,* and *bourrée* worried the elders more. And
they deemed the *bouquet* dance, which enjoyed especial popularity
toward the end of the century, completely scandalous. Whoever held the
bouquet chose a partner; thus it passed about and at the conclusion of the
ball, the last dancer was obliged to begin the process anew the next time.

[80]R. Sauzet, *Contre-Réforme et Réforme catholique en Bas-Languedoc: Le diocèse de Nîmes de 1598 à 1694* (Paris: Publications de la Sorbonne, Vander-Oyez, 1979).

[81]Huisseau, *La Discipline*, chap. 14, art. 27.

[82]A. Rulman, *Harangues*, 284, 287.

[83]BN, MS Fr. 8667, 10/12/1578.

[84]Ibid., 09/08/1581.

The accompanying instruments varied; the most common were the rebec and violin. If instruments were lacking, people improvised. Thus in 1596 four noblemen were caught dancing; one of them had sung a tune "without any instrument."[85] The occasions for dancing varied, beginning with the traditional festivals. The period around carnival or the feast of Saint John the Baptist occasioned the most censures. Private balls were more difficult to detect and, typically, were only discovered when one of the participants informed. Then came public balls such as those organized by the innkeeper Nadal Séverac and Captain Barral.[86] Musical corteges and wedding dances did not appear until the seventeenth century. The head of household was, of course, held responsible for the behavior of others in the family. In 1599, the consistory instructed the widow of Pierre Martin to hold her children "captive" at home to prevent them from going out and dancing. Despite the strictures placed on her, Claire Richard climbed out on the roof to go dancing.[87] Appeals to heads of household did not always work, for it sometimes seemed that as soon as they turned their backs, everyone began to dance. Still, the consistory was not taken in by a parent's convenient absence, seeing it as an attempt to turn a blind eye and thereby blunt consistorial condemnation.

As dancing became increasingly restricted at Nîmes, people resorted to visiting neighboring villages. The staunchly Catholic community of Marguerittes soon became a veritable den of iniquity. Altogether, the consistory chastised Nîmois for attending thirty-four balls at nearby hamlets between 1578 and 1600; Marguerittes hosted ten of them.

Beyond the fact of individual enjoyment, the urban elite felt that attendance at or participation in a ball was an obligation, a social duty that was very difficult to evade. But the consistory made no distinction between dancing, which led to licentiousness, and the convivial activity of polite society. Thus it refused to tolerate the presence of an Italian dance master, Signor Baptiste, in the home of Monsieur Pascal in 1595.[88] There were no exceptions. The consistory even reproached the prince de Condé for giving a ball. Similarly, it summoned the highly placed Messieurs de Brissac and de Noailles. Brissac was accused of having organized

---

[85]BN, MS Fr. 8667, 14/05/1578. AD, Gard 42 J 31, 27/03/1596, fol. 49.

[86]AD, Gard 42 J 31, 24/08/1598, fol. 232.

[87]Ibid., 42 J 31, 07/04/1599; 42 J 38, 01/09/1638.

[88]Ibid., 42 J 30, 10/05/1595, 19/08/1595.

a *bouquet* dance; Noailles of having attended. As a consequence, Brissac was suspended from reception of the Holy Sacrament.[89]

Censure for dancing was not, in general, well received; far from it. In 1580, the consistory failed to find a single witness willing to name those who danced at the home of Monsieur de La Croix. Sometimes, the dancers took care to don masks to avoid recognition. Citations to appear before the consistory occasionally led to very direct remarks. Monsieur de Montelz retorted that it would be better to pursue night prowlers than summon his wife for dancing.[90] In no other area was there so wide and enduring a gulf between the faithful and the consistory.

Games were, besides excesses of fashion and dancing, another vice characteristic of the upper social strata of Nîmes. Receiving guests, offering them hospitality, and maintaining a pleasant home obliged the host to offer entertainment. Games and dances were not, however, merely the pastime of the elite. If Monsieur de Nages regularly amused himself at home with backgammon, the municipal gatekeepers played cards in the guardhouse.[91] The *Discipline* forbade all games prohibited by royal edict: cards, dice, and other games of chance. It also specified the dangers, which, in turn, prompted the consistory to action: avarice, lewdness, the waste of time, quarreling, blasphemy, immoral monetary winnings, and aggravating circumstances such as playing games during the Sunday worship.[92] It bears remarking that if the condemnation of dancing occurred principally in the early seventeenth century, the condemnation of games was a sixteenth-century phenomenon.

Table 8: Games

	1578–1584	1585–1594	1595–1604	1605–1624	1625–1684
Games of chance	70	120	80	47	16
Games of skill	28	20	7	1	4

---

[89]BN, MS Fr. 8667, 21/12/1580. AD, Gard 42 J 31, 28/05/1599, fol. 284.

[90]BN, MS Fr. 8667, 27/01/1580, 01/02/1581, 07/02/1582.

[91]AD, Gard 42 J 28, 18/02/1587, 31/12/1587.

[92]Huisseau, *La Discipline*, chap. 14, art. 29.

The elders and pastors treated athletic games, especially deck tennis, more benignly, so long as the participants did not blaspheme, wager, or play on Sunday or any other day devoted to worship or the Communion service. The same was true for various kinds of ball games.[93]

The consistory feared the accompanying disorders as much as the games themselves. The game of skittle between Jean Gaillard and Carbonnel ended in stone throwing and an exchange of curses. A backgammon game in de Nages's home was the origin of the duel between Sibert and Nicolas.[94] The card game known as *brelans* was minutely watched. Regular inspection tours were organized each Sunday to put a stop to it. Merchants who sold the cards were ordered to quit doing so and burn the merchandise.[95] Wagering on a game was strictly forbidden, no matter how insignificant, even if it was only a matter of betting chestnuts.[96] Persons of higher social rank, on the other hand, laid out considerable sums. In 1586, the judge Gallopin was accused of having lost forty-two écus, a huge amount, to Blaise Baudan. A few years later, Antoine Reynaud, a merchant, admitted having lost, after three long nights of checkers, fifty-four écus and five gold rings.[97] On the other hand, the *jeu de la blanque*, a game of chance utilizing lots, did not appear until after 1600, judging by consistorial demands that the magistrates put an end to it.[98]

These various measures fell short of the complete eradication of transgressions. They only succeeded in achieving a precarious truce during the worship, lest the prayers of the entire community be polluted. The elders and pastors urged the consuls and magistrates to be vigilant, yet this amounted to asking that, in effect, some of the principal players endeavor to eliminate the most innocent games. The consistory excommunicated only the seven most recalcitrant players, individuals whose faults also included quarreling and blasphemy.

Discipline and Sociability: Farces and Comedies
Banishing vice and profligacy meant, first off, the elimination of external agents of disorder from the community. Consuls and judges were

---

[93]AD, Gard 42 J 31, 26/11/1597, fol. 199.
[94]BN, MS Fr. 8667, 19/10/1583. AD, Gard 42 J 28, 18/02/1587.
[95]BN, MS Fr. 8667, 26/10/1580. AD, Gard 42 J 31, 13/01/1595, 13/09/1600.
[96]AD, Gard 42 J 28, 01/10/1583, fol. 59; 42 J 30, 02/12/1592.
[97]Ibid., 16/04/1586, fol. 222; 42 J 30, 25/03/1592, fol. 46; 27/03/1592, fol. 52.
[98]Ibid., 42 J 31, 01/09/1600, fol. 365; 06/09/1600, fol. 365; 06/09/1603.

requested, in their capacity as temporal administrators of the city, to prevent traveling jugglers and tumblers from giving shows and to run them
out of town.[99] The consistory listened in shock when two actors from
Paris, Mathieu Leffebvre and Jacques Morin, requested authorization to
participate in the Lord's Supper. It summarily refused them because of
their profession.[100]

Some farces were, nonetheless, publicly performed by residents of
Nîmes. Radel, a legal professional, donned a faded red bonnet and dress
and set about duping the father-in-law of the bride in the "farce of the
marriage of Monsieur Roquete." Milhau, a goldsmith, who was to play in
a comedy, refused to call off a performance scheduled before the *Juge-
Criminel* and other "considerable" personages. He persisted in declaring
that, having slandered no one, this business was not subject to repri-
mand.[101]

The consistory proved particularly severe when farces and comedies
took their inspiration from the sacred texts, because Scripture, according
to the *Discipline*, was intended for the pulpit. Its action on this point
accorded with Catholic prohibitions, notably the ban by the Council of
Milan in 1566, against performing mystery plays and "sacred dramas."[102]
These theatrical activities, which corrupted and profaned the Gospel,
unfolded at Nîmes principally during the last decade of the sixteenth century.[103] The law clerks and carders had their own specialties. In 1591, the
clerks took inspiration from the beheading of Saint John the Baptist; the
carders from the sacrifice of Abraham, and five years later, the story of
Holofernes and Judith.[104]

Comic actors were occasionally welcomed into private homes. Monsieur de Favier allowed a performance by some Italian buffoons; Mademoiselle de Robert sponsored a tragedy. The *Juge-Criminel*, at his wedding
in 1596, entertained his guests with a comedy. The consistory finally
decided in 1600 to summon the heads of offending households.[105]

---

[99]AD, Gard 42 J 31, 05/05/1599; 42 J 33, 27/04/1607; 42J 34, 26/08/1609; 42 J 35, 08/01/
1614; 42 J 37, 03/01/1625.

[100]AD, Gard 42 J 33, 24/05/1606, fol. 97.

[101]Ibid., 42 J 30, 15/05/1592; 42 J 37, 10/04/1624, fol. 36.

[102]Huisseau, *La Discipline*, chap. 14, art. 28. J. Delumeau, *Naissance et affirmation de la
Réforme*, 2d ed. (Paris: Presses Universitaires de France, 1973), 358.

[103]Seventy-two censures in 1590–99; forty-two in 1600–1669.

[104]AD, Gard 42 J 31, 29/05/1596, fol. 86.

[105]AD, Gard 42 J 29, 05/06/1591, p. 667; 42 J 31, 07/02/1597, fol. 163; 29/02/1596; 10/
05/1600, fol. 347.

The municipal college was another site for the performance of plays, in this instance inspired by classical antiquity. The masters organized these affairs and the students assumed the various roles. In 1599, the consistory requested Professor Pacius to forbid the students to attend comedies. Despite the warnings, he and members of his family performed a play a few weeks later.[106] Four years afterward, Cheyron, the college headmaster, appeared before the consistory along with the Scottish master Adam Abrenethée for having performed an unauthorized comedy. To add insult to injury, they had printed announcements and even posted one on the door of the Protestant temple. The pastor, Ferrier, personally tore it up.[107]

Finally, the consistory saw in these farces and comedies a dangerous and pernicious cooperation with members of the opposing religion. In 1596, a Catholic played the role of Judith's servant woman,[108] and Cheyron was scolded for having recruited two priests for a comedy, along with a pair of choir boys to sing. The Catholic Church was equally adamant. The councils of Bourges in 1584, Aix-en-Provence in 1585, and Bordeaux in 1588 forbade clerical participation in theatrical productions.[109]

Collective and Organized Misconduct: Charivaris and Carnivals
Youthful excesses such as the charivari or carnival presented many of the same problems as dancing, games, and immodest dress. In addition, whether spontaneous or organized, these activities were always popular. They were an acute source of disorderliness. Shouts, noise, music, and disguises worsened the matter. The consistory took a dim view of these traditional structures for collective social control. It defended the interests of the family and the individual, while opposing any and every form of "ransom" as practiced in the charivari.[110] In this sense, the consistory did no more than apply and instill respect for the prohibitions enacted by the Parlement of Toulouse no less than four times beginning in 1535.[111]

For the first offense, a person might reasonably claim ignorance. Jacques Blanc and Jacques Galoffre said that they participated in a chari-

---

[106]AD, Gard 42 J 31, 05/05/1599, fol. 279; 19/05/1599, fol. 280.

[107]Ibid., 42 J 32, 05/11/1603, fol. 189; 12/11/1603, fol. 191.

[108]Ibid., 42 J 31, 05/06/1596, fol. 93.

[109]Delumeau, *Naissance et affirmation de la Réforme*, 358.

[110]J. Le Goff and J. Schmitt, *Le charivari* (Paris: Mouton, 1981).

[111]D. Fabre, "Familles: Le privé contre la coutume," *Histoire de la vie privée*, vol. 3, *De la Renaissance aux Lumières*, ed. P. Ariès and G. Duby (Paris: Seuil, 1986), 568.

vari because they "thought it was the custom of the region." Still, the consistory listened with dismay upon learning that the Saturday before the Christmas Communion service, a group of eighty to a hundred people had raucously serenaded the court clerk, Jean Petit. He bought them off with two écus, a not insignificant sum; and the soldiers of the municipal watch received fifteen sous to look the other way.[112]

Masquerades were an additional aspect of this overindulgence that the consistory sought to discourage. In 1583, on the occasion of the marriages of the sieurs Favier, twenty or so young men disguised themselves as savages, wearing nothing more than some paint on their bodies. All were suspended from the sacrament.[113] The consistory had little taste for these corporeal masquerades, seeing them as reflections of deeper spiritual pretenses, and the source of countless disturbances. Masks also allowed those who wore them to act with impunity. As with playing cards, merchants were requested to burn masks and costumes. Yet in 1594, an informer caught the goldsmith, David Jomard, lending a "savage" costume to Monsieur de La Calmette.[114]

The condemnation of masquerades also involved a ban on carnival or *Caramantran* (Mardi Gras). Carnival was a special tradition among students and a major cause of censure each year. Even Professor Pacius gave them leave to celebrate in 1599; and theology students still relished carnival as late as 1675.[115]

The consistory similarly disapproved of the "revues" sponsored by the guilds of law clerks, cobblers, and carders. These parades took place the day of the election of the corporate masters, the so-called captains and seneschals, or more commonly on the feast day of the guild's patron saint. A great deal of gunfire accompanied the revues as the members of these corporations had the right to carry arms.[116] Beginning in the 1590s, the revue organized at Pentecost by the law clerks and their "seneschal" became an important occasion for dancing. In the face of the determined resolve of this official body, the consistory found its rulings ineffective.

---

[112]BN, MS Fr. 8667, 04/01/1581, 29/12/1581.

[113]AD, Gard 42 J 28, 06/04/1583.

[114]BN, MS Fr. 8667, 01/02/1581, 27/11/1581, 06/12/1581. AD, Gard 42 J 30, 23/02/1594, fol. 256.

[115]AD, Gard 42 J 31, 24/02/1599. L. Guiraud, *Julius Pacius en Languedoc, 1597-1616* (Montpellier: Valat, 1910).

[116]A woman and child were injured in this way in 1591. AD, Gard 42 J 29, 19/06/1591.

The *papegai*, or "parrot," was a time-honored contest that annually bestowed the title of "king" or ruler of youth. The honor went to the best shot. The target, naturally enough, was in the form of a parrot. The competition provided yet another opportunity for festivities. Although the consistory never directly censured these practices, it did warn against the attending excesses.

Finally, consistorial disapproval of these traditional popular festivals even extended to the seemingly innocent practice of the *"roi boit"* (the king drinks). The custom centered on the Epiphany meal. The person who found the special bean baked in the Epiphany cake became the king or queen and had to empty his or her glass in a single gulp. The elders objected to the Epiphany celebration—the festival of the Three Kings—and to the drunkenness which sometimes accompanied its celebration. The consistory voiced the prohibition repeatedly.[117]

All youthful roamings and rovings about the streets, whether by day or night, were suspect. Offenders were labeled street "pounders" or pavement "polishers." Jacques Auffanty had his violin confiscated for having played a noisy song one Sunday at Nîmes. Antoine Fontfroide was scolded for doing much the same with a bagpipe, tambourine, and oboe.[118] A consistory session of 1596 specifically deplored the frequency of these performances.

CONCLUSION

Consistorial action met with success in the construction of a modern society, especially the promotion of the family unit. In the pacification of society, the elders realized even more striking results. The consistory made itself indispensable, and complementary to judicial institutions, as the sole authority capable of resolving common disputes and restoring to each his rights while safeguarding the honor of the parties. It did not, however, find as much approval or facility in the attempt to dissuade the faithful from worldly dissoluteness. It came up against the twin barriers of popular custom and the incoercible needs of human sociability, joviality, and exuberance. People refused to gather only for worship and otherwise remain totally inactive each Sunday. In the sphere of sociability,

---

[117]Ibid., 42 J 31, 05/01/1599.

[118]BN, MS Fr. 8667, 12/01/1583. AD, Gard 42 J 31, 18/09/1596, fol. 127; 42 J 32, 27/11/1602, fol. 125.

members of the well-to-do urban classes inclined to move about more often and, as a result, tended to have family in the neighboring towns. They could hardly not entertain; such a display of a cold severity would have been perceived as offensive and insulting. Maintenance of their station and simultaneous respect for the precepts of the *Discipline* presented grave difficulties. The youth groups and professional corporations who organized and codified their relationships and entertainment within the very heart of the city were extremely reluctant to abandon their traditional festivities.

In imposing the prescriptions of the Decalogue, the consistory infringed upon the realm of the temporal powers. In accord with the attributions that the ecclesiastical *Discipline* settled upon it, the consistory sought to maintain respect for "civil decency." Whether cooperating with the civic authorities or exhorting them to greater diligence, it assumed a precursory role in the establishment of a new moral and social order, one already favored by royal legislation. The battle against popular custom was a task common to both the Protestant and Catholic Reformation. In assuming this role, the consistory was far ahead of the priests newly trained by the Counter-Reformation seminaries.[119] Anne Rulman, in 1605, saw in this new social order the conditions necessary for progress by the subjects of the king of France. Moderation of the base impulses that threatened an orderly society was the foundation for the modern state:

> foreign nations have taken note and prophesy that the general brutality of duels, amorous liberties, indecent dancing, dissoluteness of dress, immensity of expenditures, and unbridled license of games of chance have checked the course of prosperity and hastened the ruin of the French.[120]

Reforming the individual and reforming society constituted a vast, sweeping project. The consistory recognized this solemn burden when it warned Renaud de Frontigny, a soldier from the Ile de France who presented himself as a convert, of "the great difficulties one must bear to follow Jesus Christ."[121]

[119]D. Fabre, "Familles," 574ff.
[120]Rulman, *Harangues*, 291, discourse delivered in 1605.
[121]AD, Gard 42 J 28, 28/03/1587, fol. 271.

Chapter 4

Marking the Taboo: Excommunication in French Reformed Churches

Raymond A. Mentzer

A deep-seated collective desire to classify, organize, and regulate society permeated the Calvinist Reformation of the sixteenth century. Churches within this tradition undertook, for example, innovative comprehensive efforts in the area of vital statistics, where the pastors, elders, and deacons, who gathered weekly in the consistory, developed and maintained uniform registers for baptisms, marriages, and burials.[1] A vigorous concept of election surely reinforced the penchant for arranging and defining the community. After all, these reformers were the saints, active in the creation of a new godly order, nothing less than the holy commonwealth.[2] They also wished to distinguish themselves unequivocally from the "papists." In France, particularly during the first decades of the Reformation, each local consistory kept a record of converts, persons who "renounced idolatry" and joined the true church. There were, in addition, detailed rosters of poor persons entitled to assistance, children under obli-

---

[1] A recent historical study, albeit for a slightly later period, vividly points up the value of the Protestant *état-civil*. Philip Benedict, *The Huguenot Population of France, 1600–1685: The Demographic Fate and Customs of a Religious Minority*, Transactions of the American Philosophical Society, vol. 81, pt. 5 (1991).

[2] Perhaps the most forceful expression of this point of view is Michael Walzer, *The Revolution of the Saints: A Study in the Origins of Radical Politics* (Cambridge: Harvard University Press, 1965).

The author thanks the American Philosophical Society and the Research/Creativity Committee of Montana State University for support of his research. His appreciation also extends to Professor Barbara Davis for her helpful critique of this essay.

gation to attend catechism lessons and regular worship, suspected wrongdoers whose presence the consistory demanded at its next meeting, and
disreputable women who had to be expelled from town. Other lists
methodically enumerated the relatively affluent who made pious testamentary donations for the poor, or whom the church taxed for the maintenance of the pastor, upkeep of buildings, and support of social welfare
programs.[3]

The consistory also kept account of worthy communicants, members of the congregation whose good character, correct behavior, and sat-
isfactory understanding of the faith as verified by the elders entitled them
to share in the Lord's Supper. This sacred communal celebration took
place four times each year, on Easter, Pentecost, early September, and at
Christmastide. The pastor usually announced the service two weeks in
advance, allowing everyone ample time to undertake the necessary spiritual preparation. To avoid profanation of the Eucharist, the elders subsequently distributed entry counters, often ornately decorated metal tokens,
to those persons whom they deemed qualified.[4] Each participant then presented the token to an elder at the entrance to the temple or when he or
she approached the Lord's Table, and no one could receive without doing
so. Altogether, it made for a very well regulated affair. Most churches
maintained registers of the men and women who participated; some—that
of Nîmes, for example—even prepared rolls of those who failed to do so.
The elders then questioned each to learn the reasons behind her or his
delinquency. Above all, these custodians of public well-being and promot-

---

[3]Archives départementales (hereafter AD), Gard, 42 J 28, registre du consistoire de
Nîmes, 1583–1588, fol. 81, 84, 158v, 160v, 203v, 205v, 206v, 207v, 210v, 225, 228v, 233,
233v, 240, 244, 251, 258, 306v, 311v, 329, 330v, 343v, 355v, 372–375; 42 J 29, registre du
consistoire de Nîmes, 1588–91, fols. 28, 95, 121, 286–287, 339; 42 J 30, registre du consistoire de Nîmes, 1591–95, fols. 122v–123v, 136; AD, Hérault, E Dépôt, Ganges GG 24, Actes
du consistoire de Ganges, fols. 35–36v, 77–77v, 127; AD, Tarn, I 8, registre du consistoire de
La Bastide de Saint Amans, le 28 mars 1604; AD, Tarn-et-Garonne, I 1, registre du consistoire
de Montauban, fols. 15, 29v, 106, 155v, 157v, 215v, 263v, 285, 299, 328, 339v; Bibliothèque de l'Arsenal, Paris (hereafter Arsenal), MS 6563, registre du consistoire de Pont-de-
Camarès, 1574–1578, fols. 5, 24v, 26, 39–42, 60v, 87v–88; Bibliothèque de la Société de
l'histoire du Protestantisme français, Paris (hereafter SHPF), MS 222/1, registre des du consistoire de Castelmoron, fols. 69, 85v, 109; MS 453, registre du consistoire de Meyrueis, fol.
83v; Bibliothèque Nationale (hereafter BN), MS fr 8667, registre du consistoire de Nîmes,
1578–83, fols. 140, 142v, 165v, 330v.

[4]The elders of Coutras, for instance, reported to the consistory on the "manner of living, morals, and other things" for each member of the congregation on the Sunday preceding the celebration of the Lord's Supper. Arsenal, MS 6559, fol. 13.

ers of the common good kept lists of the unworthy, rosters of those whom they had excommunicated and thereby barred or "suspended from the Holy Sacrament" (*suspendus de la Cène*).[5]

These procedures were, without question, useful for the control and discipline of the congregation. Lists of communicants and an elaborate token system designed to screen out dishonorable persons were essential to the regulation and encouragement of proper conduct. Such actions also helped to designate the community with far greater precision than had been customary, or perhaps possible, in pre-Reformation society. Records of christenings and conversion lists marked entry into the group; the registration of marriages and deaths noted additional rites of passage; Communion rosters recognized persons in good standing. In short, the records provided a meticulous catalogue of those individuals who were an integral part of the collectivity and, by extension, those who were not. The many lists, particularly the rosters of excommunicates, were more than a matter of record keeping. They were, in briefest terms, what we might dub sorting devices, useful for categorization, classification, and hierarchization.[6] Indeed, to borrow an obsolete meaning of the word "list," they specified the boundaries and defined the limits of the community as well as behavior acceptable to it, and nowhere is this more apparent than in excommunication.

Excommunication was the gravest of all ecclesiastical punishments. It was a last resort, used when pastoral counsel and consistorial admoni-

---

[5]AD, Gard, 42 J 28, fols. 372–375; 42 J 29, fols. 751, 754, 755. AD, Tarn-et-Garonne, I 1, fols. 29v, 269v, 271v, 296, 333. Arsenal, MS 6563, fol. 79v, 81v; Archives Nationales (hereafter AN), TT 234, dossier 6, registre du consistoire de Bédarieux, fols. 833, 836, 839, 842a; TT 269, dossier 25, registre du consistoire de Saint-Gervais, fols. 967–968; BN, MS fr 8666, registre du consistoire de Nîmes, 1561–63, fols. 13, 31, 77, 85, 94, 101v, 105, 111, 111v, 112, 119, 120, 120v, 137, 157, 161v, 176, 177v, 181, 182, 182v, 183v, 204; MS fr 8667, fols. 116, 200v, 321; Janine Garrisson-Estèbe, *Protestants du Midi, 1559-1598* (Toulouse: Privat, 1980), 229–236 and 241–246; Henri Gelin, *Le méreau dans les églises réformées de France et particulièrement dans celles de Poitou* (Saint-Maixent: Reversé, 1891), 12–17; François Martin, "Ganges, action de son consistoire et vie de son église aux 16e et 17e siècle," *Etudes évangéliques* (Revue de théologie de la faculté libre de théologie protestante, Aix-en-Provence), 2 (1942):27–28; Raymond A. Mentzer, Jr., "*Disciplina nervus ecclesiae*: The Calvinist Reform of Morals at Nîmes," *The Sixteenth Century Journal* 18 (1987):95–96; Maurice Oudot de Dainville, "Le consistoire de Ganges à la fin du XVIe siècle," *Revue d'histoire de l'Eglise de France* 18 (1932):472; Gaston Serr, *Une église protestante au XVIe siècle: Montauban* (Aix-en-Provence: La Pensée Universitaire, 1958), 97–103.

[6]A helpful discussion of lists and their significance is Jack Goody, *The Domestication of the Savage Mind* (Cambridge: Cambridge University Press, 1977), 80–111.

tion failed to bring about reconciliation and reform. Simply put, excommunication barred an individual from the company of the faithful and participation in the sacraments of the church, especially the Lord's Supper. It could also isolate her or him from ordinary social and business relationships, and during the Middle Ages, an excommunicate suffered certain civil disabilities too.[7] As a starting point, it seems only reasonable to ask what exactly was excommunication, and what sort of taboo conduct resulted in its application? Historians today are likely to focus on various sociological and anthropological concerns relating to the violation of communal standards of belief and behavior, sexuality and sociability. What, beyond these vital issues, was the enunciated aim of excommunication? Was it regularly achieved? How did the larger community interpret the religious and social ostracism expressed in the action? What were the rituals for reintegration of the excommunicate? How, in short, was this severe measure understood and utilized?

With an eye to the scrutiny of these questions, I have selected ten Protestant sites, two substantial urban centers, and eight lesser towns and villages, for which significant portions of the Reformed consistory's deliberations survive from the latter half of the sixteenth century. All are in the French southwest, an area stretching from the Rhône river to the Atlantic coast, and where Protestantism had extremely strong roots. By the time of the Edict of Nantes of 1598, the majority of French Protestants probably lived in the southern provinces. The larger cities in the survey, along with the inclusive dates of extant documentation, are Montauban (1595–98) and Nîmes (1561–63 and 1578–83). The Protestant population of each city stood at between eight and ten thousand persons during the Wars of Religion. The smaller towns and hamlets are Bédarieux (1579–86), Castelmoron (1597–1604), Coutras (1581–84 and 1589–91), Ganges (1587–92 and

---

[7]The literature on excommunication in the medieval world is substantial. Among the more helpful English language studies are: Richard H. Helmholz, "Excommunication as a Legal Sanction: The Attitudes of the Medieval Canonists," in *Canon Law and the Law of England*, ed. R. H. Helmholz (London: The Hambledon Press, 1987), 101–117; Rosalind Hill, "The Theory and Practice of Excommunication in Medieval England," *History* 42 (1957):1–11; Francis E. Hyland, *Excommunication: Its Nature, Historical Development and Effects* (Washington: Catholic University of America, 1928); Henry C. Lea, *Studies in Church History: The Rise of the Temporal Power—Benefit of Clergy—Excommunication* (Philadelphia: Henry C. Lea; London: Sampson Low, Son, and Marston, 1869); F. Donald Logan, *Excommunication and the Secular Arm in Medieval England: A Study in Legal Procedure from the Thirteenth to the Sixteenth Century* (Toronto: Pontifical Institute of Mediaeval Studies, 1968); idem, "Excommunication," *Dictionary of the Middle Ages*, ed. Joseph R. Strayer, 13 vols. (New York: Scribners, 1982–1989), 4:536–538; Elisabeth Vodola, *Excommunication in the Middle Ages* (Berkeley and Los Angeles: University of California Press, 1986).

1596–1603), Meyrueis (1587–92), Pont-de-Camarès (1574–77), Saint-Amans (1587–1604), and Saint-Gervais (1564–68).

The Reformed churches of France had explicit, mutually agreed upon rules for excommunication. Calvin himself in the *Institutes of the Christian Religion* firmly and pointedly argued for the necessity of church discipline to include censure and excommunication.[8] The *Discipline of the Reformed Churches of France* adopted by the first national Synod at Paris in 1559 also addressed this critical matter. The version subsequently published by the authors of the *Histoire ecclésiastique des Eglises réformées au Royaume de France* in 1580, and again by Jean Aymon in the early eighteenth century, contains forty separate, succinct articles.[9] Articles 27 through 30 treat ecclesiastical correction in its most solemn form; they regulate excommunication. During the years that followed, successive national synods modified and expanded the *Discipline* first adopted at Paris. By the seventeenth century, a lengthy series of provisions addressed the many and complex issues surrounding excommunication.

The articles relating to excommunication in the national *Discipline* provided uniformity of practice and overall guidance. A sentence of excommunication, if it were to have force, required agreement among all Reformed churches in France. To begin, it could not be limited geographically; restricting the ban to a single community would seriously impede its severity and application. When the consistory of Saint-Amans, for example, learned that two men whom it had barred from the Lord's Supper, subsequently went to the nearby town of Castres for the apparent purpose of receiving Communion, it immediately notified the church of Castres. Troubled by rumors that a woman recently arrived from Geneva had been excommunicated by the consistory there, the pastors and elders of Nîmes wrote to the Genevan church before permitting her to receive. They also barred a man from participation in the Lord's Supper upon hearing that the church at Le Vigan had suspended him.[10] In similar fash-

---

[8]Calvin's principal arguments can be found in book IV, chapter XII. John Calvin, *Institutes of the Christian Religion*, ed. John T. McNeill, trans. Ford Lewis Battles, 2 vols. (Philadelphia: Westminster, 1960), 2:1,229–1,254. See also, Patrick Le Gal, *Le droit canonique dans la pensée dialectique de Jean Calvin* (Fribourg: Editions Universitaires, 1984), 142–161.

[9][Jean] Aymon, *Tous les synodes nationaux des Eglises réformées de France*, 2 vols. (The Hague, 1710), 1:1–7; *Histoire ecclésiastique des Eglises réformées au Royaume de France*, ed. G. Baum, E. Cunitz, and R. Reuss. 3 vols. (Nieuwkoop: B. de Graaf, 1974, Reprint of Paris 1883–1889 edition), 1:215–220.

[10]AD, Tarn, I 8, le 20 janvier 1602; BN, MS fr 8666, fols. 49v, 56v, 93.

ion, excommunication was usually not bound by limitations of time. It applied until lifted by the ecclesiastical authorities.[11]

The *Discipline* established two different kinds of excommunication: temporary suspension from the Lord's Supper and full exclusion from the church. The difference between the two roughly corresponded to the medieval church's differentiation between minor and major excommunication. The former deprived a person of reception of the Eucharist. The latter added the full public weight of social and, in pre-Reformation Europe, legal exclusion. It was excommunication in the strict sense. An individual was literally "cut off from the church" (*retranché de l'église*). While the French consistories imposed both sorts, they used them with differing intent and frequency. These coercive measures were part of a graduated system of sanctions and shaming techniques. The successive steps included private fraternal admonition, censure before the entire consistory, temporary suspension from the Lord's Supper, and full excommunication. The *Discipline* urged pastors and elders "to use prudence and to distinguish between one and the other" so that they might wisely and judiciously apply the appropriate censure.[12]

The Reformers saw in minor and major, or lesser and greater excommunication a distinct progression of gravity. At Nîmes, for example, they suspended a woman from the Eucharist because of her adultery and then threatened major excommunication if she returned to her sinful ways. The consistory of Pont-de-Camarès treated another adulterous woman in identical fashion. Two persons who had engaged in a vicious exchange of insults received severe censure and the same counsel: temporary suspension from the sacrament and a warning of full excommunication if the incident were repeated.[13]

---

[11]François Méjan, *Discipline de l'Eglise Réformée de France annotée et précédée d'une introduction historique* (Paris: Editions 'Je Sers,' 1947), 300–307; Michel Reulos, "l'organisation des Eglises réformées françaises et le Synode de 1559," *Bulletin de la Société de l'histoire du Protestantisme français* (hereafter *BSHPF*) 108 (1959):20–22; "Les sources du droit ecclésiastique des églises réformées de France aux XVIe et XVIIe siècles: Ecriture et Discipline," in *Etudes d'histoire du droit canonique dédiées à Gabriel Le Bras*, 2 vols. (Paris: Sirey, 1965), 1:349–350.

[12]Aymon, *Tous les synodes*, 1:59–61; Méjan, *Discipline*, 232–233. Alfred Soman and E. Labrousse, "Le registre consistorial de Coutras, 1582–1584," *BSHPF* 126 (1980):198; Vodola, *Excommunication*, 36, 41–42.

[13]Arsenal, MS 6563, fol. 71–71v; BN, MS fr 8666, fols. 37v–38, 156v. For other examples, see: Arsenal, MS 6559, fol. 32; BN, MS fr 8666, fol. 156v.

The mere threat of excommunication, whether major or minor, was always a powerful instrument for promoting correct conduct or dissuading offenders from a repetition of their sinful ways. The pastors and elders of Nîmes exhorted a man who had put off his marriage for a year because of economic difficulties to resolve the matter promptly on pain of excommunication and banishment from the town. These same men examined a woman's refusal to abide by written promises to marry a goldsmith. They concluded that the betrothal promises were binding and gave her twenty-four hours to "change her mind." Otherwise, they would bar her from Communion. The Consistory of Montauban, reinforced by the colloquy of Bas-Quercy, threatened the elders at the nearby church of Meauzac with lesser excommunication when they balked at paying a former pastor's back salary. Perhaps more typical is an incident that occurred at Ganges. Ecclesiastical officials admonished a woman for dancing at a Catholic votive festival at an adjacent village and then threatened suspension from the sacrament if she repeated the offense. This same group, after censuring a man for blasphemy and gambling, warned that he would be publicly excommunicated if he continued these activities.[14] Though these stern cautions may have been effective, they were hardly welcome. When church authorities at Nîmes threatened to excommunicate a woman for sending her son to the Jesuit *collège* at Tournon, her annoyance was unmistakable. She replied that they should "excommunicate whores and not respectable persons."[15]

The French Protestants administered full excommunication, a stern measure that separated a person from the "comfort" of the faithful in addition to precluding the reception of the Holy Sacrament, far less often than simple suspension (minor excommunication). The pastors and elders reserved complete excommunication for serious sins and egregious breaches of behavior. They never imposed the penalty indiscriminately, certainly not without serious reflection. The church at the remote mountainous village of Saint-Gervais, for example, routinely consulted the regional colloquy whenever it contemplated applying this severe punishment.[16]

[14]AD, Gard, 42 J 29, 177; AD, Hérault, E Dépôt, Ganges GG 24, fols. 89, 143v–144; AD, Tarn-et-Garonne, I 1, fols. 304–304v, 309v, 311–311v, 313, 315v–316v, 327, 332; BN, MS fr 8666, fols. 141, 162v.

[15]BN, MS fr 8667, fol. 353v.

[16]AN, TT 269, dossier 25, fols. 961v, 962; Méjan, *Discipline*, 303.

The French Calvinists expanded the medieval church's concept of minor or lesser excommunication by applying it often, and for a broad spectrum of offenses. Major excommunication was a far rarer occurrence. Over a period of seven years between 1579 and 1586, the consistory at the town of Bédarieux in the Cévennes mountains mentioned the word "excommunication," meaning major excommunication, but once and then merely to threaten an especially hardened multiple offender who steadfastly refused to submit to correction. During the same time, it suspended twenty persons from participation in the Lord's Supper and threatened the action in a number of additional instances. The actions of other churches were analogous (see Table 1). At Castelmoron, a town along the Lot river north of Agen, the minister and elders suspended 47 men and women over eight years between 1597 and 1604, while excommunicating only 1 person. The church of Pont-de-Camarès in the Rouergue suspended 17 persons and fully excommunicated 3 others during a four-year span in the mid-1570s. The consistory of Saint-Amans, whose records are remarkably continuous, suspended 136 persons over the course of eighteen years beginning in the late 1580s, but did not fully excommunicate a single individual.

Table 1: Sentences of Major and Minor Excommunication

Location	Minor Excommunication	Major Excommunication
Urban Centers		
Montauban	73	7
Nîmes	99	5
SUBTOTAL	172 (93%)	12 (7%)
Rural World		
Bédarieux	20	0
Castelmoron	47	1
Coutras	22	3
Ganges	76	2
Meyrueis	17	1
Pont-de-Camarès	17	3
Saint-Amans	136	0
Saint-Gervais	2	0
SUBTOTAL	337 (97%)	10 (3%)
TOTAL	509 (96%)	22 (4%)

The data from several other towns, though fragmentary, confirm the pattern: many more suspensions than full excommunications. The tiny church at Saint-Gervais—the elders there recorded only ninety-three communicants—suspended two men and threatened another with major excommunication during a five-year period in the late 1560s. The consistory of Coutras, far to the west in the vicinity of Bordeaux, suspended twenty-two individuals and completely excommunicated three others over the span of eight years in the 1580s and early 1590s. Sporadic registers from the church at Ganges, located in the rugged uplands north of Montpellier, indicate that its consistory, at a minimum, suspended seventy-six individuals and fully excommunicated two others from the late 1580s through the early 1600s.

The pattern of excommunications at Montauban, a major population center that was home to some ten thousand Protestants, suggests much the same. Over three and a half years from mid-1595 to late 1598, the consistory issued seventy-three sentences of lesser excommunication and seven of the greater type. Practice within the Reformed Church of Nîmes, a town of analogous size, was similar. Over some two years beginning in 1561, the consistory temporarily prohibited thirty-three persons from participating in the approaching Communion service and fully excommunicated another four. A few years later, between 1578 and 1583, this same consistory suspended sixty-six persons from the Lord's Supper, while issuing but a single sentence of major excommunication. Altogether, fewer than one in twenty excommunications (4 percent) were major; the overwhelming majority (96 percent) were minor.

The consistories in the ten towns and villages encompassed by the present study issued a total of 531 sentences of excommunication, both major and minor. The reasons for the sentences break down into sixteen principal categories (see Table 2). Nearly three-quarters of all excommunications fall into the first five classifications (see Graph on page 107). Disputes and quarrels—boisterous verbal confrontations and, occasionally, bodily injuries—make up the largest category. The second leading reason for excommunication was illicit sexual activity, either adultery or fornication. Together, these two categories account for 40 percent of the total. The findings are not surprising on several counts. To begin, bickering and squabbling were the most prevalent of all transgressions (not merely those deserving excommunication) that the French consistories sought to correct. It seems only natural that some of these disputes resulted in excommunication. In addition, quarrels were the principal reason for excommunication

Table 2: Reason for all Excommunications

	Montauban	Nîmes	Bédarieux	Castel-moron	Coutras	Ganges	Meyrueis	Pont-de-Camarès	Saint-Amans	Saint-Gervais	Total	Percent of Total
Disputes & Quarrels	22	22	3	16	2	10	8	7	26	0	116	22
Adultery & Fornication	12	34	5	5	3	14	3	2	20	0	98	18
Dancing	1	0	0	1	4	31	0	0	27	0	64	12
Contact with "Popery"	16	16	1	8	3	3	0	0	13	2	62	12
"Rebellion" & Contumacy	6	12	2	7	2	8	1	6	10	0	54	10
Marriage Difficulties	9	4	3	1	0	4	3	0	0	0	24	4
Gaming & Gambling	0	0	2	0	0	0	0	0	15	0	17	3
Blasphemy	1	6	0	0	0	0	0	0	6	0	13	2
Pending Criminal Actions	2	5	0	0	0	1	0	1	1	0	10	2
Refusal to Contribute	6	0	0	2	0	0	0	1	0	0	9	2
Resort to Sorcery	1	1	3	0	0	0	0	0	0	0	5	1
Apostasy	1	0	0	0	2	0	0	0	0	0	3	1
Drunkenness & Indolence	0	0	0	1	2	0	0	0	0	0	3	1
"Idolatry" on Benefice	2	1	0	0	0	0	0	0	0	0	3	1
Miscellaneous	0	2	0	0	0	0	0	0	5	0	7	1
Unknown	1	1	1	7	7	7	3	3	13	0	43	8

Reasons for all
Excommunications

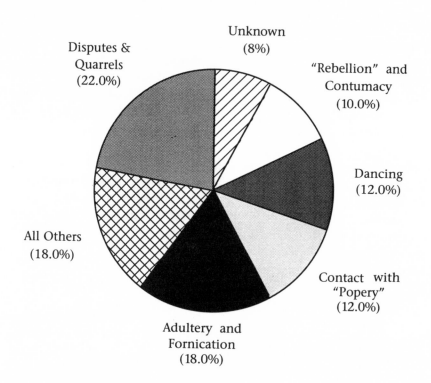

Disputes &
Quarrels
(22.0%)

Unknown
(8%)

"Rebellion" and
Contumacy
(10.0%)

Dancing
(12.0%)

All Others
(18.0%)

Contact with
"Popery"
(12.0%)

Adultery and
Fornication
(18.0%)

in other Calvinist communities, notably the city of Geneva during the late 1560s.[17] Sexual offenses, while less common, were nonetheless a transgression that consistories everywhere took seriously.[18] Matters such as adultery and fornication violated rudimentary Scriptural injunctions as contained in the Decalogue. They also seemed to threaten primary social

[17]E. W. Monter, "The Consistory of Geneva, 1559–1569," *Bibliothèque d'Humanisme et Renaissance* 38 (1976): 479.

[18]Mentzer, "*Disciplina nervus ecclesiae*," *The Sixteenth Century Journal* 18 (1987): 108–109; idem, "Le consistoire et la pacification du monde rural," *BSHPF,* 135 (1989): 378–384.

institutions such as marriage and the family, which were themselves deemed fitting structures for leading a moral and useful life.

The dimensions of the next three classifications—dancing, contact with "popery," and "rebellion" and contumacy—are roughly equivalent. Each was 10 to 12 percent of the total. Together, they constitute another third of all excommunications. This second echelon of excommunicable offenses reveals, in part, the persistence of contaminating associations with Catholicism. Dancing, for example, frequently took place within the context of Protestant participation in votive festivals and traditional folk celebrations held in Catholic communities. Other, more explicit contacts with "popery" focused on marriage to a Catholic or involvement in Catholic religious rites. Although a different sort of offense, "rebellion" and contumacy, which is to say, failure to submit to the authority of the consistory, led to excommunication with roughly the same frequency.

The remaining categories for excommunication cover a sizable assortment, even though they account for only a quarter of the total cases. They include marriage problems, gambling, blasphemy, suspension pending criminal process, refusal to contribute to the church, recourse to sorcery and magic, apostasy, drunkenness, and allowing Catholic services on ecclesiastical benefices that had been leased by Protestants. Finally, there are a fair number of excommunications, 8 percent, for which the specific reason is unknown. As we proceed to careful examination of these causes, let us differentiate them according to sentences of major and minor as well as public and private excommunication.

The Reformed churches employed major excommunication in cases of apostasy and heresy and, more commonly, outrageous adultery. Excommunication for heresy was rare. Sensational examples, such as the apostate pastor Gaspard d'Olaxe at Castres or Jérémie Ferrier at Nîmes, are well known, but exceptional.[19] There were very few excommunications of this nature. The consistory of Coutras excommunicated François Delagarde and Jehan Desalles for their "apostasy." Delagarde, in an unusual reversal of gender roles, married a Catholic woman and "returned to popery." In

[19]On the subject of Olaxe and Ferrier, see: Jacques Gaches, *Mémoires sur les guerres de religion à Castres et dans le Languedoc (1555-1610)*, ed. Charles Pradel (Geneva: Slatkine, 1970; reprint of 1879-94 Paris edition), 440-451; Camille Rabaud, *Histoire du Protestantisme dans l'Albigeois et le Lauragais*, 2 vols. (Paris: Fischbacher, 1873 and 1898), 1:182-187, 472-475; P. Koch, "Jérémie Ferrier, pasteur de Nîmes (1601-13)," *BSHPF* 89 (1940):9-21, 152-163, 237-261, 341-370; Joël Poivre, *Jérémie Ferrier (1576-1626). Du Protestantisme à la raison d'état* (Geneva: Librairie Droz, 1990).

the only other instance of apostasy from this survey, Marie de Bruguier, who had been "baptized, nourished, and raised" in the Reformed Church of Montauban, abandoned Protestantism at the moment of her marriage to a Catholic man, declaring that she wished to "live and die in the papist religion." Despite pleas for understanding by her distraught sisters, the consistory fully and publicly excommunicated the woman.[20] The sisters' distress took place on several levels: They lamented the harsh punishment inflicted upon an immediate blood relative; normal social dealings with a sibling were now forbidden; finally, the whole family shared the public disgrace.

Adultery and fornication were the second leading grounds for excommunication in both its greater and lesser forms. For one or two churches this was an especial concern. A third of all excommunications at Nîmes resulted from improper sexual behavior. Many cases involved women who had given birth to a child out of wedlock, an action that endangered the orderliness and stability of marriage and family structure, which pastors and elders sought so ardently to maintain. Flagrant sexual misconduct, moreover, invariably led to major excommunication. The consistory of Nîmes fully excommunicated Jacques Ursi for carrying on an adulterous relationship with a married woman over a period of seven or eight years. The same sanction befell a woman who invited a neighbor's "papist" servant into her bed while her husband was out of town. The consistory excommunicated a teenage schoolboy and the mother of a classmate after the unlikely pair had spent several hours alone in a weaver's bedroom. It also publicly excommunicated the weaver for permitting such conduct in his house.[21]

Temporary suspension from the Lord's Supper, like the lesser excommunication that the medieval church had defined and recognized by the early thirteenth century, was intrinsically corrective and penitential.[22] A person could not participate in one of the four annual Communion services but remained a part of the community. According to the *Discipline,*

---

[20]AD, Tarn-et-Garonne, I 1, fols. 134, 135v–136, 137–136v, 144, 145, 148–149, 150–150v, 153–153v; Arsenal, MS 6559, fols. 29v, 32.

[21]BN, MS fr 8666, fols. 19, 20, 26v, 77v–80, 103v.

[22]Neither "major" nor "minor" excommunication was official terminology. In the case of the latter, most consistories borrowed the medieval expression *suspensio*. Thus the consistory of Nîmes would declare a person "suspended" (*suspendu*) from participation in the Lord's Supper. The consistory of Montauban, on the other hand, preferred the word "prohibited" (*interdit*). Serr, *Montauban*, 100–101; Vodola, *Excommunication*, 42 n. 55.

the intention was to "humble sinners and move them to a more profound sense of their failings."[23] Consequently, the suspension, its cause, and the brief ceremony that reconciled the repentant offender to the church were usually private matters limited to the consistory and the wrongdoer.

The two great exceptions to the rule of confidentiality, as outlined in the *Discipline*, involved persons who participated in Catholic marriages or baptisms, and individuals accused of criminal acts where conviction entailed corporal punishment. Their behavior heaped scandal upon the church and the consistory publicized these suspensions, usually from the pulpit at the Sunday worship, in order to absolve the church of any reproach and to remind the faithful of the danger of these transgressions. Religiously mixed marriages, in particular, amounted to a kind of confessional miscegenation and were regarded as extremely dangerous. They threatened the faith in a manner unlike any other action. There was always a risk that a person would apostatize and join the spouse's faith. Given a husband's domination as head of the household, women appear to have been under greater pressure than men in this regard.[24] More important, mixed unions jeopardized the spiritual welfare of the next generation— the children born to the marriages. Again, women who married Catholic men likely acquiesced to their spouses in the religious upbringing of their offspring. These various concerns prompted the Nîmes consistory to bar a carder, his wife, and his daughter from the Lord's Supper because of the young woman's marriage to a Catholic. The pastor, moreover, announced their punishment to "the people" to set an "example" for other folk lest they succumb to the same fault. Antoine Bergier and his spouse as well as a carter of Montauban and his wife were similarly suspended from the sacrament and made to perform public reparation after they allowed their daughters to wed papists.[25]

[23]Méjan, *Discipline*, 233.

[24]See, for example, AD, Tarn-et-Garonne, I 1, fol. 134.

[25]The Nîmes church made a general announcement that persons "who married papists will perform public reparation." BN, MS fr 8667, fols. 42v, 104v, 105–105v, 121v; AD, Hérault, E Dépôt, Ganges GG 24, fol. 21v; AD, Tarn-et-Garonne, I 1, fols. 324v–325; Aymon, *Tous les synodes*, 1:203; Janine Estèbe and Bernard Vogler, "La genèse d'une société protestante: Étude comparée de quelques registres consistoriaux languedociens et palatins vers 1600," *Annales: Économies, sociétés, civilisations* 31 (1976):372; Martin, "Ganges," *Etudes évangéliques* 2 (1942):24; Méjan, *Discipline*, 233, 237. For other examples, see: AD, Tarn, I 8, le 20 décembre 1600, le 1 septembre 1601; Arsenal, MS 6559, fol. 43v; AD, Tarn-et-Garonne, I 1, fols. 140v, 227v–228, 307.

The consistory treated persons charged with grave criminal acts, roughly the equivalent of felony offenses, in analogous fashion. These accusations and subsequent trials disgraced the church and, as a result, called for firm action and public acknowledgment. The consistory of Pont-de-Camarès enjoined a nobleman from receiving the sacrament on account of a murder charge lodged against him; he needed first to establish his innocence. Two men were immediately and publicly excluded from the sacrament when brought to trial in the presidial court of Nîmes on charges of forced abduction. Several other men and women suffered similar public exclusions until they "purged" themselves of accusations of battery and murder. A notary at Montauban took his wife to court, accusing her of adultery. The consistory prohibited her from reception of the sacrament until she cleared herself of the charge.[26]

As a practical matter, the consistory sometimes publicized suspensions for other reasons as well. When two men from Pont-de-Camarès quarreled to the point of open violence and bodily injury, the consistory restored peace between them, barred them from participating in the Easter Communion service, and then announced the penalty to the entire congregation. The church of Bédarieux openly proclaimed the suspension of an unmarried pregnant woman. The visible evidence of her sin—swollen belly and eventual infant—demanded a public declaration. The consistory thereby advised everyone that it had dealt firmly with these obvious and disgraceful deeds, scandals that, if left uncorrected, reflected badly on the entire community.[27]

What were the precise grounds for minor excommunication or, as it was commonly labeled, suspension? In reality, there appears to have been considerable interpretative latitude. Bernard Constans, the unyielding and legalistic pastor of Pont-de-Camarès during the 1570s, attempted to prescribe and compel a stern moral order that, not surprisingly, irritated many townsfolk. With the assistance of the elders, he composed a series of articles plainly stipulating the transgressions for which a person could be "suspended from the Lord's Supper and, if need be, expelled from the church." This litany of sins, which he subsequently promulgated from the pulpit, encompassed refusal to take instruction in proper prayers, God's

---

[26]AD, Hérault, E Dépôt, Ganges GG 24, fol. 4v; AD, Tarn-e-Garonne, I 1, fols. 82v, 342; Arsenal, MS 6563, fol. 10; BN, MS fr 8667, fols. 112, 137, 211, 212, 253, 288v, 330v, 332, 335, 351, 372.

[27]AN, TT 234, dossier 6, fol. 827; Arsenal, MS 6563, fols. 4v–5.

commandments, the sacraments, and the "rudiments of Christianity."
Other wrongs were blasphemy, playing dice and cards, disobedience
toward the consistory or the civil authorities, battering one's relatives or
neighbors, commission of violent crimes, and in general leading a "scandalous life."[28] Although not all ecclesiastical officials shared Constans'
probing sense of human culpability, they did bar individuals from
Communion.

The occasion for many suspensions was similar to the case of a
butcher who squabbled with another man and then refused to make up.
He was barred from Communion until he agreed to reconciliation. In a
more serious vein, a man clashed violently with a soldier. He wounded the
man with a sword blow to the head and, showing no sign of remorse, was
suspended.[29] Quarreling, both oral and physical, was never-ending and
ubiquitous. It was the leading reason for all excommunications, account-
ing for 22 percent of the total (see Table 2). Although disputes were
extremely common and the consistory everywhere sought to restore harmony,[30] the offense did not usually result in excommunication. The
exceptions were those instances in which feuding parties refused to make
up or where the dispute was extreme and led to bloodshed.

Another frequent cause of suspension—one suggested earlier—was
sexual scandal. Examples abound: the proprietor of a cookshop fathered a
child out of wedlock, a merchant of Bédarieux committed fornication and
then adamantly refused to submit to correction, a woman at Nîmes had an
illicit sexual relationship with a Catholic priest. At Meyrueis, the consistory suspended a man from the September celebration of the Eucharist for
having gotten a young woman pregnant.[31]

---

[28]Arsenal, MS 6563, fols. 62v–63; Frank Delteil, "Institutions et vie de l'Eglise réformée
de Pont de Camarès," in *Les églises et leurs institutions au XVIe siècle: Actes du Ve Colloque de
Centre d'Histoire de la Réforme et du Protestantisme,* ed. Michel Péronnet (Montpellier: Université Paul Valéry, 1978), 96–97, 102–105.

[29]BN, MS fr 8667, fols. 161v, 166, 169, 178v.

[30]Half of all offenders (not merely excommunicates) who appeared before the consistories of Nîmes and Meyrueis were chastised for disputes and quarrels. The proportion was
one-third at Castelmoron and one-quarter at Montauban. Throughout southern France,
quarrels averaged about one-third of all infractions that the Reformed consistories sought to
correct. Mentzer, *"Disciplina nervus ecclesiae,"* *The Sixteenth Century Journal* 18 (1987):108–
109; Estèbe and Vogler, "La genèse d'une société protestante," *Annales: Économies, sociétés,
civilisations* 31 (1976):378–379; Garrisson-Estèbe, *Protestants du Midi,* 244–245.

[31]AN TT 234, dossier 6, fols. 812, 828a, 829a, 830; BN, MS fr 8666, fols. 104, 121v, 126,
162, 187, 190; MS fr 8667, fols. 330, 332, 334; SHPF, MS 453, fols. 56–56v.

A substantial number of persons found themselves placed under minor excommunication for dancing. The instances tended, however, to be concentrate at two towns—Ganges and Saint-Amans—during the early seventeenth century, which is to say, toward the end of the present survey. In 1600, the consistory of Ganges suspended ten men and twenty women from the Pentecost Communion service for having danced at the nearby village of Laroque on the first of May, a traditional occasion for festivities welcoming the change of season. The following year, the pastor and elders of Saint-Amans suspended several men for having danced and celebrated Mardi Gras "in papist fashion."[32] On other occasions, the consistory suspended members of the faithful for dancing at votive festivals in nearby Catholic towns. Dancing was indecent and polluting. It was the foul distraction of "pagans and idolaters." Such debauchery, wholly unsuited to "Christians," reflected the blasphemous attachment that "pagans and infidels" had for their "idols."[33] The offense, in these instances, was worse because of its association with "superstitious" popish customs, which the Reformers regarded as profane and ardently sought to eradicate. According to the Reformers, medieval folk and religious festivities, and the dancing that regularly accompanied them, were completely immoral.

A related reason for minor excommunication is one that I have designated "contact with 'popery.'" It generally fell into one of two categories: marriage to a papist in a Catholic ritual, or attendance at Mass and other rites while visiting a Catholic town or village. Protestant ecclesiastical authorities, as already noted, had little tolerance for persons who took a Catholic spouse and celebrated their marriage before a priest. Several individuals were excommunicated merely for being present at such a marriage ceremony. Any involvement with the Catholic liturgy was, if judged by consistorial inclination to excommunicate, a dangerous breach of behavior. Thus, the minister and elders of Castelmoron denied Communion to a man who heard Mass while visiting Agen. The Nîmes consistory suspended an attorney for going to Mass while a student at Toulouse, a woman for doing the same while visiting Avignon. The church of Saint-Amans excommunicated a miller for attending a "papist" funeral at a

---

[32]AD, Hérault, E Dépôt, Ganges GG 24, fols. 123–124v; AD, Tarn, I 8, le 31 août 1601, le 1er septembre 1601.

[33]According to the church of Saint-Amans, dancing "n'appartient pas à ung crestien fors sulement aux payens et ydolattres." AD, Tarn, I 8, le 29 et 31 mai 1602. See as well the admonition to Paul Vinhele; AD, Tarn, I 8, le 10 janvier 1604.

neighboring hamlet, and a woman for taking part in a Catholic baptism.[34]

The consistory also took seriously any attempt to defy or ignore its authority, an offense it labeled "rebellion." A woman was excommunicated for her absolute unwillingness to answer any of the consistory's questions, other folk for denying misconduct of which the consistory apparently had ample evidence. An altogether more common aspect of rebellion, essentially insubordination toward the consistory, was contumacy. Much as the medieval jurists had defined it, excommunication here resulted from the failure of the incorrigible to turn up when summoned. The consistory could, in following the advice of the *Discipline*, declare a person contumacious upon failure to heed three summonses. A law clerk insulted and even slapped a pastor. When, following three requests to appear, he obstinately refused to submit to correction, the consistory excommunicated him. The pastor and elders of Saint-Amans asked Daniel Dougados to come before them and explain reports that he lit a large bonfire on the eve of the feast of Saint John the Baptist, a traditional midsummer festival that the reformers viewed as another superstitious "papist" practice. The man refused to comply, and after he ignored three successive summonses, the consistory suspended him from the sacrament. Church officials could, nonetheless, be more lenient. As an extreme example, the Nîmes consistory summoned a woman for malicious slander and repeated the call more than a dozen times before losing patience and excommunicating her.[35]

The use of excommunication in these latter cases was similar to its employ during the Middle Ages. Under medieval canon law (although there were some inroads on the principle, and many abuses), a sentence of excommunication was meant to compel the stubbornly obstinate or contumacious to appear and answer to the charge at hand. Its purpose, in this respect, was more corrective than punitive. The intention was to induce a

---

[34]AD, Tarn, I 8, le 2 juin 1599, le 15 décembre 1602; BN, MS fr 8667, fols. 297, 366v; SHPF, MS 222/1, fol. 94.

[35]AD, Gard, 42 J 28, fols. 372–375; 42 J 31, fol. 98v; AD, Hérault, E Dépôt, Ganges GG 24, fol. 83; AD, Tarn, I 8, le 27 juin, 4 juillet, 11 juillet, 5 décembre, and 29 décembre 1599, le 20 septembre 1603; AD, Tarn-et-Garonne, I 1, fol. 298; BN, MS fr 8666, fols. 15v, 20, 22, 43, 44, 50, 77v–80, 89, 95–96v, 99, 103v, 128, 132v; MS fr 8667, fols. 199, 206, 207, 210, 213v, 215, 220, 221v, 222v, 226v, 229v, 232, 237, 238, 355; Helmholz, "Excommunication as a Legal Sanction," 106; Logan, *Excommunication*, 15; Méjan, *Discipline*, 233–234; Vodola, *Excommunication*, 36–37.

person to reconciliation and repentance. The excommunicate's willingness to accept the judgment of the church would itself normally entitle her or him to a lifting of the sentence. The same applied to those Calvinists who, though initially recalcitrant, eventually submitted to the will of the church and made the required appearance before the consistory. On the other hand, the French Reformers sometimes altered medieval practice and made minor excommunication a penal sanction in, say, the modern sense of imprisonment. These persons had to accept a term of suspension from the Lord's Supper—typically from one specified service—for having committed a sin. It was itself a penalty. Thus, the church of Pont-de-Camarès punished two quarrelsome men by prohibiting them from receiving Communion "for a single time." Ecclesiastical officers at Ganges barred a woman from the upcoming September celebration of the Eucharist, after she scandalized the town by receiving a man into her home one evening during her husband's absence. They similarly excluded two ambitious noblewomen from the Christmas Communion service, because they had previously engaged in a shoving match, each trying to get ahead of the other in the Communion line and, accordingly, display superiority of social position. The consistory of Saint-Amans suspended a pair of men from the next Lord's Supper following their involvement in a bloody brawl. It acted likewise with a man and two women who danced at Catholic festivities at a neighboring village on the feast of the Virgin Mary.[36]

As noted earlier, the major categories of offenses—quarrels, sexual faults, dancing, association with Catholicism, and contumacy—account for nearly three-quarters of all excommunications (both minor and major) in this study (see Table 2). The remaining sentences, again mostly suspensions, stemmed from a wide range of infractions. There were, for example, a variety of difficulties relating to marriage. Suspension sometimes occurred when one or another participant balked at honoring betrothal vows, the binding promises to wed. The consistory of Ganges suspended Jehan Séguy, his parents, and his fiancée because of their recalcitrance in proceeding with the couple's wedding. Despite the young man's claim of financial insolvency, the consistory insisted upon solemnization of the marriage and barred the responsible parties from the Eucharist until settlement of the union.[37]

[36]AD, Hérault, E Dépôt, Ganges GG 24, fol. 9v, 116v, 117v; AD, Tarn, I 8, le 5 septembre 1587, le 10 septembre 93; Arsenal, MS 6559, fols. 4v–5, 42v, 44v.

[37]AD, Hérault, E Dépôt, Ganges GG 24, fols. 72v–73.

Ecclesiastical officers at Bédarieux and Saint-Amans temporarily excluded seventeen persons for their habitual playing of games and gambling. In late 1594, for instance, the consistory of Saint-Amans lost patience with three incorrigible men whom it had repeatedly censured for card playing. It finally suspended them in the expectation that this severe measure would induce a change of behavior. Grievous blasphemy sometimes elicited a similar response. The pastors and elders of Montauban suspended Jehan Latapie until he atoned for his irreverent utterances. Those at Nîmes barred a cobbler from Communion after he blasphemed "against Christ," another man when he invoked the devil. The consistory of Pont-de-Camarès had explicit rules for dealing with repeated blasphemy: private rebuke in the consistory's chambers for the first offense, punishment before the entire congregation for the second, and excommunication in the event of a third infraction.[38]

The Reformed consistories occasionally suspended individuals, invariably men, for failure to pay the monetary "contribution" that the church assessed them for the pastor's salary, poor relief, building maintenance, and so forth. The elders and pastor at Coutras pointedly warned the faithful to meet their obligation, lest they be excommunicated; those of Castelmoron, Montauban, and Pont-de-Camarès made good the threat and suspended several delinquents. Much as the church excluded persons for moral and religious failings, so it excluded them for neglect of what it perceived to be their legitimate financial responsibilities.[39] The language of the consistory suggests its viewpoint. It labeled these men "ingrates." They had thanklessly disregarded their basic obligations to a church that endeavored to assist them in the struggle for eternal salvation. A related evasion of duty, and possible cause for excommunication, centered on reluctance to accept ecclesiastical office. Pierre Jourdain declined election as deacon in the Church of Coutras. The consistory responded that he had no valid excuse and ordered him to agree to the charge or suffer censure and suspension from the Lord's Supper.[40]

Finally, there was a handful of lesser excommunications for dabbling in magic, recurrent drunkenness, tolerating "idolatry," and the like. Three women from Bédarieux were suspended after consulting a sorceress. At

[38]AD, Tarn, I 8, le 21 décembre 1594; AD, Tarn-et-Garonne, I 1, fols. 215v–216; Arsenal, MS 6563, fol. 30; BN, MS fr 8666, fols. 94, 101; MS fr 8667, fol. 37v.

[39]AD, Tarn-et-Garonne, I 1, fols. 280, 282, 283–283v, 292v, 357v; Arsenal, MS 6559, fols. 40v, 43v; SHPF, MS 222/1, fols. 42v, 50v; Martin, "Ganges," *Etudes évangéliques* 2 (1942):32–35.

[40]Arsenal, MS 6559, fol. 38v.

Nîmes, a peasant suffered the theft of some money. When he consulted an "enchanter" to divine the identity of the robber, the consistory suspended him from the September celebration of the Lord's Supper. A man from Castelmoron was barred from Communion for chronic drinking, another at Coutras for his unrestrained fondness for hunting, even to the point of Sabbath breach. The consistories of Montauban and Nîmes suspended several businessmen, who held lease to ecclesiastical benefices, for failing to eradicate "idolatry"—the celebration of the Mass—on these lands. [41]

Not all excommunications, incidentally, sprang from the violation of a strict moral and religious code. Some sentences focused on matters of societal custom, public decency, and simple human understanding. The consistory of Saint-Amans suspended a woman for arranging her hair in an intricate twisted style. Though this was typically a minor affront, the woman's behavior in this instance touched a deeper nerve within the social mores. She was supposed to be in mourning for her recently deceased father. Another woman approached the communal oven of Saint-Amans one wintry day, only to find a dying beggar lying in her path. She cursed the sick pauper, took hold of his feet, and dragged him aside where he could "croak" out of sight. Her lack of compassion—"cruelty" according to the pastor—earned an immediate suspension from the sacrament. [42]

In all of this, the strength and effectiveness of excommunication flowed from the theological and social significance attached to the Lord's Supper and its reception, the absolute necessity of remaining in the good graces of the church for a variety of services (above all those pertaining to baptism and marriage), and the ostracism of excommunicates from normal social and economic relationships. The Lord's Supper held a pivotal position in the life and worship of all members of the congregation. Baptism and the Eucharist were the only two sacraments in the Calvinist tradition. They were signs and tokens, "pledges and seals of God's grace," which served to "aid and comfort" the faithful. The Lord's Supper, in particular, witnessed the union of the faithful with Christ. It was the "spiritual nourishment" that strengthened those who received the bread and wine in faith. [43] On a different level, the Eucharist had potent social con-

---

[41] AD, Tarn-et-Garonne, I 1, fols. 290v–291; AN, TT 234, dossier 6, fols. 847a–848; Arsenal, MS 6559, fols. 30v–31v; BN, MS fr fols. 124, 195; MS fr 8667, fol. 353; SHPF, MS 222/1, fol. 79.

[42] AD, Tarn I 8, le 15 août, le 23 décembre 1594, le 19 et 23 décembre 1601, le 3 et 5 avril 1602.

[43] See the Confession of Faith, especially articles 34–38, approved by the National Synod at Paris in 1559; *Histoire ecclésiastique* 1:201–215.

notations; it conveyed notions of fellowship, peace, and concord. The religious ceremony could be construed as a meal of reconciliation. The sharing of food is an intimate human activity, which can serve to define a moral community. Excommunication, exclusion from the celebration of the sacramental meal, followed from some rupture of the moral code. Subsequent readmittance to the Eucharist and the reconciliation implicit in eating the bread and drinking the wine depended upon the restoration of proper social relations, the repair of imperfections in the intricate fabric of public conduct. Thus, the Lord's Supper, exclusion from it, and readmission to it became powerful symbols for establishing the moral and social body, fixing its borders, and setting the terms of entry and exit.[44]

The activities of the consistory confirm the notion of the shared sacramental meal as an opportunity for reconciliation in another important way. The period of two weeks or so between the pastor's announcement of the service and its actual conduct was the specific occasion for settling unresolved conflict and contacting wrongdoers who had thus far failed to make amends. The church of Ganges, for example, pointedly invited the recalcitrant to appear before the consistory in order to end their factious disputes, propel them to solemnize marriages that they had vowed to undertake, accept censure for misdeeds such as gambling or dancing, and demonstrate penitence by performing the required reparation. Other churches also seem to have used the time immediately before the Lord's Supper as an occasion for contrition and communal reconciliation.[45] The clear incentive to comply was the promise of admission to the upcoming Lord's Supper. This was an appropriate and favored moment for repentance and the restoration of communal harmony. And some excommunicates did use this opportunity to reclaim their place within the congregation.

The faithful generally understood and took seriously the standards of comportment necessary for participation in the Lord's Supper. There

[44]John Bossy, "The Mass as a Social Institution 1200-1700," *Past and Present* 100 (August 1983):29-61; David W. Sabean, *Power in the Blood: Popular Culture and Village Discourse in Early Modern Germany* (Cambridge: Cambridge University Press, 1984), 43, 46, 59, 209.

[45]See, for example, AD, Hérault, E Dépôt, Ganges GG 24, fols. 19v, 25v-26, 68v-69, 73-73v, 98, 103-105v, 113, 116-117, 120, 142-143. The registers of the consistory of Bédarieux (AN, TT 234, dossier 6), Coutras (Arsenal, MS 6559, fol. 13), Meyrueis (SHPF, MS 453, fol. 85v), and Saint-Amans (AD, Tarn, I 8) suggest practices similar to those at Ganges. The church of Nîmes, given its much larger congregation, began reviewing its "list of excommunicates" about a month before the communion celebration. AD, Gard, 42 J 28, fols. 372-275.

were, to be sure, the incorrigible. On the other hand, men and women sometimes acted from a personal sense of worthiness or unworthiness without specific direction from the consistory. At Nîmes, a man hesitated to receive Communion because of a "heavy conscience." When the pastor and elders of Castelmoron inquired why Guirauld Trabuchet had not participated in the recent Communion service, the man responded that he had absented himself "voluntarily." It seems that he was engaged in acrimonious litigation with another member of the congregation. An inhabitant of Saint-Amans refrained, on his own accord, from the Lord's Supper while in a lawsuit against his brother. Pierre Montignac, also from Castelmoron, Antoine Vezin of Ganges, and Catherine de Court of Montauban, to cite but a few, absented themselves because of ongoing quarrels and rancorous legal squabbles with business associates, neighbors, and relatives. Jehanne Treilles could not forgive a cobbler for "gravely offending and injuring" her. Unable to "soften her heart," she returned her Communion token to the elders and began a self-imposed suspension. A soldier from Bédarieux declined Communion after he mortally wounded a fellow townsman.[46]

The consistory sometimes appealed to this personal sense of right and wrong. Rumors circulated about Ganges that Jehan Taudou had committed adultery with a cobbler's wife. The outraged husband added to public suspicion by declaring his intent to avenge the wrong and slay Taudou at the point of a sword. When summoned before the consistory, Taudou asserted complete innocence in the matter, and absent "proof" to the contrary, the minister and elders allowed him to take Communion, "if his conscience permitted him." In an analogous case, the consistory of Montauban reproached a man for having gotten his servant woman pregnant. Faced with the suspect's vigorous denial, the officials allowed him to receive Communion, if he had a "clear conscience."[47] Finally, people

---

[46]AD, Hérault, E Dépôt, Ganges GG 24, fol. 5. AD, Tarn, I 8, le 8 avril 1588; for the examples of Laurens Flottes, le 12 janvier 1591, Jehan Moulinier, le 12 septembre 1593, and Pierre Landes, le 22 décembre 1601. AD, Tarn-et-Garonne, I 1, fols. 32v, 308. SHPF, MS 222/1, fols. 34–34v, 82v–83; AN, TT 234, dossier 6, fols. 813, 828; BN, MS fr 8666, fol. 140v, and other examples: fols. 112, 113; MS fr 8667, fols. 9, 117v, 168v, 174, 201, 214v, 216, 218v, 240v, 248, 250–251, 341v, 358, 359v; Sabean, "Communion and Community: The Refusal to Attend the Lord's Supper in the Sixteenth Century," in *Power in the Blood*, 37–60, examines similar reluctance among parishioners in the duchy of Württemberg to attend communion during the 1580s.

[47]AD, Hérault, E Dépôt, Ganges GG 24, fol. 136v; AD, Tarn-et-Garonne, I 1, fol. 342v. For the case of a student left to "his conscience": BN, MS fr 8666, fol. 104; and a clerk: MS fr 8667, fol. 181.

stood ready to report potential excommunicates when the consistory seemed to overlook the facts. A maidservant, angered by her dismissal, lodged a complaint with the consistory, accusing her former mistress of malice and slander. The offended woman demanded that the consistory refuse her erstwhile employer admission to the Lord's Supper until she had restored the servant's damaged honor. Two women of Saint-Amans tangled in a fierce argument; one called the other a "drunk and a whore." The aggrieved woman then appealed to the consistory, demanding the suspension of her insulting detractor and, once more, the repair of injured pride and tarnished reputation.[48] The faithful, at least in these examples, considered the consistory an appropriate forum for redress; it mediated conflict and offered satisfaction for injuries sustained.

Besides exclusion from the Eucharist, a sentence of excommunication had consequences relating to baptism and marriage. As in the medieval church, an excommunicate could not be admitted as a baptismal sponsor, nor could her or his infant be baptized in the church.[49] On several occasions, the church of Saint-Amans prohibited fathers, namely heads of household, from presenting their infants for christening until they "submitted to the judgment of the consistory" and had their suspensions from the sacrament lifted. At Montauban, the pastor declined to baptize the child of Jehan Peyrusse because of the man's excommunication; the pastor at Nîmes similarly refused baptism to an excommunicate's infant. Finally, a couple could not marry in the church if one of the contracting parties was excommunicated. Thus, the pastor at Ganges refused to marry Estienne Maury and his fiancée because the young man had been excommunicated.[50]

Because the French Reformed Churches enjoyed less than full support from the state, they did not have the means necessary to influence the legal status of excommunicated persons or restrict their exercise of judicial rights. The consistories could not prevent them from bringing certain civil and criminal actions as was possible under the medieval canon law system, where the state recognized the sentence of excommunication and aided the church in its enforcement. This aspect of excommunication

---

[48]AD, Tarn, I 8, le 16 décembre 1590, le 9 janvier 1591, le 5 avril 1602, le 28 août 1602.

[49]According to the church of Saint-Amans, he "who is suspended from one of the sacraments is suspended from the other." AD, Tarn, I 8, le 6 février 1591.

[50]AD, Hérault, E Dépôt, Ganges GG 24, fol. 11v, and fol. 138 for the case of Jaquette Vincente; AD, Tarn, I 8, le 13 mai 1588, le 6 février 1591; AD, Tarn-et-Garonne, I 1, fols. 223–224; BN, MS fr 8667, fol. 351; Hyland, *Excommunication*, 125–126 and 132–134; Méjan, *Discipline*, 262–265 and 284–285.

assumed a unity of interest and purpose between church and civil society. The sharp division between the French monarchy and the Protestant community limited, at least in this regard, the effect of excommunication. The Reformers, however, retained the practice of denying excommunicates the benefit of friendship and common social relationships. A person was not supposed to consort with these errant members of the congregation and, say, dine or work with them. The consistory of Nîmes severely admonished a couple for "eating and drinking . . . ordinarily and familiarly" with an excommunicate. The prohibition on hospitality also followed earlier medieval guidelines as it applied only to individuals who had been fully excommunicated, and not to those temporarily excluded from reception of the Eucharist.[51] This special aspect of major excommunication separated an offender from the community, and unquestionably reinforced the sense that he or she had violated, perhaps even rejected, the standards of society.

Reintegration of the excommunicate into the church—the vital and indispensable process of reaggregation—came in a ceremony of repentance. Persons suspended from the sacrament without publicity made amends in the privacy of the consistory chambers. A farmer from Saint-Césaire near Nîmes, excluded for reason of his dreadful blasphemy, knelt before the assembled pastors, elders, and deacons, begging God's forgiveness. In exceptional cases, the consistory carried the process a step further. Jehan Amalric, an inveterate card player, came before the consistory of Saint-Amans and repented. The members, in view of the man's past conduct, harbored doubts concerning the steadfastness of Amalric's contrition, and accordingly continued the suspension until he displayed "improvement" in his daily life.[52]

Individuals whose suspensions were public or who had been fully excommunicated suffered the stigma of a humiliating ordeal in the presence of the entire congregation. They performed public penance to restore public harmony.[53] Claude Costeplane's association with "papists" had dis-

---

[51]BN, MS fr 8666, fols. 23v, 159v; Hyland, *Excommunication*, 124–125; Vodola, *Excommunication*, 48–54, 70–73, 164–180.

[52]AD, Tarn, I 8, le 26 avril 1596. See also le 6 septembre 1596, le 2 avril 1598; BN, MS fr 8666, fols. 153v, 156, 163v.

[53]In the words of the consistory of Montauban, "d'aultant que l'escandalle est publique aussi la reparation sera faicte publiquement." AD, Tarn-et-Garonne, I, 1, fol. 82; Or at Castelmoron: "il la repareroit publiquement puisque le scandale estoit public." SHPF, MS 222/1, fol. 5. The consistory of Saint-Amans used similar language: "depuis que sa faulte estoit publique qu'il faloit faire reparation publique." AD, Tarn, I 8, le 24 décembre 1593. A woman of Ganges made public amends because her fault was "publicly known." AD, Hérault, E Dépôt, Ganges GG 24, fol. 19v.

honored the Protestants of Pont-de-Camarès and led to his full excommunication. Accordingly, reentry into the community required that he ask forgiveness of God and all the faithful who had assembled for Sunday worship. A young couple of Castelmoron, suspended for fornication, was made to do public reparation, because the "scandal was public."[54] The consistory demanded public atonement for what it regarded as especially outrageous wrongdoing. It invariably insisted upon an open ceremony of contrition at the Sunday service from women who had become pregnant out of wedlock, even when they had merely been suspended from the sacrament. The existence of an illegitimate child accentuated the disgrace of their misbehavior and, in the eyes of the consistory, necessitated public expiation. Thus, Alaisette Ribarde, whose fornication had led to the birth of a "bastard," endured a ceremony of public repentance in the presence of the full congregation on Sunday morning before the consistory admitted her to the Lord's Supper.[55] Other women, cast in similar circumstances, suffered the same painful process.

Calling attention to one's own faults and openly begging forgiveness in the presence of fellow townsfolk or villagers—a person's neighbors and kin, close friends, and sworn enemies—cannot have been a pleasant experience. The daughter of a leading magistrate on the Nîmes presidial court, was ordered to appear at the principal Sunday worship and ask pardon for having married a Catholic. She pleaded to have the embarrassing and humbling ritual moved to a less well attended service, but to no avail. A notary complained bitterly that public reparation was nothing but a "human invention" and could not be found in Holy Writ. Pierre Boudon, a headstrong excommunicate, appeared before the Consistory of Ganges in 1597 and asked permission to participate in the Lord's Supper. It seems that he had been barred from Communion "four or five years" earlier because of "contumacy and fornication." To compound the difficulty, the woman with whom he "lived carnally" had borne him a son, a fact that openly advertised his sin. For its part, the consistory demanded public reparation on the day of the Communion service. Boudon responded that he would rather "change religion" than suffer the humiliation. Another five years passed before he finally bowed to the consistory's demand and confessed his faults publicly on the same day as the September celebration of the Lord's Supper. The loss of dignity and sense

---

[54]Arsenal, MS 6563, fol. 6v; SHPF, MS 222\1, fol. 5.
[55]AD, Hérault, E Dépôt, Ganges GG 24, fols. 94v–95.

of shame associated with public reparation unquestionably reinforced the disgraceful social exclusion of excommunication. Public repentance may also have compensated, however unintentionally, for the consistory's inability to restrict the legal rights of excommunicates.[56]

Not all persons, as we have observed, accepted these penitential and reintegrative rites without argument, and sometimes modifications occurred. A few objected strenuously to being made to fall to their knees, especially in public. When the pastors and elders of Nîmes ordered a merchant's wife to kneel before them and ask forgiveness for having returned to "papal superstitions" and heard Mass, she objected to being made to go to her knees. The consistory reluctantly agreed and accordingly the woman stood for the repentance ceremony. Roland Valat went further and appealed to the regional colloquy when required to kneel in a public demonstration of remorse. In the end, the consistory allowed him to remain standing and agreed that a brief ritual in his own house, the site of the offense (wife beating), would be sufficient. The presence of two or three witnesses satisfied the demands of publicity. Antoine Fraissinet balked at the demand that he kneel and publicly confess his fault to the congregation in conjunction with the celebration of the Lord's Supper at Saint-Gervais. The consistory subsequently "moderated" the requirement to a private recognition of culpability in the presence of three elders. The church apparently found room for the occasional compromise.[57]

It bears noting that the French consistories excommunicated far more men than women. Men dominated the public sphere and, given the fact that excommunication was often the result of "public scandal," it is not surprising that men offended more frequently. In addition, the strongly patriarchal consistory generally held fathers, husbands, and brothers accountable for the behavior of other members of the family.[58] A man had substantial power over his spouse and offspring, especially in the household's relationship with the exterior world. He stood watch over

---

[56]AD, Hérault, E Dépôt, Ganges GG 24, fols. 79, 136; BN, MS fr 8666, fol. 31v; MS fr 8667, fols. 56, 58, 59, 62.

[57]AN, TT 269, fols. 959v, 964v; BN, MS fr 8666, fol. 121v, 123, 161, 187v, 190; MS fr 8667, fol. 141v.

[58]See the remarks of Gregory Hanlon, *L'univers des gens de bien: Culture et comportements des élites urbaines en Agenais-Condomois au XVIIe siècle* (Talence: Presses Universitaires de Bordeaux, 1989), 98–99; Estèbe and Vogler, "La genèse d'une société protestante," *Annales: Économies, sociétés, civilisations* 31 (1976):377; Mentzer, "*Disciplina nervus ecclesiae*," *The Sixteenth Century Journal* 18 (1987):109–111.

family members and was, in many ways, responsible for their actions. The consistory routinely suspended fathers for allowing their daughters and, less often, sons to marry "papists" in Catholic ceremonies. When, after four or five summonses, Donna Laurence still refused to come before the Nîmes consistory, it instructed her brother "to make her appear," or she would be excommunicated for contumacy. The consistory at Saint-Amans debated whether it should excommunicate men who "married papists" on the understanding that these women would convert to Protestantism, and then "permitted their wives to return to idolatry." This same body summoned the wife of the Sieur de Landes and accused her of participating in "debauched" balls and other "foolishness." She denied the entire matter and refused to submit to correction. Such defiance and insubordination led to her immediate suspension from Communion. The consistory instructed her husband, himself an elder, to take control of this disobedient wife and ensure her appearance before the consistory. Otherwise, he too would be suspended from the sacrament and dismissed from the office of elder.[59]

The Protestant consistories of southern France directed about two-thirds of their sentences of excommunication against men, the remainder against women (see Table 3). The proportions are close to the overall ratio

Table 3: Gender Differences in Excommunications

Location	Men	Women
Urban Centers		
Montauban	45	35
Nîmes	63	41
SUBTOTAL	108 (59%)	76 (41%)
Rural World		
Bédarieux	13	7
Castelmoron	38	10
Coutras	21	4
Ganges	37	41
Meyrueis	11	7
Pont-de-Camarès	19	1
Saint-Amans	105	31
Saint-Gervais	2	0
SUBTOTAL	246 (71%)	101 (29%)
TOTAL	354 (67%)	177 (33%)

[59]AD, Tarn, I 8, le 3 juin 1603, le 20 septembre 1603; BN, MS fr 8667, fol. 127v.

of men and women appearing before these same consistories for all offenses, not merely excommunicable matters.[60] The data, furthermore, point toward a slight variation between the larger urban centers and the rural world. At Montauban and Nîmes, women account for some two-fifths (41 percent) of excommunicates. Yet they represent a smaller proportion (only 29 percent) in the lesser towns and villages. The difference likely underscores a conservative tendency within the more traditional countryside—an inclination to disregard and neglect women in religious affairs, if not in all facets of public activity.

Another question that weighs heavily in the popular view of excommunication among Calvinists everywhere in Europe is the frequency of its application. E. William Monter calculates that, in the years between 1564 and 1569, the Genevan consistory excommunicated approximately 2,500 persons—1,906 municipal residents and 530 peasants and other rural dwellers from the surrounding countryside. In this city of 25,000, five persons per week or one in twenty-five adults each year were excommunicated during the late 1560s.[61]

For comparison, let us return to the examples from the southern French provinces. At Meyrueis, a small rural community in the Cévennes, an average of 481 persons participated in each of the Communion services during the five-year period between 1588 and 1592.[62] The number of communicants provides a crude measure of the size of the congregation, or at least the adult portion that is this essay's principal interest. A communicant had to be at least twelve years old and, in general, to have taken some Catechism instruction.[63] Over the course of these same years, the local consistory suspended or excommunicated a total of 18 persons. The single greatest annual number of excommunicates was 6; this occurred in 1589. The average number of communicants that same year was 468. Accordingly, 1 in approximately 80 adults was excommunicated. We can observe a similar order of magnitude at Saint-Gervais, where the elders noted that 93 men and women took Communion at a single service during the late 1560s. During the same period, the consistory excommunicated less than

[60]Mentzer, "*Disciplina nervus ecclesiae*," *The Sixteenth Century Journal* 18 (1987):109–110; idem, "Le consistoire et la pacification du monde rural," *BSHPF* 135 (1989):378–379, 388.

[61]Monter, "The Consistory of Geneva," *Bibliothèque d'Humanisme et Renaissance* 38 (1976):471, 479–480, 484; idem, "Women in Calvinist Geneva (1500–1800)," *Signs: Journal of Women in Culture and Society* 6 (1980):189–191.

[62]SHPF, MS 453, fols. 57v, 60v, 61, 72, 78v, 86.

[63]Méjan, *Discipline*, 275.

1 person per year. The church of Montauban, to take a third example, was significantly larger. The town likely had a total Protestant population of roughly 10,000 by the 1590s. At the 1596 Easter celebration of the Lord's Supper, 4,380 adults participated. The following year, the pastor remarked that "more than four thousand persons" received.[64] During each of these same years, the consistory excommunicated less than 30 persons or, for comparison's sake, about one in 140 to 150 adult members of the congregation.

Information from still other towns confirms the overall impression. The consistory at Castelmoron, a town whose population hovered around 1,500 persons[65] (though not all were Protestant), excommunicated but 48 persons during the eight years between 1597 and 1604. The average was 6 excommunications per year. Over a half-dozen years in the early 1580s, the consistory at Bédarieux, a small town with fewer than 1,000 inhabitants, issued twenty sentences of suspension, fewer than three annually. At Nîmes, a considerably larger city whose total Protestant population was likely about 8,000, the consistory excommunicated 37 persons during a two-year period in the early 1560s and 67 individuals over some five years between 1578 and 1583. The annual average was less than 15 persons. While these data are far from conclusive, they point toward considerably less regular utilization of excommunication than by the Genevan Consistory.

On the other hand, excommunication within the Reformed churches of France, if not nearly so common as at Geneva, was likely applied more often than in pre-Reformation times.[66] This situation resulted, in part, from the fact that the French Protestant churches lacked state support and thus had a smaller array of penalties at their disposal. The consistory could not imprison, banish, or inflict corporal punishment, and those

---

[64]AD, Tarn-et-Garonne, I 1, fols. 132, 242v–243.

[65]Estèbe and Vogler, "La genèse d'une société protestante," *Annales: Économies, sociétés, civilisations* 31 (1976):363.

[66]There were, of course, complaints that the medieval church inflicted the sentence of excommunication without proper distinction, far too often, and for trivial offenses. The sporadic nature of the data makes such claims difficult to evaluate. Julius Goebel, Jr., *Felony and Misdemeanor: A Study in the History of Criminal Law* (1937; reprint, Philadelphia: University of Pennsylvania Press, 1976), 308–309; Hill, "The Theory and Practice of Excommunication," *History* 42 (1957), 8–11; Logan, *Excommunication*, 23–24. For the comments of the medieval southern French bishop William Durant, see: Constantin Fasolt, *Council and Hierarchy: The Political Thought of William Durant the Younger* (Cambridge: Cambridge University Press, 1991), 199–200.

sanctions that it did impose were without civil consequences. At the same time, the church sought to strengthen control over the faithful and did so through the conscious elaboration and amplification of a measured sequence of shaming procedures involving censure, private and public reparation, and excommunication. Shame, a strong sense of guilt and embarrassment, and the accompanying dishonor and disgrace proved a potent means of discipline, especially when done artfully and systematically.

Why, finally, were these offenders expelled from the sacraments of the church and, in the gravest instances, subjected to total social and economic ostracism by the rest of the community? How were their situations distinct from those of other wrongdoers, whose deeds merited simple censure or some other punishment that fell short of excommunication? The actions of the French Reformed churches suggest three general sets of circumstances that warranted excommunication. First, the consistory excommunicated persons for egregious misbehavior, conduct that was so heinous that it deserved excommunication. Some offenses, apostasy and scandalous sexual misconduct for example, warranted full excommunication, and a variety of lesser wrongs led to simple suspension from the Lord's Supper. Indeed, suspension from the Lord's Supper on a single occasion became a familiar, albeit severe, punishment for sinful conduct. Secondly, excommunication resulted from persistent delinquency, after the church had exhausted all other means of correction. These were often cases of lesser shortcomings aggravated by recidivism, inuredness to consistorial directives, or an unwillingness to submit to correction. A baker and his spouse were suspended until they settled their quarrel with another couple, a group of men until they stopped their endless gambling.[67] Finally, the consistory excommunicated the insubordinate and contumacious, those who "rebelled" and failed to appear when summoned.

In all of this, the consistory carefully sought to balance several objectives. To begin, it corrected misbehavior as it promoted virtuous conduct. The elders and pastors wished to bring the guilty to a recognition of their faults and to punish them. They also sought to pacify, control, and supervise, to put an end to disorderly and unrestrained activity— unregulated human sociability. Excommunication delineated the margins of appropriate behavior as understood by church officials: what was

---

[67]AD, Tarn, I 8, le 19 décembre 1601; BN, MS fr 8667, fols. 314, 350.

allowable and legitimate, what was not. The ecclesiastical guardians of communal authority, in marking the limits of acceptability, strove to establish a highly structured and explicit moral universe. There are, moreover, good reasons to think that most members of the community readily grasped and generally agreed with these standards, though they did not always abide by them. At the same time, the consistory wished to defuse conflict, maintain harmony, and foster cohesion within society. The public and private ceremonies of atonement that every excommunicate underwent were a ready vehicle for remedying deficiencies in the code of conduct even as they emphasized the boundaries of morality and social comportment. These actions repaired the honor of the community and preserved the bonds of amicability, all the while laying bare the rich texture and complex structures of early modern society.

The practices associated with excommunication also prompt questions about the underlying nature of Reformed communal structures in France. The Protestants were highly self-conscious in the way they articulated a set of goals and elaborated an identity that separated them from the surrounding Catholic world. Yet why did they choose excommunication as so fundamental a means to cement identity and community? Here a function explanation may be in order. Catholics possessed a rich variety of ways to reaffirm the unity of a spiritual community and continued to develop new civic and religious rituals. Lay activism in the form of pious confraternities, penitential processions, and other devotional observances springs to mind. Did the French Protestants emphasize and even reinvigorate excommunication because they too needed ceremonial and liminal ways of temporarily restoring unity in the face of continual erosion of their community? The Reformed world had few choices at its disposal, certainly far fewer than Catholics. Excommunication, though antithetically related to the Eucharist, accentuated the Lord's Supper as the centerpiece of a civic and religious experience for Protestants. Taken together, the sacral meal and the ability to exclude persons from it gave powerful definition to the activities and influence of the French Reformed churches.

Chapter 5

Social Discipline In Scotland, 1560–1610

Michael F. Graham

And this our weak begynnyng [in 1558] God did so bless, that within few monethis the hartes of many war so strenthned, that we sought to have the face of a Church amanges us, and open crymes to be punished without respect of persone. And for that purpose, by commoun electioun, war eldaris appointed, to whome the hole brethren promissed obedience

—John Knox, *History of the Reformation in Scotland*[1]

Becaus thai heve not a pastor and also thair kirk [is] al[to]gether decayit, thair is na eldaris, deacones nor forme off disciplein in this congregatione quhairthrow sin and vyce gretlie abundis amangis thame

—Visitor's report from parish of Port of Menteith (Stirlingshire)
August 19, 1586[2]

I f John Knox seems overly confident about the speed with which Scotland embraced reform, particularly the reformation of behavior that he expected would result from the imposition of the disciplinary process recommended in Matt. 18:15–19, this is due to his polemical purpose. To him, the Reformation in Scotland was an early spring, nipped in the bud and permanently stunted by the corrupting frost accompanying the return of the Catholic Mary, Queen of Scots, from France in August 1561. In 1566, he recalled the early period of 1558-61 with the rhetorical question: "to what confusion and fear war idolateris, adulteris, and all pub-

[1]David Laing, ed., *The Works of John Knox*, 6 vols. (Edinburgh Wodrow Society edition of 1846-64; reprint, New York: AMS Press, 1966) (hereafter cited as Knox), 1:300.
[2]James Kirk, ed., *Visitation of the Diocese of Dunblane and Other Churches, 1586-1589* (Edinburgh: Scottish Record Society, 1984), 11.

lict transgressoris of Goddis commandimentis, within short tyme brought?" But after the queen's return, he lamented, "suddandlie the most parte of us declyned from the puritie of Goddis word, and began to follow the warld, and so again to schaik handis with the Devill, and with idolatrie."[3]

Knox's version of events, so influential in Scottish Reformation historiography, posits a quick, comprehensive revolution in doctrine and behavior, later sabotaged by "flatterers of the court"—his general label for all who opposed his brand of reform. But if one uses the practice of congregational discipline as a yardstick, (recalling that the *Scots Confession* of 1560 made it the third mark of the true Church) one wonders if Knox was drunk on his own vitriol.[4] The Scottish Kirk was hardly reformed when the queen returned. The goals had been set in the first *Book of Discipline* (1560)[5] and elsewhere, but the process of erecting the new order had only just begun. In fact, the parish of Port of Menteith, which so troubled its visitor in 1586, was not unusual. Numerous examples could be cited, even in fairly populous lowland regions, of communities which still lacked working kirk sessions (the Scottish version of the Calvinist-style consistory) twenty-five to fifty years after the religious revolution of 1560.[6] As late as 1596, the General Assembly felt compelled to remind ministers that they were expected to form sessions in their parishes.[7] This can hardly be blamed on the Catholic queen, deposed in 1567. Rather, Scotland, particu-

[3]Knox, 2:263–265.

[4]G. D. Henderson, ed., *The Scots Confession, 1560 and the Negative Confession, 1581* (Edinburgh: Church of Scotland, 1937), 75.

[5]James Cameron, ed., *The First Book of Discipline* (Edinburgh: Saint Andrew Press, 1972), esp. 165–179.

[6]E.g., Haddington in 1590, Newtown (near Edinburgh) in 1586, Crail (south coast of Fife) in 1605 (although this session had probably functioned earlier), Fossoway, Kincardine, Fowlis Wester, Tullibole, and Alva (all near Stirling) in 1586, Strowan (Clackmannanshire) in 1588, Falkirk and Tullibole (again) in 1591, Muckhart (Clackmannanshire) in 1592, Aberfoyle (Stirlingshire), and Port of Menteith (again) in 1593. See Kirk, ed., *Dunblane Visitation*, 15, 29, 33, 35, 43, 79; ibid., ed., *The Records of the Synod of Lothian and Tweeddale, 1589–1596, 1640–1649* (Edinburgh: Stair Society, 1977), 27–28; Mark Smith, ed., *The Presbytery of St. Andrews, 1586–1605: A Study and Annotated Edition of the Register of the Minutes of the Presbytery of St. Andrews* (Saint Andrews University Ph.D. Thesis, 1986), 422–424; Scottish Record Office (Edinburgh) MS CH2/121/1, 12v; West Register House (Edinburgh) MS CH2/722/2, (microfilm copy of unfoliated original deposited in Central Regional Archives, Stirling), June 22 and September 21, 1591, February 13, 1592, August 21, 1593.

[7]Thomas Thomson, ed., *Acts and Proceedings of the General Assemblies of the Kirk of Scotland*, 3 vols. (Edinburgh: Bannatyne and Maitland Clubs, 1839–45) (hereafter referred to as BUK), 3:865.

larly rural Scotland and the north, was slow to adopt the disciplinary system, because of both the weakness of the Kirk's position and the ways in which Reformed discipline was incompatible with the traditional ordering of Scots society.

BACKGROUND AND EARLY HISTORY

Recent historiography has emphasized the regional nature of the Scottish Reformation,[8] and there appears to have been a geographic pattern to the spread of kirk sessions as well. All evidence of functioning sessions in the decade after 1560 comes from the lowland coastal regions surrounding the firths of Forth and Tay, in the southeast. Records survive for the Saint Andrews session beginning in 1559, the Monifieth session from 1562 (although these are fragmentary until the late 1560s), and the session of the Canongate (Edinburgh's eastern suburb) for the period 1564–67.[9] Other evidence suggests the existence of kirk sessions elsewhere. Dundee, the 'Geneva of Scotland,' apparently had a functioning session from mid-1559, at least.[10] Edinburgh had, according to Knox, a "Privie Kirk," with an elected session, meeting during the 1550s in "secreit and privie conventiounis in Houses, or in the Feilds."[11] Unfortunately, this session left behind no records, and the earliest surviving register of Edinburgh's kirk session does not commence until 1574.[12]

[8]Ian Cowan, *Regional Aspects of the Scottish Reformation* (London: The Historical Association, 1978); Michael Lynch, "Calvinism in Scotland, 1559-1638," in *International Calvinism, 1541-1715*, ed. Menna Prestwich (Oxford: The Clarendon Press, 1985), 225-255, at 229; Frank Bardgett, *Scotland Reformed: The Reformation in Angus and the Mearns* (Edinburgh: John Donald, 1989).

[9]D. Hay Fleming, ed., *Register of the Ministers, Elders and Deacons of the Christian Congregation of St. Andrews, 1559-1600*, 2 vols. (Edinburgh: Scottish History Society, 1889-1890), (hereafter referred to as StAKS); A. B. Calderwood, ed., *The Buik of the Kirk of the Canagait, 1564-1567* (Edinburgh: Scottish Record Society, 1961) (hereafter referred to as BKC); New Register House (Edinburgh) MS OPR 310/1. All quotations from manuscripts in the OPR (old parish registers) series are made with permission of the Controller of Her Britannic Majesty's Stationery Office.

[10]Iain E. F. Flett, *The Conflict of the Reformation and Democracy in the Geneva of Scotland, 1443-1610: An Introduction to Edited Texts of Documents Relating to the Burgh of Dundee* (Saint Andrews University M.Phil. Thesis, 1981), 83-86, 98.

[11]Knox, 2:151-152; James Kirk, "The 'Privy Kirks' and Their Antecedents: The Hidden Face of Scottish Protestantism," in *Voluntary Religion*, ed. W. J. Sheils and Diana Wood (Oxford: Basil Blackwell, 1986), 155-170, at 167-168.

[12]Scottish Record Office MS CH2/450/1.

Of course, the simple existence of registers does not prove much. The northeastern coastal burgh of Aberdeen established a kirk session in 1562, for which records survive, but all they reveal is a burgh oligarchy more concerned with demonstrating 'godliness' than disciplining sinners. In fact, the town's magistrates, most of them still Catholic, created the session to distance themselves from the rebellion of their powerful Catholic neighbor, the earl of Huntly. They hoped to convince the Calvinist Lord James Stewart (later earl of Moray) to spare them from punishment as he made a retributive tour of the northeast on behalf of his half sister the queen. This session passed sternly worded ordinances based on the Ten Commandments, banished one brothel keeper, and then stopped meeting once the political storm had passed.[13] Further uncertainty following the queen's deposition spurred the session to revive for two months in 1568, but it did not begin to meet regularly or seriously attempt to regulate residents' behavior until late 1573.[14]

The records of the urban kirk sessions are scanty enough, but there is even less evidence regarding discipline in rural parishes (where the vast majority of the population lived), before the creation of the first group of intermediate presbytery courts in 1581. Indeed, the failure of the parochial reformation in rural areas, due to a shortage of qualified ministers or enthusiastic lay elders, was one of the reasons given by the *Second Book of Discipline* (1578) for the establishment of the "commoun eldarschip," or presbytery.[15] Only two pre-1581 registers from predominantly rural parishes have survived in any condition, and their irregularity makes it difficult to use them quantitatively.[16] Of course, the paucity of surviving material may be evidence that relatively few rural parishes had sessions. Doubtless some rural registers have been lost, but how many? The Saint

---

[13]Scottish Record Office MS CH2/448/1, 1–11 (manuscript paginated rather than foliated). Some extracts from these records are given in John Stuart, ed., *Selections from the Records of the Kirk Session, Presbytery and Synod of Aberdeen* (Aberdeen: Spalding Club, 1846), but they should be used with caution, as they contain several significant errors in dating. For more on the reaction of the burgh magistrates to the Huntly rebellion, see Allan White, "The Impact of the Reformation on a Burgh Community: The Case of Aberdeen," in *The Early Modern Town in Scotland*, ed. Michael Lynch (London: Croom Helm, 1987), 81–101, at 86.

[14]Scottish Record Office MS CH2/448/1, 13–20.

[15]James Kirk, ed., *The Second Book of Discipline* (Edinburgh: Saint Andrew Press, 1980), 199.

[16]The registers are Monifieth (Angus), New Register House MS OPR 310/1 and Anstruther Wester (Fife), New Register House MS OPR 403/1. Anstruther Wester was, technically, a burgh, but it was tiny, and many of the parishioners came from the surrounding countryside or the equally tiny neighboring burghs of Anstruther Easter, Pittenweem, or Kilrenny.

Andrews Kirk Session sent a letter in 1560 "to all ministeris, eldaris and diacons of the congregatioun of Anstruthir," and its minutes make reference to the existence of elders at Crail in 1565, but these scraps of evidence do not prove the existence of a working session in either parish.[17] The Saint Andrews session did feel the need to take up quite a few cases from the villages of eastern Fife, and in many of them there is no reference to local disciplinary proceedings. Firm conclusions are impossible, but any case for widespread rural disciplinary practices before the advent of the presbyteries would have to rely on faith more than reason.[18]

Attempts to establish rural sessions were bound to encounter difficulties not found in cities. For example, larger burghs such as Edinburgh, Saint Andrews, or Aberdeen already had governing institutions, such as burgh councils and craft guilds, which were accustomed to collective responsibility for civic affairs. These could lend experience, authority, and membership to newly established kirk sessions. Many of these bodies had exercised some control over their urban churches even before the Reformation, so ecclesiastical administration was not foreign to them. But in rural areas, barony courts were generally dominated by an individual—the superior or his representative—and their jurisdictional boundaries were not necessarily coterminous with those of the parish. At Monifieth in Angus, for instance, several estates in the parish were part of the Angus Douglas regality of Kerriemuir, while two others—Ardownie and the subdivided Ethiebeaton—were not, being held instead either under the earl of Crawford or directly from the crown.[19] The parish of Anstruther Wester in 1580 contained four tiny burghs in three different baronies, plus at least one additional lordship. The minister took a peripatetic approach to this problem, convening two or even three sessions (with different memberships) at various locations throughout the parish. One laird (roughly the Scots equivalent of the English squire) was given a free hand to choose all the elders and deacons from within his lordship.[20] But where one laird

[17]StAKS, 1:22–23, 258–259.

[18]Faith like that of G. D. Henderson, who made the rather bizarre claim that "the eldership had been more or less accepted in Scotland before Knox arrived in 1559. . . ." See G. D. Henderson, *The Scottish Ruling Elder* (London: James Clarke, 1935), 30.

[19]J. Malcolm, *The Parish of Monifieth in Ancient and Modern Times* (Edinburgh: William Green, 1910), 31; Bardgett, *Scotland Reformed*, 99.

[20]The burghs were Anstruther Wester and Pittenweem, belonging to the abbey of Pittenweem, Kilrenny, belonging to the family of Beaton of Balfour, and Anstruther Easter, belonging to John Anstruther of that ilk. In addition, the parish contained the lordship of Caiplie and several other rural estates. See New Register House MS OPR 403/1, 12r, 22r–24v, 27r, 28r.

held the right of ministerial patronage while several others held many of the estates in the parish, the former was bound to chafe at sharing ecclesiastical authority with the latter group, whose members might be at odds with one another over land or jurisdictional disputes.

By the late 1580s and the 1590s, however, rural kirk sessions were becoming more common, if the survival of records is any index. Registers exist, for example, for Errol (Angus) beginning in 1583 and Saint Monance (Fife) in 1597.[21] The creation of the presbyteries was probably the major factor in this development; the General Assembly of the Scottish Kirk set up thirteen "model" presbyteries in 1581, and at least a couple of others had begun operating by 1584, when political backlash due to the association between the Kirk and the recently ousted Ruthven faction caused the crown and Parliament to abolish the lot.[22] They were revived permanently in 1586, however. It is probably no coincidence that Errol and Saint Monance were both attached to presbyteries founded in 1581. The presbyteries were the most effective vehicle for the translation of the policies of the national Kirk into local practice.

In addition to disseminating policy and policing the ministry, the presbyteries were disciplinary courts, initially including both ministers and lay elders, just as local kirk sessions did. Lay elders never really returned to them after the interlude of 1584-86,[23] but presbyteries continued to handle disciplinary cases from communities that had no kirk sessions, or difficult cases involving particularly stubborn or prominent sinners which local sessions had been unable to resolve. Any complete study of social discipline in the early Scottish Reformed Kirk would have to examine the role of the presbyteries as well as the kirk sessions. In addi-

---

[21]New Register House MS OPR 351/3; Scottish Record Office MS CH2/1056/1.

[22]BUK, 2:482-487; Acts of the Parliaments of Scotland, 1124-1707, 12 vols. (London: HMSO, 1814-75) (hereafter referred to as APS), 3:293; David Calderwood, History of the Kirk of Scotland, 8 vols. (Edinburgh: Wodrow Society, 1842-49), 4:491-494. For a good account of the events of 1582-86, including the Ruthven Raid and its aftermath, see Gordon Donaldson, All the Queen's Men: Power and Politics in Mary Stewart's Scotland (London: Batsford, 1983), 132-151.

[23]For example, the Stirling Presbytery had enjoyed the regular participation of several lay elders during the period 1581-84, but no lay elders were listed in sederunts between September 6, 1586, and October 31, 1592, and the presence of two on the latter date was not soon repeated, even at half strength. In 1587, the Edinburgh Presbytery lamented the absence of the "baronis and gentilmen" who had helped found the presbytery, but had little luck in getting them to return to meetings. See West Register House MS CH2/722/2, October 31, 1592; Scottish Record Office MS CH2/121/1, 29v.

tion, it would require evidence from both rural and urban communities, and should represent all geographic regions from which records survive. As part of such a project, I have been collecting disciplinary cases from various Scottish kirk sessions and presbyteries between 1560 (when the Roman Catholic Church was officially overthrown and the *First Book of Discipline* accepted by the General Assembly and a number of Scots noblemen), and 1610 (when control over the ultimate sanction of excommunication was taken away from the disciplinary courts and given to the Jacobean bishops). Recording as much information as possible on each case and coding it into a computerized database has made it possible to look at the evidence from several angles, and to assess the practical implementation of the Scottish Reformation at the parish level. Of particular interest are: (1) the breakdown between different categories of offenses, (2) the relative abilities of the church courts to make sinners appear before them and carry different types of cases through to conclusion, (3) gender- and class-based differences in offenses and treatment,[24] and (4) the ways in which these factors changed over time, as the Reformed Kirk sought to establish itself. Table 1 presents some of the data from kirk sessions, and Table 2 from presbyteries.[25]

[24]For a discussion of the way in which the disciplinary courts handled prominent sinners and how this differed from the treatment of the general population, see Michael Graham, "Equality before the Kirk? Church Discipline and the Elite in Reformation-era Scotland," *Archiv für Reformationsgeschichte* 84 (1993):289–310.

[25]The kirk sessions, years tabulated, and sources are as follows: (1) Aberdeen, 1562-63, 1568, 1573-78 (460 cases) Scottish Record Office MS CH2/448/1; (2) Anstruther Wester (Fife) 1583-85, 1588-98 (546 cases) New Register House MS OPR 403/1; (3) Canongate 1564-67 (287 cases) Alma B. Calderwood, ed., *The Buik of the Kirk of the Canagait, 1564-1567* (Edinburgh: Scottish Record Society, 1961); (4) Dundonald (Ayrshire) 1602-10 (644 cases) Henry Paton ed., *Dundonald Parish Records: The Session Book of Dundonald, 1602-1731* (Edinburgh: Bute Society, 1936); (5) Edinburgh General Session 1574-75 (321 cases) Scottish Record Office MS CH2/450/1; (6) Monifieth (Angus) 1579-81, 1593-94, 1600-1, 1603-6 (105 cases) New Register House MS OPR 310/1; (7) Rothiemay (Banff) 1605-6 (75 cases) New Register House MS OPR 165/3; (8) Saint Andrews (Fife) 1559-1600 (2,156 cases) D. Hay Fleming, ed., *Register of the Minister, Elders and Deacons of the Christian Congregation of St. Andrews 1559-1600*, 2 vols. (Edinburgh: Scottish History Society, 1889-90). The presbyteries, years tabulated, and sources are: (1) Edinburgh, 1586-90 (138 cases) Scottish Record Office MS CH2/121/1; (2) Saint Andrews, 1586-1605 (329 cases) Mark Smith, ed., *The Presbytery of St. Andrews, 1586-1605: A Study and Annotated Edition of the Register of the Minutes of the Presbytery of St. Andrews* (Saint Andrews University Ph.D. Thesis, 1986); (3) Stirling, 1581-94 (724 cases) James Kirk, ed., *Stirling Presbytery Records, 1581-1587* (Edinburgh: Scottish History Society, 1981), and then West Register House MSS CH2/722/1-2.

Sin and the Calvinists

Table 1: Disciplinary Cases from Scottish Kirk Sessions, 1560–1610

Sin class	Cases	Male	Female	No-shows
Sexuality	2,523 (55%)	1,234	1289	403 (16%)
Breach of Sabbath	485 (11%)	406	79	98 (20%)
Church/Communion attendance	244 (5%)	154	90	83 (34%)
Extrafamilial verbal disputes	207 (4.5%)	102	105	31 (15%)
Religious dissent/practices	178 (4%)	145	33	26 (15%)
Marriage questions	136 (3%)	101	35	8 (6%)
Political offenses	116 (2.5%)	114	2	9 (8%)
Violent attacks	114 (2.5%)	98	16	20 (18%)
Domestic disputes	103 (2%)	56	47	17 (17%)
Dealings with outcasts	93 (2%)	52	41	33 (35%)
Disobedient to Kirk	64 (1.5%)	45	18	14 (22%)
Magic, witchcraft	43 (1%)	11	32	10 (23%)
Dancing, gaming	33 (0.5%)	23	10	5 (15%)
Totals*	4,594	2,710	1,881	831 (18%)

Listed categories do not add up to totals because additional cases are scattered through other categories. Total "No-show" percentages calculated for within each offense type.

Table 2: Disciplinary Cases From Scottish Presbyteries, 1581–1605

Sin class	Cases	Male	Female	No-shows
Sexuality	572 (48%)	314	258	141 (25%)
Religious dissent/practices	175 (15%)	132	43	75 (43%)
Disobedient to Kirk	64 (5.5%)	40	24	33 (52%)
Violent attacks	59 (5%)	58	1	28 (47%)
Breach of Sabbath	56 (4.5%)	55	1	43 (78%)
Church/Communion attendance	52 (4.5%)	28	24	38 (73%)
Magic, witchcraft	35 (3%)	10	25	14 (40%)
Extrafamilial verbal disputes	34 (3%)	31	3	22 (65%)
Dealings with outcasts	31 (2.5%)	26	5	10 (32%)
Marriage questions	25 (2%)	16	9	8 (32%)
Totals	1191	777	414	453 (38%)

Listed categories do not add up to totals because additional cases are scattered through other categories. Total "No-show" percentages calculated for within each offense type.

SEXUALITY AND MARRIAGE

The most striking element in these tables is the large proportion of offenses involving sexuality, either fornication, adultery, or incest. Other historians have noticed this fixation, and sought to explain it in terms of a prudery thought to be native to the Scots.[26] Since there is strong sentiment in western societies today that governments should stay out of the private lives of citizens, the church courts seem nosy, or even voyeuristic to our modern eyes. But this was no all-powerful neighborly Big Brother peering into bedroom windows (where, indeed, bedrooms or windows existed). Rather, the Kirk's obsession with sex was more a reflection of its weakness than its strength. The need to discourage illicit sexuality was accepted by nearly all powers—Reformed, half-reformed, or tenaciously Catholic—even when they could agree on little else. As population grew, resources shrank, and beggars crowded the roads, even the most tradition-alist elders were happy to seize the untraditional reins of church discipline to attack the social problem of bastardy, although they had little interest in the rest of the Kirk's program.

This was particularly true in rural parishes such as Monifieth and Anstruther Wester, where kirk sessions functioned for several years after their foundations without showing interest in anything but sex. The Monifieth session was founded in 1562, but handled only sexuality cases until the 1590s.[27] Anstruther Wester's session took up ninety-three cases during the period 1583-85 (earlier records are too fragmentary to be used quantitatively), and all but two involved sexual misbehavior.[28] At Roth-iemay in the northeast (dominated by the crypto-Catholic Lord Salton and his relatives) 80 percent of cases involved sex as late as 1605-6.[29]

It was only when the disciplinary system was on firm footing locally that ministers and elders began to show much interest in other aspects of the disciplinary agenda, such as enforcement of the Sabbath, church atten-dance, religious orthodoxy, or making peace between bickering neigh-

---

[26]John Bossy has confidently asserted that "at least" two-thirds of the cases handled by Scottish kirk sessions in the first fifty years of the Reformation involved sexuality, though offering no documentation for the claim. See John Bossy, *Christianity in the West, 1400-1700* (Oxford: Oxford University Press, 1985), 130. For a more cautious discussion, see T. C. Smout, *A History of the Scottish People, 1560-1830* (Glasgow: William Collins, 1969), 75–76.

[27]Damage to the record makes certainty impossible, but the first nonsexual case I was able to find was that of Henry Howat and Andrew Good, forced to make peace and end their feud in May 1593. See New Register House MS OPR 310/1, 83v.

[28]New Register House MS OPR 403/1, 33r–42v.

[29]New Register House MS OPR 165/3, 14r–24v.

bors. Thus at Dundonald in Ayrshire, where the reform effort had powerful local patrons dating back to the early 1560s, sexuality had shrunk to 36 percent of the recorded disciplinary caseload by 1602–10.[30] At Anstruther Wester, it had declined to the remarkably low level of 10 percent by 1597–98, and at Monifieth 46 percent by 1600–1.[31] This usually was not just a matter of the addition of other cases, either; numbers of sexuality cases shrank both proportionally and absolutely.

The most obvious explanation for the decline (and the one of which historians are likely to be the most suspicious) is that strict enforcement of the sanctions of ritualized public repentance and fines simply forced people to change their behavior and have fewer children out of wedlock.[32] There may be some truth to this, but it seems more plausible that two other things happened. First, as kirk sessions became more entrenched locally, they could rely on civil magistrates (some of whom were elders themselves) to enforce secular laws against sexual impropriety. Habitual offenders who seemed immune to the Kirk's techniques of behavioral modification might then be punished by magistrates without any kirk session proceedings. Second, as local attitudes hardened against unwed mothers, they were more likely to flee to more tolerant locales, perhaps seeking their children's baptisms from unlicensed readers or recusant priests. The Stirling Presbytery in the late 1580s became concerned that the latter were seeking converts among those who were fugitives from Reformed parochial discipline.[33]

Those eager to brand the Scots as sexually obsessed should also consider the extent to which irregular marriage may have contributed to the sexual caseloads. The church throughout western Europe had been trying to gain control over the institution of marriage since the eleventh century,[34] and Scotland was one of the final frontiers in this effort. There is

---

[30]Henry Paton, ed., *Dundonald Parish Records: The Session Book of Dundonald 1602–1731* (Edinburgh: Bute Society, 1936), 1–220 passim. John Fullarton of Dreghorne (d. 1587), an influential local laird, had been an active Protestant since at least 1562, and had attended early general assemblies. See BUK, 1:61; James Paterson, *History of the County of Ayr with a Genealogical Account of the Families of Ayrshire* (Ayr: John Dick, 1847–52), 2:22.

[31]New Register House MS OPR 403/1, 106v–121v; MS OPR 310/1, 98r–106r, although the overall caseload at Monifieth was still low enough to make wide fluctuations in annual figures possible.

[32]Geoffrey Parker has hypothesized that this took place at Saint Andrews, where sexual cases dipped to very low levels in 1595–96. However, this requires an explanation of why sexual cases returned in large numbers thereafter. See his contribution to this volume.

[33]West Register House MS CH2/722/1, May 14, 1588, May 6, 1589 (no folio markings).

[34]Georges Duby, *The Knight, the Lady and the Priest* (New York: Pantheon Books, 1983); Bossy, *Christianity in the West*, 21–24.

some debate on the prevalence of "handfast" marriage—in which couples would seal their alliances outdoors or at home, before witnesses but not necessarily clergy—in sixteenth-century Scotland. The authors of one recent study have opined that it was certainly dead by the mid-seventeenth century, except perhaps in the Highlands.[35]

Attitudes in some of the lowland communities I have examined were clearly changing in the late sixteenth century; the clerk of the Anstruther Wester session (possibly the minister himself) had no qualms about the use of the term "concubine" in 1583, suggesting a local recognition of cohabitation arrangements, but the word disappeared from the register within a few years.[36] In 1573-74, the kirk session of Aberdeen—hardly in the vanguard of the movement to instill social discipline—launched a campaign against couples who were betrothed and living together, but who had never formalized the arrangement. Those called before the session were generally given a deadline by which to marry, or face a fine. Because marriage was a legal issue, involving transfer of property and support of offspring, as well as a religious matter, the Aberdonian city fathers wanted relationships defined more precisely. The fact that these unions previously had been accepted locally is verified by the session clerk's occasional tendency to refer to the woman in these couples as the "wife."[37] Since slowness to marry was obviously the main issue here, I have classified these as marriage cases, but many other offenses, in which long-standing unmarried couples were disciplined for producing children, appear as sexuality cases when unofficial marriage was probably the real problem.

THE SABBATH

Beyond sexual misdeeds, the Kirk's disciplinary courts were most interested in preserving the Sabbath.[38] But this was an effort largely postponed until the late 1580s. Of the 485 Sabbath-breach cases in the database from kirk sessions between 1560 and 1610 (see Table 1), only 72 predate 1580,

---

[35]Rosalind Mitchison and Leah Leneman, *Sexuality and Social Control: Scotland 1660-1780* (Oxford: Basil Blackwell, 1989), 101-102.

[36]New Register House MS OPR 403/1, 33r, 34r, 35v.

[37]Scottish Record Office MS CH2/448/1, 31, 68 (paginated rather than foliated).

[38]For general discussions of sabbatarianism in early modern Scotland (but whose authors curiously make no use of sixteenth-century kirk session or presbytery registers), see Leah Leneman, "'Prophaning' the Lord's Day: Sabbath Breach in Early Modern Scotland," *History* 74 (1989):217-231; and R. D. Brackenridge, "The Development of Sabbatarianism in Scotland, 1560-1650," *Journal of Presbyterian History* 42 (1964):149-165.

and 66 of those come from the Saint Andrews session, which seems to have been precocious in this respect. Some of the leading burghs had ordinances enforcing Sabbath observance early on—such as Edinburgh, whose magistrates in October 1560 ordered that merchants close their booths on Sundays and that all Sunday markets be moved to another day—although it is not clear that these pious resolutions were strictly enforced.[39] The Sabbath proved even more difficult to maintain outside the major burghs.

Sunday markets were lucrative for those in whose bailiwick they took place, so many local authorities happy to combat illegitimacy dragged their feet when it came to enforcing the Sabbath. The Scots Parliament lamented in 1579 that "sabboth dayis ar now comounlie violat and brokin alsweill w[i]t[h]in burgh as to landwart," and ordered that all goods put up for sale on Sundays be confiscated. In addition, it instituted fines against those who worked, played games, or patronized taverns on the Sabbath, as well as those who did not attend sermons.[40] But such legislation always required the cooperation of local authorities for enforcement, and this was often lacking. When a commissioner from the Stirling Presbytery in 1586 requested James Chisholm, bailie of Dunblane, to close the Sunday market there, Chisholm said he could not "becaus the pepill wald in nawys consent to change the same off that day. . . ." Chisholm was not even willing to order a break in the market for sermons, and the market was still said to be thriving in 1593.[41] When the Stirling Presbytery was in the midst of a long campaign to close his Sunday market at Falkirk in 1591, Lord Livingston complained that similar enterprises under the protection of noblemen were tolerated elsewhere.[42] Lord Somerville protested to the

---

[39]*Extracts from the Records of the Burgh of Edinburgh, 1557-1571* (Edinburgh: Burgh Records Society, 1875), 85–86. The fact that the burgh council had to make another proclamation against Sunday markets in July 1563 suggests that the earlier regulation was not being observed. Likewise, tavern keepers were reminded to close during preaching in January 1569, as were those in the neighboring Canongate. See ibid., 165, 259; "Extracts from the Records of the Burgh of the Canongate," in *Maitland Club Miscellany* (Edinburgh: Maitland Club, 1840), 2:281–359 at 317. Dundee prohibited trading during preaching times in late 1559, and in January 1569 closed its port from 10 p.m. Saturday until 4 p.m. Sunday. See Flett, ed., *Conflict of the Reformation*, 87, 99–100. Aberdeen's council did not pass a Sabbath ordinance until 1576. See John Stuart, ed., *Extracts from the Council Register of the Burgh of Aberdeen, 1398-1625* (Aberdeen: Spalding Club, 1844, 1848), 2:27–28.

[40]APS, 3:138. The act was repeated in 1593 with the additional stipulation that presbyteries were to see that local magistrates enforced it. See ibid., 4:16.

[41]West Register House MS CH2/722/2, August 21, September 4 and 18, 1593; Kirk, ed., *Dunblane Visitation*, 37–38.

[42]West Register House MS CH2/722/2, April 6, 1591.

General Assembly in 1590 that his enfeoffment guaranteed him the right to hold a market.[43] When it came to sexuality, the moral interest of the Kirk coincided with the financial interests of local powers, but this was not the case with Sabbath enforcement.

Violators of the Sabbath were most often men (85 percent), and were usually charged with working, rather than recreation. Thus, John Logan admitted to the Rothiemay Kirk Session in October 1605 that he and his son had loaded a horse early one Sunday morning, but "thay thocht it had bein na fault to haif done any thing befoir ye sun ryising." The elders assured him that predawn activities were just as forbidden as those after sunrise, and warned him not to repeat the offense.[44] James and John Brown granted to the session of Anstruther Wester in November 1590 that they had operated a mill on the Sabbath, but pleaded that they had done so on the orders of their master, the laird of Abbotshall, and could not stop unless ordered to by him. The mill was still running on Sundays two years later.[45] A powerful individual such as Abbotshall, whose lands were on the fringe of the parish anyway, could be difficult to bring to heel. Humbler masters were more pliable, and the kirk session of Dundonald was able to make the widow Marion Smelie answer for having forced her servant to work on the Sabbath in May 1605.[46]

Of course, many were summoned for working on their own behalf, because servants or tenants often did not have any day but Sundays free from labor obligations to work their own plots or cattle. The Stirling Presbytery displayed some sympathy for those faced with this dilemma in November 1590, when it urged local gentlemen to give their tenants another day free for their own labors, so they would not be forced to violate the Sabbath.[47] Max Weber might have shuddered upon encountering such an anticapitalist proposal from an undeniably Calvinist body, but local landowners appear to have paid it little heed.

For those with a bit more leisure, Sabbath breach could be recreational. The Stirling Presbytery in August 1581 ordered Stirling's kirk session to "tak ordur with sic personis as dansis on the sabboth day, speciallie with thai that dansit within the nycht in Robert Wysis hous on Sonday

[43]BUK, 2:769.
[44]New Register House MS OPR 165/3,17r.
[45]New Register House MS OPR 403/1, 66v–67r, 76r.
[46]Paton, ed., *Dundonald Parish Records*, 80. Smelie was able to clear herself on the grounds that the work was necessary.
[47]West Register House MS CH2/722/2, November 3, 1590.

last."[48] Janet Hog and Isobell Gibson were fined by the Anstruther Wester session in November 1595 for hosting Sunday drinking parties, and the same session gave Andrew Craig and Alan Cook a stern warning in February 1598 not to play golf on the Sabbath again.[49] Ten men, including an elder, faced fines for having attended a joust in a nearby village.[50] Others played "kyles" (ninepins), or hunted rabbits or foxes.[51]

Just as the percentages of cases involving Sabbath breach increased dramatically in the 1590s and after 1600, so did the punishments doled out for the offense. The Aberdeen session slapped Thomas Parry with a five-shilling fine for working on the Sabbath in 1576, and let the barber William Gerard off with a warning for the same offense two years later.[52] Neither of these punishments was particularly severe, and the Anstruther Wester session likewise extracted nothing more from Richard Anderson in Pittenweem in 1588 than a promise not to repeat his sin.[53] The session may have been hesitant to push matters too far, because it was having considerable difficulty getting those it charged with Sabbath breach even to appear when summoned.[54] As late as 1593, those who answered the summons and admitted the offense in Anstruther were simply told to ask God's forgiveness.[55] But this changed within a few years, and the treatment given the golfers mentioned above was in fact quite lenient relative to that given others. William Trumbull had to pay a twenty-shilling fine in August 1596, and John Fogow had to pay a fine and make a public confession of his sin the following year.[56] The elders of Anstruther Wester may have become eager to collect fines in the 1590s because by then they were using the local church treasury as a kind of municipal credit bank, loaning money to the burgh and its burgesses, including some of their own number.[57] But the trend toward more severe treatment of Sabbath-

[48]Kirk, ed., *Stirling Presbytery Records*, 4.

[49]New Register House MS OPR 403/1, 95v–96v, 114v.

[50]Ibid., 117v, 120v.

[51]Ibid., 98r–v; Paton, ed., *Dundonald Parish Records*, 33, 41, 110, 141.

[52]Scottish Record Office MS CH2/448/1, 89, 129. The value of Scots money relative to English was sinking throughout the sixteenth century. Around 1575 the ratio was six pounds Scots per pound Sterling, and it slid to twelve to one by century's end.

[53]New Register House MS OPR 403/1, 59v.

[54]E.g. five men (one of them a repeat offender) on October 15, 1588, a couple on January 28, 1589, and seven women and two men on August 12, 1589. See ibid., 61r, 62v, 64v.

[55]Ibid., 76v–77r.

[56]Ibid., 102v, 113v.

[57]E.g. ibid., 89r. The Dundonald session also loaned money, using suspension from Communion as a sanction against those who did not pay it back in a timely fashion. See Paton, ed., *Dundonald Parish Records*, 159.

breakers was visible elsewhere as well; violators in Dundonald after 1602 usually paid fines of a mark or more and performed public repentance.[58] The session at Monifieth was by then even prepared to make Sabbath-breakers do their public repentance in linen clothing, a penitential garb normally reserved for those guilty of more serious sins, such as adultery or slaughter.[59]

We can therefore conclude that by 1600 Sabbath enforcement was a live issue in those lowland communities where kirk sessions and/or presbyteries were active. In addition to trying to keep Sunday free for religious observances, the disciplinary courts of the Kirk were also by then seeking to force everyone to participate actively in Reformed worship. Sabbath breach was a sin of commission, but sins of omission, such as absence from sermons, Communion, or pre-Communion examinations or ignorance of doctrine, were becoming common in disciplinary caseloads nearly everywhere by 1600.

INDOCTRINATION AND MANDATORY PARTICIPATION

Some urban kirk sessions had pursued these matters practically from the start: the Canongate session reminded the burgh's craftsmen in September 1564 that their prior attendance at Communion represented a commitment to the local congregation, and that they were expected to continue to attend sermons and participate in Communion, rather than Sunday recreation.[60] The craftsmen simply wanted to enjoy their day off, but others declined to participate for more serious reasons, such as the session elder John Murdo, who would not take Communion because of his enmity against another parishioner who had wounded him in a fight. Told by his fellow elders to let bygones be bygones, Murdo refused, saying "my concience will nocht, nour I can nocht cum to the tabill, nour play the ipocreit."[61] In terms of the progress of reform, the Canongate was advanced; examinations of doctrine before Communion, for example, had apparently been held there as early as December 1561.[62]

---

[58]E.g. Paton, ed., *Dundonald Parish Records*, 82, 84, 102–103, 106, 109, 149–150, 153–154.
[59]New Register House MS OPR 310/1, 99r.
[60]Calderwood, ed., *Buik of the Kirk of the Canagait*, 6–7.
[61]Ibid., 16.
[62]Assertion based on conviction by assize of William Balfour in Leith (part of the Canongate parish) for, among other things, disrupting the examination. See Robert Pitcairn, ed., *Criminal Trials in Scotland* (Edinburgh: William Tait, 1833), pt. 1:416–418.

Rural parishes lagged several decades behind. Thomas Worthy was deposed from the beadleship of Saint Ninians Kirk (near Stirling) in November 1592 for refusing reconciliation with Patrick Hodge and because he had "manie yeirs bygane absented him self fra receaving of ye holie comunione to ye evill exampill off uyers."[63] Examples could be extremely important. Two leading lairds in Monifieth parish were summoned to a presbyterial visitation in August 1603 for declining to participate in Communion. One of them, William Durham of Grange, was the patriarch of a family that had led local reform efforts from the beginning.[64] His flagging interest may account for the fact that the local session, which typically handled an average of ten disciplinary cases a year, only took up three in 1603, two of them involving the absent lairds.

In addition to teaching by example, the Kirk also sought to bring religious instruction to all, and punish those who did not participate in or profit from the exercise. Alexander Young and his wife, charged with violating the Sabbath at Anstruther Wester in January 1589, were said to be "ignorant of all christian Doectrin," but examinations before Communion were introduced there the next month. Later that year the session ruled that couples seeking to have their banns read were first to be tested for their knowledge of doctrine.[65] Thus, in 1594 William Fogo and Girsall Bissie had to delay their wedding and pledge to "get the knalledg of the heades of the religion" within forty days or pay a twenty-shilling fine.[66]

Likewise, the elders of Anstruther pledged that they would begin noting sermon absences in early 1589, including instances in which people left the kirk before the final blessing.[67] The first charges of absence came in August 1589, but of twenty-one people summoned for the offense that year, only two bothered to appear before the kirk session. They were both told to perform public repentance.[68] By the mid-1590s, the session was much more successful at getting such offenders to show up, but it

---

[63]West Register House MS CH2/722/2, November 28, 1592.
[64]New Register House MS OPR 310/1, 111r, 113v. His grandfather William had attended the first General Assembly of the Kirk in 1560, and was active in the national Kirk until his death in 1574. See BUK 1:3; Calderwood, *History*, 2:45, 289, 293–294, 378–383; Gordon Donaldson, *Scottish Church History* (Edinburgh: Scottish Academic Press, 1985), 116–117; Frank Bardgett, *Scotland Reformed: The Reformation in Angus and the Mearns* (Edinburgh: John Donald, 1989), 99–100.
[65]New Register House MS OPR 403/1, 62v–63r.
[66]Ibid., 86r.
[67]Ibid., 62v, 65r.
[68]Ibid., 64v.

generally let them off with warnings, perhaps sensing that local opinion would not accept the harsher punishment.[69] By that time the Dundonald session was keeping close track of its parishioners' participation as well. William Hobkin was fined five shillings for missing an examination in 1596, but had it refunded in 1602 because he faithfully attended every examination in the interim.[70] Careful notation of attendance was not necessarily accompanied with effective enforcement, though. Bessie Blair attended neither examination nor Communion for five years before the Dundonald elders caught up with her in late 1604 and ordered her to perform public repentance in linen. John Findlay was given the same punishment for a similar term of absence the next year; not surprisingly, he did not even know the Lord's Prayer.[71]

RELIGIOUS DISSENT AND UNORTHODOX PRACTICES

People might decline to participate in the religious life of their parishes due to lack of interest or enmity with neighbors, as we have seen. Another possible reason was religious dissent, although where this was clearly the issue I have placed the offense in a separate category. Dissent was particularly common whenever the Reformed disciplinary regime was relatively new to a burgh or area. In some cases it involved explicit Catholicism, and in others simply adherence to traditional practices that the Reformed Kirk had defined as "idolatrous." Rare individuals might be suspected of non-Catholic heterodoxy as well, such as Alexander Thomson in Dundonald parish, accused of denying the existence of eternal life (he claimed innocence), or the vagrant Margaret Underwood, who granted that she had said "Christ vald not bein sa daft as to haif died for hir."[72] Some dissent appears to have been a reaction against discipline, as in Edinburgh in 1575, when Neil Laing, ordered to perform public repentance for orchestrating "pompous convoy and supperflowis banketting" at his sister's wedding, declared "he rather wald be of the devillis Kirk [than] be of ye Kirk of this burgh and that he sould nevir be ane member tharof and wald nocht knaw ye same as ye Kirk and that ye elderis and deaconis wer bot fallowis. . . ."[73]

---

[69]E.g. ibid., 94r–v, 98r, 100r.

[70]Paton, ed., *Dundonald Parish Records*, 25.

[71]Ibid., 61, 84.

[72]Ibid., 46, 48–49. Underwood said she made the statement on account of her "witlesnes," and the matter was dropped.

[73]Scottish Record Office MS CH2/450/1, 42r, 50v.

Among communities studied here, Catholicism per se was mostly an issue around the capital, in the regions north and west of Stirling that bordered on highland country, and in Aberdeen. The session of Aberdeen made a number of accusations of Catholicism in the period 1573–78, but handled the problem with kid gloves, because many of the burgh's leading families, including the Menzies, who controlled the provostry, remained Catholic or had Catholic branches.[74] In fact, five of the thirteen elders elected in 1573 can be identified as having actively opposed the Reformation locally in 1559–60.[75] Men who were themselves Catholics, crypto-Catholics, or who had Catholic wives could hardly spearhead an orthodoxy crusade that might find a target too close to home. The session decided on November 12, 1573, that those "transgressors againis ye Religion" who did not attend sermons "be first handillit & travellit w[i]t[h] gentilly, gif be ony meanis possiblie yai may be von."[76] One Catholic was summoned and appeared immediately, but there was no action even attempted against any others until the following April.[77] The case of Marjorie Urquhart was not unusual. Examined on her religious beliefs in March 1575, she refused to promise she would attend the Reformed Communion, saying she "had sic ane pyk on hir c[on]science yat show culd not be fulle of yis p[rese]nt religione now in Scotland." No action was taken against her, and several months later she did sign the confession of faith.[78] Thomas Menzies, son of the provost, was certainly treated gently; first summoned in April 1574, he declined to appear before the session until June, and then simply refused to say whether he would join the Reformed congregation. Nothing more was said on the matter.[79]

Church courts in and around Edinburgh also had to proceed carefully with Catholics, many of whom were associated with the royal court. The queen's chapel provided a Catholic alternative in the early and mid-1560s, and local elders could not be too severe with those who chose to worship with their sovereign. William Anis admitted to the Canongate elders in 1566 that he had been married and had his child baptized by

---

[74]For a discussion of lingering Catholicism in the burgh, see Allan White, "The Impact of the Reformation on a Burgh Community: The Case of Aberdeen," in *The Early Modern Town in Scotland*, ed. Michael Lynch (London: Croom Helm, 1987), 81–101, at 96–97.

[75]Scottish Record Office MS CH2/448/1, 19; Stuart, ed., *Extracts from the Records of the Burgh of Aberdeen*, 1:315–19.

[76]Scottish Record Office MS CH2/448/1, 25.

[77]Ibid., 25, 34.

[78]Ibid., 66, 71.

[79]Ibid., 34, 40.

Reformed rites, "bot my hart gevis me to the mes [Mass], and thairfor I can nocht come to the commonion." The session denounced him as "ane promis braker to the eternall God," and suspended him from the sacraments, but could do little else for the time being.[80] This sanction probably bothered Anis little. The queen's deposition and the victory of the boy-king James VI's supporters in the 1567-73 civil war made Catholicism more difficult to maintain in the capital, and there are some examples in the register of the Edinburgh Kirk Session from the mid-1570s of former Catholics seeking admittance to the Reformed Kirk. They were told to perform a ritual involving a public confession and four sessions of public repentance in sackcloth during church services.[81]

The Kirk at the national level in the late 1580s and early 1590s became very concerned about the perceived Catholic threat, and the General Assembly was forever issuing dire warnings about the infiltration of Jesuits and "papists."[82] The sixth earl of Huntly, implicated in intrigue with Phillip II of Spain, was its most prominent target, but there were others as well.[83] The ministers were concerned that the nobility in particular was abandoning the Reformed faith,[84] and the royal court again appeared, as it had under Mary, as a den of idolatry. The Edinburgh Presbytery summoned several courtiers, but had little luck with them; delays in proceedings and royal intercession generally prevented any clear outcome in such cases.[85] By threatening excommunication of Catholic courtiers, the Kirk was in effect claiming the right to ban them from the royal presence, but James was determined to choose his companions, regardless of ministerial complaints. In 1596 he told a delegation of ministers that the disciplinary courts should not meddle in politics, "but upon fornicatioun, and suche like slanders."[86]

---

[80]Calderwood, ed. *Buik of the Kirk of the Canagait*, 38.

[81]Scottish Records Office MS CH2/450/1, 10v, 11v, 12v-13r.

[82]E.g. BUK, 2:719-722, 724, 738, 784; 3:796-799, 846-847, 876; Calderwood, *History*, 4:666, 691; 5:134-135, 241.

[83]For actions against Huntly, see Scottish Record Office MS CH2/121/1, 43v; BUK, 3:821, 918-922, 1,048; Calderwood, *History*, 5:263-268, 289, 309; 6:758-759; Robert Pitcairn, ed., *The Autobiography and Diary of Mr. James Melvill, minister of Kilrenny* (Edinburgh: Wodrow Society, 1842), 309-310, 318-322, 374.

[84]Keith M. Brown, "In Search of the Godly Magistrate in Reformation Scotland," *Journal of Ecclesiastical History* 40 (1989):553-81, at 566.

[85]Scottish Record Office MS CH2/121/1, 47v-49v, 50v-51v, 52v, 54r, 56v, 65r.

[86]Calderwood, *History*, 5:451.

Humbler people were rarely charged with Catholicism per se. Instead, they would be accused of engaging in "superstitious" practices such as celebrating Christmas or making pilgrimages. When the earl of Morton, regent from 1572–78, paid a visit to Aberdeen in the summer of 1574, he ordered the burgh council to redesign the interior of the burgh church, remove its organ, and prevent "the superstitious keping of festivall days usit of befor in tyme of ignorance & papistrie." Morton was thus challenging the burgh oligarchy, whose loyalty to his regime was in doubt, to demonstrate political conformity by enforcing religious orthodoxy. The local session, which included several burgh councillors, responded the following December and January, summoning a number of residents who had allegedly celebrated Christmas by, among other things, "plaing, dansink & singin off fylthy karrells."[87] The group was treated gently, let off with a warning, and enforcement was thereafter left to the burgh's deacons of crafts.[88] Any zeal to eradicate vestiges of Catholicism in Aberdeen faded with the memory of Morton's visit.

Christmas died hard elsewhere as well; local authorities in rural areas were slow to accept such an attack on tradition, leaving most commoners to observe the old liturgical calendar undisturbed. Alexander Wallace, minister of Clackmannan, was accused in the spring of 1588 by his fellow ministers in the Stirling Presbytery of having had bells rung in his church "upone yt day callit of awld Iull day" the previous December. He said he did so under heavy pressure from the laird of Clackmannan "quha menasit & co[m]pellit him siclyk agains his will," so he ordered the bells rung "for feir of his lyf." The presbytery accepted this excuse, and proved equally unsuccessful in efforts to discipline residents of Dunblane who celebrated Easter in traditional fashion in April 1589.[89] By 1605, though, the elders of Dundonald, where the Reformed Kirk had been established for several decades, were able to force residents to admit that keeping Christmas was a sin. Two local farmers even requested an investigation of several of their laborers who had refused to yoke ploughs on December 25, and those accused felt compelled to offer plausible excuses, such as the need to repair equipment. As the old tradition lost acceptance, Christmas celebrants changed their ways or learned discretion.[90]

---

[87]Scottish Record Office MS CH2/448/1, 58–59; Stuart, ed., *Selections from the Council Register of Aberdeen*, 2:25–26.
[88]Scottish Record Office MS CH2/448/1, 107.
[89]West Register House MS CH2/722/1, April 16, 1588, April 15, 1589.
[90]Paton, ed., *Dundonald Parish Records*, 69–70.

It was in a similar spirit that the Monifieth session in 1600 ordained that those who practiced "anie auld superstitioun not admit[ted] be goddis word" such as "superstitious dayes . . . bainfyeris or the lyk" would have to perform public repentance in linen and pay ten shillings to the poor, although the session register does not reveal any examples of this regulation's enforcement.[91] The presbyteries of Stirling and Edinburgh also railed against midsummer bonfires, but were apparently unable to prevent them as late as the mid-1590s.[92] By the end of the century, the king was issuing proclamations in support of May games, giving popular culture reinforcement from above.[93]

The populace probably clung to many holidays out of the need for social recreation. Pilgrimages, on the other hand, offered physical remedies in a world full of unpredictable and debilitating ailments. The Reformed Kirk could bring regular preaching, discipline, and even religious instruction into the lives of the people, but had no alternative medicine available. May pilgrimages to the well at the "Preistis hauch" near Peebles, just twenty miles south of Edinburgh, were still common in 1596, with the Peebles Presbytery either unable or unwilling to do anything about them.[94] The Stirling Presbytery did make a concerted effort against pilgrimages to Christ's Well, a site within its bailiwick, but it was apparently unable to stamp them out. In late May 1583, after unsuccessful prodding of local secular officials to stop the "papisticall" pilgrimages that it had first denounced two years earlier, the presbytery decided to take matters into its own hands. It commissioned several ministers to hide near the well on a Saturday evening and take down the names of pilgrims. These were given in, and a dragnet followed.[95] In June and July, thirty-eight people (thirty-two of them women) were summoned for making the pilgrimage.

The statement by Elizabeth Lennox, one of the accused, that "scho past to Chrystis will becaus hir foirbearis past thair and becaus scho hade ane sair leg," indicates that making pilgrimages to the well was not a new practice, despite the presbytery's characterization of it as something begun "at leat."[96] Rather, it was a venerable aspect of local piety that the

---

[91]New Register House MS OPR 310/1, 99v.

[92]West Register House MS CH2/722/1, June 25, 1588; CH2/722/2, May 22, 1593; Scottish Record Office MS CH2/121/1, 42v, 43v, 44v–45r.

[93]Calderwood, *History*, 5:735–736.

[94]James Kirk, ed., *The Records of the Synod of Lothian and Tweeddale, 1589-1596, 1640-1649* (Edinburgh: Stair Society, 1977), 38–39, 81, 88, 100.

[95]Kirk, ed., *Stirling Presbytery Records*, 4–5, 115–116, 120.

[96]Ibid., 150.

Kirk was only just beginning to combat. Margaret Downy and Jonet Allane must have been surprised when, just shy of the well, they were met by "ane certane halbert men" (one of the presbytery elders?) who "struik them away," and prevented them from reaching its healing waters. Although the presbytery concluded that they had not succeeded in committing idolatry, they still had to perform public repentance for the attempt.[97]

Those who had made it to the well were asked specific questions about what they did there, and their responses testify eloquently to their fears and uncertainties, as well as their faith in folk remedies. Janet Harvie confessed that she poured the water over her shoulders "becaus sho was seik in hir hairt and in her hed and lipnit that the woll sould have helpit hir seikness." William Kay testified that his baby son was ill, and that he had left an apron string from the boy's clothing at the well, taking some of its water for him to drink in the hope that it would cure him.[98] Agnes Blair said she washed her sickly child with water from the well, believing that it would bring him either a speedy recovery or a speedy death.[99]

The presbytery's attack on this local tradition certainly aroused opposition; later that summer a resident of a nearby village was ordered to do public repentance for having proclaimed the medical efficacy of the well's waters at Stirling's "mercat cross." He admitted having said "gif he wist to gait his haill [health] at Chrystis Woll he wald pas thair quha wald quha wald nocht."[100] The disciplinary campaign did not stop the pilgrimages, either. In 1586, some parishioners at Port of Menteith reported that there was still "ane universall abuse rinnyng to Chrystis well fra all places in May time," but would not name guilty individuals.[101] The presbytery summoned more pilgrims in May 1593; James Baird said he had seen many people there, and that David Morris, who sold aquavit, had reported "thair was many broght to yat well quha gangs hame on yair feit." Baird was ordered to do public repentance in sackcloth, but many local residents were clearly still willing to risk such a penalty in order to partake of the superior magic of the well.[102]

[97]Ibid., 140.
[98]Ibid., 135.
[99]Ibid., 150.
[100]Ibid., 147.
[101]Kirk, ed., *Dunblane Visitation*, 12.
[102]West Register House MS CH2/722/2, May 22, 1593, May 29, 1593.

Another traditional religious practice which disciplinary courts, particularly presbyteries, sought to eliminate in the late sixteenth century was burial within churches. Leading families customarily buried their departed beneath the kirk floor, but by the late 1580s, the Scots Reformers were seeking to preserve the Kirk for the edification of the living, rather than the commemoration of the dead. That these could be viewed as competing interests is plain from the case of John Christie and John Henderson, parishioners of Logie, who admitted in 1593 to sneaking into the kirk on a Saturday night, removing the pew of David Balfour, a local laird, and breaking it up. Henderson claimed they had done so because the pew "stude on yair foirbears beans [bones]."[103]

The Stirling Presbytery charged thirteen men with burying relatives in kirks between 1589 and 1593, requiring most of them to perform public repentance. Not surprisingly, some were slow to accept that it was now sinful to inter parish notables alongside their ancestors. The entire kirk session of Logie parish faced censure in February 1593 for having allowed Margaret Alexander's family to bury her within Logie Kirk. The elders and deacons were made to promise "not to burie any of yair freinds in ye kirk frathymefurt and [not to] give consent to burie any p[er]son yair in tymis cu[m]ing undir ye paine of ten punds money to be payit be everie one of yame that dois in ye contrar." One elder from the Alexander family who refused to grant that the practice was sinful was deposed from the eldership.[104]

The campaign against burial in kirks was not unique to the Stirling Presbytery. The bailies of the Canongate were summoned to appear before the Edinburgh Presbytery twice in the late 1580s for allowing the practice in their parish, and at least one laird from the rural area around Edinburgh was charged with supervising a burial within a kirk.[105] The presbytery of Saint Andrews also dealt with the offense a number of times, and in October 1595 the Synod of Lothian vowed that those who buried relatives in kirks in the future would be forced to dig up the corpses and do public repentance.[106]

---

[103]Ibid., August 21 and 28 and September 11, 1593.

[104]West Register House MS CH2/722/2, February 6, March 13 and 20, and May 29, 1593.

[105]Scottish Record Office MS CH2/121/1, 7r–8r, 61r–v, April 8 and 29, 1589. On the other hand, there was apparently no protest over the 1588 burial of the countess of Argyll next to the remains of her husband, the popular earl of Moray, in Saint Giles Kirk. Moray, in death even more than in life, was much beloved by the leadership of the Kirk. See *Selections from Burgh Records of Edinburgh*, 4:525.

[106]Smith, ed., *Presbytery of St. Andrews*, 189–191, 205, 232, 251–252, 254, 260, 263, 265, 267, particularly the 1598 case of Robert Bruce of Pitlethie; Kirk, ed., *Records of the Synod of Lothian and Tweeddale*, 99.

This was a classic example of an effort by the presbyteries and higher courts of the Kirk, on which ministers predominated, to seek change in local religious practices that prominent laymen had tolerated or encouraged. Kirk sessions often resisted reform. The elders of Rothiemay simply used the new policy as a fund-raising ploy; in June 1606 they declared that those who buried relatives in the kirk would thenceforth pay a forty-shilling fine, surely not a prohibitive sum for the prominent families of the parish. The families of those interred since the 1599 arrival of Minister Alexander Smart were to pay a retroactive fine of twenty shillings.[107] The old ways also continued at Monifieth, where the Durhams of Grange covered one wall of the kirk's choir with their family monument around 1600.[108]

PEACEMAKING

While kirk sessions were often unenthusiastic about efforts to reform religious practices, by the end of the sixteenth century most of them had become active as peacemakers. Like enforcement of the Sabbath, this was an aspect of the disciplinary program that was slow to take hold. As the obsession with sexuality faded, however, elders spent increasing amounts of time mediating disputes so that the Communion celebration (which generally took place one to four times a year) would not be contaminated by rancor between participants.

The Scots of the sixteenth century were blunt in speech and quick to violence, particularly when they felt their honor had been threatened. Men often went about armed with a "quhinger" (a short sword), and were constantly in a state of armed readiness.[109] This bellicosity knew no social boundaries, not even those that defined kirk session membership. Thus Simon Wallace, a deacon on the Dundonald session, took offense when John Dickie, with whom he had a long-standing feud, arrived at Communion in April 1602 with a band of armed followers. The result was a brawl, with drawn swords, in the kirkyard. Wallace later told the elders (among

---

[107]New Register House MS OPR 165/3, 21r. The session of Anstruther Wester in Fife, probably urged on by the ministers James Melville and Robert Durie, passed a resolution in 1590 against burial in the kirk, however. See New Register House MS OPR 403/1, 65v.

[108]Malcolm, *Parish of Monifieth*, 82–83.

[109]For the role played by violence, see Keith M. Brown, *Bloodfeud in Scotland, 1573–1625: Violence, Justice and Politics in an Early Modern Society* (Edinburgh: John Donald, 1986).

whom were several of his kinsmen) that "he tuik [Dickie and the others' arrival in church] as done in contempt of him." The session investigated the incident for over a year, trying to determine who had first resorted to violence, before finally finding both parties equally culpable and ordering both to perform public repentance on two consecutive Sundays.[110] In this highly ritualistic society, most people realized the importance of enmity as a personal attitude. If one gave up enmity, one was closing the door on future avenues for redress. Alan Cook faced this decision in 1598 when summoned before the Anstruther Wester Kirk Session on the charge of "setting on Patrik Mellvill, wryght, w[i]t[h] a drawin whinger." He was willing to admit that he had done so, but said he was not ready to display any repentance for the act. The session urged him "to think mair deiplie of the mater & to call to god to giv him a syght of his synne." Later, he was admonished from the pulpit, and referred to the presbytery of Saint Andrews, but proved recalcitrant. For the time being, at least, Cook was more interested in maintenance of his grudge than full membership in the Christian community.[111]

Some disputes involved only words, as in 1598 when Kate Brown was accused by the Anstruther Wester session of calling Kristin Scot "drunk harlot" just outside the kirk door in words audible to the worshipers inside. Brown claimed Scot provoked her by telling her to "kis her ers," but the session found Brown the more guilty of the two, and she had to apologize to Scot on her knees as the elders watched, "promis[in]g to walk mair warlie in tym coming."[112] This was actually lenient treatment; others (usually women) found guilty of slander in Anstruther often had to perform public repentance and either pay a fine of forty shillings or spend a couple of hours in the "branks" (an iron bridle with a gag set up in the marketplace).[113] By the early seventeenth century, kirk sessions everywhere were quick to censure the sharp-tongued woman. Janet Thain in Rothiemay denied calling George Mureson a thief, and witnesses testified only to her having used the epithets "murtherer & throtcutter." Consider-

---

[110]Paton, ed., *Dundonald Parish Records*, 16–17, 20–24, 35.

[111]New Register House MS OPR 403/1, 121r, 122r. Cook never bothered to appear before the presbytery. See Smith, ed., *Presbytery of St. Andrews*, 288, 290. For a discussion of the uses of enmity outside the Scottish context, see David Sabean, *Power in the Blood: Popular Culture and Village Discourse in Early Modern Germany* (Cambridge: Cambridge University Press, 1984), 38–41, 47–54.

[112]New Register House MS OPR 403/1, 117r–v.

[113]Ibid., 99r, 101v, 104v–105v.

ing the mitigating circumstances—Mureson, weapon in hand, had been chasing Thain's husband with apparent deadly intent—the session demanded from Thain only a private apology rather than public repentance! The elders did not take any action against Mureson.[114]

While most disciplinary courts, particularly in rural areas, were not active as peacemakers until near the end of the century, the urban kirk session of the Canongate took on this role quite early. Some mediation had occasionally taken place before the burgh council (several of whose members were session elders) in the past, so the concept was not entirely new.[115] But the need to sanctify the Reformed Communion rite through neighborly harmony, coupled with the significance of the ritual of public repentance in church, gave it a new and expanded meaning, and brought more women into the process. The session hosted a number of mass reconciliations, usually on the eve of Communion celebrations. One such session in January 1567 involved twenty-four parishioners. Usually all parties were found equally guilty, though there were exceptions, such as Bessie Rokart and her daughter Ellen, who were told to apologize to the widow Jonat Cuthbert for having called Cuthbert's late husband a thief while he lay on his deathbed.[116] Other conflicts carried the potential for bloodshed, as in August 1566 when the bailie James Wilkie complained that John Mosman was harboring a man in his house who had killed one of Wilkie's kinsmen. Such a charge threatened to draw Mosman into what was apparently a blood feud, and the session admonished him to remove the man from his house.[117]

Just as their efforts to reform sexual mores and marriage customs answered what leading laymen of all religious stripes viewed as a social need, the disciplinary courts were also well structured, both in terms of makeup and theological *raison d'être*, to play the part of peacemaker. By the late sixteenth century, the crown, the Kirk, and many leading laymen were united in the belief that the conflicts endemic to Scottish society had to be brought within the purview of the legal system.[118] At the local level,

---

[114]New Register House MS OPR 165/3, 17v.

[115]E.g. "Extracts from the Records of the Burgh of the Canongate near Edinburgh," *Maitland Club Miscellany* (Edinburgh: Maitland Club, 1840), 2:281–359, at 290–301.

[116]Calderwood, ed., *Buik of the Kirk of the Canagait*, 60–63, Rokart-Cuthbert dispute on 62.

[117]Ibid., 50.

[118]Brown, *Bloodfeud in Scotland*, 267–69.

where private justice had hitherto ruled, and where the central courts of the state had made few inroads, the church courts—theoretically impartial and representing an institution that claimed the allegiance of all—seemed the best forum for mediation.[119] Their success was limited, particularly with disputes involving those of lairdly status or higher,[120] but humbler people were usually persuaded to end their disputes or submit them to arbitration.[121]

WITCHCRAFT AND MAGIC

Another disciplinary category on which there was a broad societal consensus was witchcraft.[122] Witchcraft made up only a very small part of the caseloads of kirk sessions (1 percent) and presbyteries (3 percent), but those cases that arose were treated seriously and with a great deal of cooperation between elders, ministers, and secular magistrates. Many women and some men were executed as witches in sixteenth- and seventeenth-century Scotland, but only secular courts could impose the death sentence. Church courts generally played an advisory role, reviewing the depositions made by accused witches before secular officials,[123] or handing evidence or suspects uncovered in disciplinary proceedings on to magistrates once it seemed there were grounds for trial.[124]

There were two types of witchcraft cases that kirk sessions or presbyteries would carry through to their conclusions. First were the (surprisingly common) instances in which suspects who admitted magical practices were dismissed with a warning not to repeat.[125] In addition, there were those who had consulted with suspected or convicted witches and were told to perform public repentance. In May 1591 the Edinburgh Presbytery, responding to a query from the king, reiterated the claim of a

---

[119]For the role of church courts within the legal system as a whole in the seventeenth century, see Stephen J. Davies, "The Courts and the Legal System 1600-1747: The Case of Stirlingshire," in *Crime and the Law: The Social History of Crime in Western Europe since 1500*, ed. V. A. C. Gatrell, Bruce Lenman, and Geoffrey Parker (London: Europa, 1980), 120-154.

[120]E.g. Scottish Record Office MS CH2/121/1, February 18 and 25, 1589, January 6, 1590.

[121]E.g. Paton, ed., *Dundonald Parish Records*, 115.

[122]For Scottish witchcraft, see Christina Larner, *Enemies of God: The Witch-hunt in Scotland* (London: Chatto and Windus, 1981).

[123]E.g. Smith, ed., *Presbytery of St. Andrews*, 273.

[124]E.g. West Register House MS CH2/722/2, April 21, May 1 and 12, June 10, 1590.

[125]Ibid., July 21 and 28, August 18 and 25, September 8 and 17, 1590; New Register House MS OPR 403/1, 66r, 69r.

1563 act of Parliament that consulters of witches deserved death just as the witches themselves, but this apparently had little effect.[126] The Saint Andrews Presbytery decided in July 1598 to order consulters of witches to do public repentance in the same fashion as adulterers (another class of offender who deserved death according to statute law).[127]

The earliest example from the database of an attempt to discipline anyone for consulting a witch dates from April 1590, when James Kinnard, a resident of the remote parish of Glendevon, admitted to the Stirling Presbytery that he and his wife had consulted with the witch Isobell Watson, "to haill him of ye worme." No action was taken against Kinnard, who produced Watson herself for examination.[128] The presbytery was not so lenient two months later with William Culross, who consulted Watson (while she was imprisoned in the Stirling tollbooth) about his cow's sudden inability to give milk. Watson referred Culross to another sorceress, whose help he then sought, and he performed public repentance several times for his offense.[129] Within a few years, consulters of witches elsewhere were also forced to perform public repentance, as the Kirk sought to reduce the demand for diabolical services as well as to ferret out the providers.[130]

CONCLUSIONS

There are other aspects of the Kirk's disciplinary program, such as the attack on certain types of public performance, on excessive drinking and dance, on infanticide, and on political dissent, which have not been discussed here, because the numbers of cases involved are relatively small. Also, no attention has been given to the effectiveness of excommunication, including its civil implications. Excommunication was often threatened but was rarely invoked, and then only against the most recalcitrant of offenders. When used, it seems to have been relatively ineffective,

[126]Scottish Record Office MS CH2/121/1, May 4, 1591; APS, 2:539.

[127]Smith, ed., *Presbytery of St. Andrews*, 272.

[128]West Register House MS CH2/722/2, April 21, 1590. Watson was later put to an assize, although the outcome is unclear. See ibid., June 10, 1590.

[129]Ibid.,une 2, June 23, September 29, 1590.

[130]StAKS, 2:799-800; New Register House MS OPR 403/1, 113r-115v; Paton, ed., *Dundonald Parish Records*, 66, 109, 111, 113-114, 169-170, 236; Smith, ed., *Presbytery of St. Andrews*, 222-224, 331.

although it might have carried more sting in the close confines of urban burgh society.[131]

What should be clear from this brief examination of the first fifty years of the disciplinary regime of the Kirk is how slowly the system spread, particularly in rural areas, and the conservative outlook of many early elders, which caused them to restrict their efforts to a crackdown on illicit sexuality. It was really only in the last decade of the sixteenth century that the rest of the disciplinary program, including enforced church attendance, catechizing, Sabbath observance, and the elimination of "superstitious" holidays or practices, was introduced outside the few burghs with longer experience of the Reformed regime, such as Edinburgh or Saint Andrews. It was also only then that the rural kirk sessions and presbyteries had won enough local acceptance to serve effectively in mediating disputes and punishing slanderers. In the burghs, the disciplinary system was not universally welcomed, but existing urban institutions and habits created much better conditions for its introduction than would be found in rural areas. Even Aberdeen, with its Catholic provost and partially Catholic burgh oligarchy, was host to a functioning Calvinist-style kirk session (with several Catholic elders) by the mid-1570s. In the countryside, the courts of the Kirk developed much more slowly, and many parishes were incorporated into presbyteries before they had their own sessions. But in the slow process of gaining respect and acceptance, from wary magistrates and unruly sinners alike, the rural courts of the Reformed Kirk played a pioneering role in overcoming the fragmentation of authority that had been the legacy of medieval Scotland.

---

[131]Michael Lynch has argued that it was quite effective in Reformation-era Edinburgh. See Michael Lynch, *Edinburgh and the Reformation* (Edingurgh: John Donald, 1981), 188. See chapter 4 of this collection (pp. 97–128) for further discussion of excommunications.

Stool of Repentance

The "Kirk By Law Established" and the Origins of "The Taming of Scotland": Saint Andrews 1559–1600

Geoffrey Parker

In August 1590 Mr. James Melville, minister of the Church of Scotland, delivered a stirring exhortation to the General Assembly which called for major improvements in the condition of the Kirk. One of his principal arguments was:

> That discipline was maist necessar in the Kirk, seing without the saming, Chrysts Kingdome could nocht stand. For unles the Word and Sacraments war kiepit in sinceritie, and rightlie usit and practesit be direction of the discipline, they wald soone be corrupted. And therfor certean it was, that without sum discipline na kirk; without trew discipline, na rightlie reformed kirk; and without the right and perfyt discipline, na right and perfyt kirk.

At the end of the session, the Assembly endorsed Melville's stand and resolved that "Euerie minister sould haiff a copie of the Book of Discipline and peruse it; and euerie presbyterie sould cause thair haill members sub-scryve the sam; and the refusars to be excomunicat." Melville's autobiography, which includes the text of his speech, makes it clear that at the forefront of his mind lurked the troubles that he had witnessed for more than a decade in planting a disciplined church in the town of Saint Andrews in Fife.[1]

Saint Andrews in the age of the Reformation was the seat of both a university and the metropolitan see of Scotland; it was also a lively burgh, with considerable seaborne trade and jurisdiction over a number of outlying villages.[2] Although in the absence of contemporary registers of births and deaths, or a census, it is hazardous to offer an estimate of the parish's population, it is likely that it consisted of some four thousand people in the early seventeenth century, of whom perhaps twenty-five hundred to three thousand lived in the town.[3] But there are two reasons for thinking that the population in the previous half-century is likely to have been lower than this. On the one hand, the disruption caused by the Reformation caused both some Catholic clergy and many students to pack their bags; on the other, the plague of 1585–86 "raget till almaist utter vastation" and the principal towns of Scotland, including Saint Andrews, were

---

[1]*The Diary of Mr. James Melvill, 1556–1601*, Bannatyne Club, vol. 34 (Edinburgh, 1829), 188–189 and 195. There is another edition of Melville's holograph manuscript (in the National Library of Scotland): R. Pitcairn, ed., *The Autobiography and Diary of Mr. James Melville*, Wodrow Society, vol. 3 (Edinburgh, 1842). All citations that follow are, however, from the 1829 edition.

[2]H. Scott, *Fasti ecclesiae scotticanae* (Edinburgh: Oliver and Boyd, 1925), 5:177ff., gives the exact size of the parishes in and around Saint Andrews. Cameron was disjoined from Saint Andrews in 1646; Strathkinness and Boarhills in the nineteenth century. The parish of Saint Leonards, inside the burgh, was used by all members of the university and was entirely separate from Saint Andrews parish.

[3]The first true census for the parishes of Fife, compiled in 1755, gave Saint Andrews a population of 5,877 persons: see J. G. Kyd, *Scottish Population Statistics including Webster's Analysis of the Population since 1755*, Scottish History Society, third series, vol. 40 (Edinburgh, 1952), 38–41, combined total for Saint Andrews and Cameron parishes. Attempting a back-projection from this figure is hazardous, but might be attempted along the following lines. Webster judged that the parish in 1755 possessed 1,177 "fighting men," aged between eighteen and fifty-six years. The record of those who subscribed to the 1643 Solemn League and Covenant in the parish of Saint Andrews contains 985 names. Of these, 140 were members of the university and therefore belonged to the parish of Saint Leonards, reducing the total for Saint Andrews parish to 845. Since only adult males were included among the subscribers, it seems reasonable to suppose that the 845 might be roughly equated with Webster's category of "fighting men." Using Webster's carefully calculated ratio of fighting men to the total population (1:5), a parish of some 4,250 is indicated for the year 1643. (See the list in Saint Andrews University Archives, Typ/BE.C43 TSS2: *A solemne League and Covenant* [Edinburgh, 1643], 15–43.) Continuing backwards, the earliest surviving tax record for Saint Andrews, the burgh stent-roll for 1618, contains the names of 486 householders, but covers only the burgh, not the parish, and omits those who (like all university personnel) were exempt from taxation. If we assume five persons to have constituted the average household, the population of the burgh proper in 1618 may have approached twenty-five hundred. (Saint Andrews University Archives: MS B65/20/3.) Happily, these tentative calculations are supported by a letter from

left "almost desolat."[4] But despite these losses, and perhaps others due to a shift in Scotland's overseas trade to larger and better-appointed harbors in the vicinity, Reformation Saint Andrews remained a large parish by the standards of sixteenth-century Scotland. It therefore offered a considerable challenge to the architects of the New Jerusalem.

Ministers of the church such as James Melville had at hand three distinct weapons for enforcing their moral standards and their doctrines upon the Scots: certain teachings and traditions of the church; the active support of the secular authorities; and a new and ubiquitous hierarchy of church courts and jurisdictions. All were put to full use. John Calvin, whose example the Scottish Reformers chose to emulate, had been impressed by the evidence contained in the Acts of the Apostles and in certain Epistles of Saint Paul that the first Christian churches had strictly controlled and vigorously censured the social behavior of their members. In his Ecclesiastical Ordinances of 1541, as well as in later editions of his *Institutes of the Christian Religion*, Biblical sanction was claimed for the office of "elder," whom Calvin made responsible for overseeing the morals and manners of the community.[5]

But who, precisely, comprised the community? Here the example of the early church was less often cited. There were many in the Protestant movement who argued that, as in the time of the Apostles, only true believers should be considered full members of the church; and that therefore only they should be subject to ecclesiastical discipline. This was the stance adopted by Calvinist leaders in both the Dutch Republic and northwest Germany: only those who had placed themselves "under the

---

the ecclesiastical historian David Calderwood, written to the archbishop of Saint Andrews in 1615, which claimed "there are in fact more than 3,000 regular comunicants" in the parish (quoted by D. Hay Fleming, ed., *Register of the Minister, Elders and Deacons of the Christian Congregation of Saint Andrews, comprising the Proceedings of the Kirk-Session and of the Superintendent of Fife, Fothrik, and Strathearn, 1559–1600*, Scottish History Society, vols. 1–2 [Edinburgh, 1889–90], 2:74.)

[4]See J. M. Anderson, ed., *Early Records of the University of St. Andrews*, Scottish History Society, third series, vol. 8 (Edinburgh, 1926), 154–159 and 262–272, for matriculation and graduation rolls during the period 1556–65. These reveal no graduation ceremony in 1559–60, on account of the troubles and very few graduates from then until 1565. Matriculations were more or less halved during 1560–63, while in 1559 the record states "Hoc anno, propter tumultus religionis ergo exortos, paucissimi scholastici ad hanc universitatem venerunt" (266). The plague of 1585–86 is recorded in Melville's *Diary*, 148, 162.

[5]See the excellent discussion of the sources of the notion of "discipline" in J. K. Cameron, "Godly Nurture and Admonition in the Lord: Ecclesiastical Discipline in the Reformed Tradition," in *Die dänische Reformation vor ihrem internationalen Hintergrund*, ed. L. Grane and K. Horby (Göttingen: Vandenhoeck und Ruprecht, 1990), 264–276.

sweet yoke of our chief shepherd Jesus Christ" could be disciplined.[6] But Calvin himself had vehemently opposed this view. For him, the Christian community embraced everyone, sinners and saved alike, and in Geneva he created a special tribunal called the *consistoire*, composed of ministers and elders (some of them also magistrates), to interrogate and judge all who fell from doctrinal and moral purity. Those who erred, whoever they might be, were severely punished—whether for religious obstinacy (like Miguel Servetus, who was burned at the stake for heresy) or for moral turpitude (like those convicted of flagrant adultery, who were drowned).[7]

This uncompromising stance was fully endorsed by the leading Scottish Reformer, John Knox. Although during his ministry of the English church in Frankfurt (1554-55) and Geneva (1556-58) his elders could only deal with the "manners and disorders" of the small exile community, in a polemic written at Dieppe in 1559, just before he embarked for Scotland, Knox made a powerful defense of strong discipline, up to and including death for deviants, equally applied to all. And when, the following year, the "face of a public kirk" was at last established in his homeland, Knox ensured that the Scots Confession recognized "Ecclesiastical discipline, uprightly ministered as God's word prescribes, whereby vice is repressed and virtue nourished" as one of the three "notes, signs and assured tokens" whereby the true church might be "known from that horrible harlot" the church of Rome.[8] The reasoning and the consequences

---

[6]See A. C. Duke, "The Ambivalent Face of Calvinism in the Netherlands, 1561-1618," in *International Calvinism 1541-1715*, ed. M. Prestwich (Oxford: Clarendon Press, 1985), 109–134, esp. 130f.; and H. Schilling, "Reformierte Kirchenzucht als Sozialdisziplinierung. Die Tätigkeit des Emder Presbyteriums in den Jahren 1557-62," in *Niederlande und Nordwestdeutschland*, ed. W. Ehbrecht and H. Schilling (Cologne/Vienna: Böhlau, 1983), 261-327.

[7]See the accounts given by R. M. Kingdon, "The Control of Morals in Calvin's Geneva," in *The Social History of the Reformation*, ed. L. P. Buck and J. W. Zophy (Columbus: Ohio State University Press, 1972), 5-16; and E. W. Monter, "The Consistory of Geneva, 1559-1569," *Bibliothèque d'Humanisme et Renaissance* 38 (1976): 467-84. See also the important discussion of J. K. Cameron, "Scottish Calvinism and the Principal of Intolerance," in *Reformatio perennis: Essays on Calvin and the Reformation in Honor of F. L. Battles*, ed. B. A. Gerrish and R. Benedetto (Pittsburgh: Pickwick Papers, 1981), 113–128.

[8]"The forme of prayers and ministration of the sacraments" of 1556 was published in D. Laing, ed., *The Works of John Knox* (Edinburgh: Wodrow Society, 1855), 4:155-214—see esp. 203-206: "The order of ecclesiasticall discipline"; and the "Answer to a great nomber of blasphemous cavillations" of 1559, in ibid., 5:17-468—see 208-232 on the need to punish. See also the Scots "Confession of faith," chap. 18, in W. C. Dickinson, ed., *John Knox's History of the Reformation in Scotland*, 2 vols. (London: Thomas Nelson and Sons, 1949), 2:266-267. It is worth noting that both Luther and Calvin had identified only two "marks" of the true church—right teaching of the gospel and right administration of the sacraments—and that the

were both spelled out in chapter 7 of another of Knox's literary endeavors of 1560 entitled—perhaps ominously—*A First Book of Discipline*:

> As that no Commonwealth can flourish or long indure without good lawes and sharpe execution of the same, so neither can the Kirk of God be brought to purity neither yet be retained in the same without the order of ecclesiastical discipline, which stands in reproving and correcting of the faults which the civil sword either doth neglect or not punish. . . . Drunkenness, excesse (be it in aparel or be it in eating and drinking), fornication, oppressing of the poore, . . . wanton words and licentious living tending to slander, doe openly appertaine to the kirk of God to punish them, as God's word commands.

None were to escape scrutiny of their conduct for, the *Book* continued: "To discipline must all the estates within this Realm be subject, as well the Rulers as they that are ruled; yea and the Preachers themselves, as welle as the poorest within the Kirk."[9]

It was to enforce Mosaic Law upon all Scots, and to prepare them for the second (and more glorious) coming of the Lord, that powerful new church courts were created. At the parish level a kirk session, composed of the minister and a number of lay elders and deacons, kept an eye on church fabric and finance, and administered poor relief, but spent most of its time on discipline. The records of almost every Scottish kirk session, from the mid-sixteenth to the mid-eighteenth century, are filled with parishioners who manifestly failed to respect the Lord's Day; with neighbors who, before witnesses, quarreled and assaulted each other either verbally or physically; and, above all, with couples who admitted, more or less reluctantly, their illicit sexual liaisons. But three eventualities might cause a session to send one of its cases before a higher court—the local "presbytery" where all the ministers of a given area met together for the examination and ordination of ministers, the supervision and visitation of

---

idea of discipline as a third seems to derive from Bucer: see A. N. Burnett, "Church Discipline and Moral Reformation in the Thought of Martin Bucer," *The Sixteenth Century Journal* 22 (1991): 439–456; and J. C. Spalding, "Discipline as a Mark of the True Church in its Sixteenth-Century Lutheran Context," in *Piety, Politics and Ethics: Studies in Honor of George W. Forell*, ed. C. Lindberg, Sixteenth Century Essays and Studies, vol. 3 (Kirksville: Sixteenth Century Journal Publishers, 1984), 119–138.

[9] J. K. Cameron, ed., *The First Book of Discipline* (Edinburgh: Saint Andrew Press, 1972), 165–166, 173: "The Seventh head: Of ecclesiastical discipline."

constituent parishes, the enactment and enforcement of ordinances handed down by higher ecclesiastical tribunals, the correction of manners and morals, and the ultimate sanction of excommunication.[10] The first category of offenders referred to the presbytery were guilty of transgressions deemed to be particularly serious (any offense leading to sentence of excommunication was automatically referred). Others might be "sent upstairs" because the offender (often a local landowner) either refused to accept the session's authority or repeated their crime frequently. Finally, others still might come before the presbytery because their case offered unusual difficulties.

A case heard by the presbytery of Stirling in 1587 may serve as an example of the first variety. One of the ministers informed his brethren that "their is ane man dwelland within his said parrochun callit James Wilson . . . quha [=who] hes fallin in the fourt fault of fornicatioun with three soverall wemen, and thairfor inquyrit of the brethir quhat he sould do thairwith." (Their answer was to issue a summons against James Wilson under pain of excommunication.)[11] An example of the second category appeared in the minutes of the kirk session of Auchtermuchty in Fife in 1649. James Sibbald, a miller, was denounced for carting a load of flour on the Sabbath. He appeared before the session, but with an ill grace, and was overheard in the anteroom "saying 'I defy the minister and you and all you session and all that ye can do . . . I cair not for you.'" For this evident insubordination he was referred to the presbytery, and "depairted the session in a werrie disdainful way, muttering wordis quhilkis could not be heard."[12] A splendid example of the third variety of presbytery disciplinary business—the "difficult" case—is afforded by the remarkable saga of Janet Dick, whose apparent achievement of a virgin birth troubled the kirk session of Airth and the presbytery of Stirling on several occasions

---

[10]See the excellent summary of the duties of the presbyteries at this time in J. Kirk, ed., *Stirling Presbytery Records 1581-1587*, Scottish History Society, 4th series, vol. 47 (Edinburgh, 1981), xviii; and J. Kirk, ed., *The Second Book of Discipline* (Edinburgh: Saint Andrew Press, 1980), 102–114.

[11]Kirk, *Stirling presbytery records*, 258–259. Mr. Wilson appeared the very next week and was sentenced "to mak publict repentence, in his awin parroche kirk four soverall Sondayis in tyme of sermond, bair fuittit in linning clathis" (ibid., 260).

[12]Quoted in J. di Folco, "Discipline and Welfare in the Mid-Seventeenth Century Scots Parish," *Records of the Scottish Church History Society* 19 (1977): 169–183, at 176. Throughout the 1640s and 1650s, the burgh of Auchtermuchty was apparently riven by dissent among the elders, between the minister and some of his elders, and between the session and a group of parishioners. See further details in ibid., 176–177.

between 1656 and 1668. Janet, a spinster, "brought forth a bairn" and yet steadfastly denied ever engaging in sexual intercourse. Examination by midwives beforehand seemed to confirm her story. The kirk was not convinced, but even the most stringent questioning failed to break her story, so she was left "lying under scandal" (a verdict which virtually deprived her of all civil rights) until the explanation was produced twelve years later. A local man, after being almost killed by a bolt of lightning, admitted that he had "committed uncleanness" (as he put it) with the girl while she was so soundly asleep that she never woke up. The man was fined for his "sin," and no cult of the Virgin Janet took root in the central lowlands.[13]

Janet Dick and her clandestine lover, like countless other inhabitants of seventeenth-century Scotland, never seem to have questioned the right of the church courts to judge and to punish them. Open contempt for the system, like that of James Sibbald, was rare, and except in the 1650s, it was seldom successful. Those who would not bend the knee were relentlessly pursued and, eventually, either imprisoned or forced to flee.[14] It is worth pausing for a moment to examine why.

No doubt there was an element of fear among most ordinary lay folk that resisting or refusing the commands of the church might lead to damnation; but that alone would probably not have been enough to secure obedience—it certainly did not in England.[15] In Scotland, however, fear

[13]Scottish Record Office, Edinburgh [hereafter SRO] CH2/722/6, entries in the register of the presbytery of Stirling for October 1 and 8, 1656; January 26, 1659, March 20, 1661; and CH2/722/7, entries for September 21, 1664, and April 29, July 22, August 22, September 16, and November 18, 1668. This case was generously brought to my attention by Dr. Stephen J. Davies of Manchester Polytechnic.

[14]See the example of an Edinburgh delinquent pursued in 1653–55 by letter to Aberdeenshire whither she had fled in hope of avoiding censure, in L. M. Smith, "Scotland and Cromwell: A Study in Early Modern Government" (Ph.D. diss., University of Oxford, 1980), 236. In the eighteenth century some sessions even placed "Wanted" advertisements in newspapers requesting information about missing suspects: see R. Mitchison and L. Leneman, *Sexuality and Social Control: Scotland 1660–1780* (Oxford: Basil Blackwell, 1990), 34. See also W. Mackay, ed., *Records of the Presbyteries of Inverness and Dingwall, 1643–1688*, Scottish History Society, vol. 24 (Edinburgh, 1896), 60, 84: the case of William McPherson, in 1675, "adulterer and thereafter fornicator in Inverness, haveing appeared several yeares *in sacco*, evidenceing his publick remorse for his said gross sins, supplicated the presbytery [of Inverness] to be absolved." But the assembled ministers seemed to feel that a few further years in sackcloth were called for, and the petition was refused. So in 1677 the unfortunate man went away to Holland to become a soldier: possible death at the hands of the Catholic French must have appeared preferable to endless humiliation before his fellow parishioners.

[15]The most influential account of the "bawdy courts" of Reformation England is that of C. Hill, *Society and Puritanism in Pre-Revolutionary England*, 2d ed. (New York: Schocken, 1967), chap. 8. Subsequent research, however, has not endorsed his negative, unsympathetic

was heavily reinforced by the comprehensive support for ecclesiastical justice provided by the secular authorities. It is true that the General Assembly of the church failed to persuade the Scots Parliament in 1560 to give the Book of Discipline statutory backing; and that Parliament also declined a request in May 1562 to outlaw those "horibill vices" described in Leviticus for which "the eternal God in his Parliament hes pronounced death to be the punishment."[16] But in 1563 incest and witchcraft were declared capital offenses; while in 1567 "notoure and manifest adulterie" joined them, and fornicators were threatened with either a forty pound fine or eight days in prison. In the same year, Parliament expressly recognized the Kirk's jurisdiction in preaching of the word, administration of the sacraments, and correction of manners; and between the 1570s and the 1690s ten separate acts were passed to make blasphemy into a statutory offense, and fourteen to penalize sabbath breach.[17]

---

account. See, for example, R. B. Manning, *Religion and Society in Elizabethan Sussex* (Leicester: Leicester University Press, 1969); R. A. Marchant, *The Church under the Law: Justice, Administration and Discipline in the Diocese of York, 1560–1640* (Cambridge: Cambridge University Press, 1972); J. A. Sharpe, "Crime and Delinquency in an Essex Parish 1600–1640," in J. S. Cockburn, ed., *Crime in England 1550–1800* (Princeton: Princeton University Press, 1977), chap. 4; R. Houlbrooke, *Church Courts and the People during the English Reformation, 1520–1570* (Oxford: Oxford University Press, 1979); P. Collinson, *The Religion of Protestants* (Oxford: Oxford University Press, 1982), 62–70; S. Lander, "Church Courts and the Reformation in the Diocese of Chichester 1500–1558," in *The English Reformation Revised*, ed. C. Haigh (Cambridge: Cambridge University Press, 1987), chap. 2; and, above all, M. J. Ingram, *Church Courts, Sex and Marriage in England, 1570–1640* (Cambridge: Cambridge University Press, 1987).

[16]Quoted in *Knox's History of the Reformation*, 2:49. The petition continued with a vintage piece of Knoxian moral blackmail: "and seing that kings are but His lieutenants, having no power to give life where [God] commands death, . . . so will He not fail to punish you for neglecting his judgments." It is interesting to note that the English Parliament also refused to back a disciplinary package at this time: see J. C. Spalding, *The Reformation of the Ecclesiastical Laws of England, 1552*, Sixteenth Century Essays and Studies, vol. 19 (Kirksville: Sixteenth Century Journal Publishers, 1992).

[17]Details from T. Thomson, ed., *Acts of the Parliaments of Scotland* (Edinburgh, 1814), 2:539 and 3:24–25, 38; and B. Lenman and G. Parker, "The State, the Community and the Criminal Law in Early Modern Europe," in *Crime and the Law. The Social History of Crime in Western Europe since 1500*, ed. V. A. C. Gatrell, B. Lenman, and G. Parker (London: Europa, 1980), 11–48, at 37. Interestingly enough, persons convicted of the "sins" of sodomy and bestiality were also executed—but without the passage of any statute to that effect! It was the opinion of one great eighteenth-century Scots lawyer that they were tried and condemned solely on the basis of the book of Leviticus: see J. Erskine, *An Institute of the Laws of Scotland* (1773; revised ed., Edinburgh: Edinburgh Printing and Publishing Company, 1838), 1105.

Further down the judicial spectrum, but equally important, magistrates and landlords lent their evident support to the church courts by sitting on the local kirk session. In most burghs—including Saint Andrews—the session elders normally included at least one of the town magistrates, and sometimes the minutes note that a sentence was passed on offenders "the baillies being present," since that made the decision immediately enforceable in the secular as well as in the ecclesiastical courts. Some urban parishes, indeed, openly reserved one or more places specifically for their local law officers.[18] The interlock of church and state was equally apparent in rural areas, not least because the internal divisions of each parish normally reflected the landholding patterns within it: elders were appointed for each barony, since that organism was the basic unit of economic and social life in early modern Scotland.[19] And, as in the towns, those exercising secular jurisdiction were encouraged to participate in the disciplinary work of the church. The acts of the kirk session of the Gaelic-speaking parish of Cromdale, for example, drawn up in 1702 by the minister and elders "and with them the laird of Grant, younger, of that ilk, as civil judge, to give his concurrence," ordained that "[i]n regard there are severall scandals committed within the bounds of this pariochen, therefore the civill judge, in the parish's presence, is to be intreated to every session, and his concurrence to suppress immorality is to be required by the minister and elders."

---

[18]From 1599 onwards, for example, the kirk session of Glasgow resolved that the persons elected as provost and bailies of the burgh should always be enrolled among the elders. See G. Donaldson, *Scotland: James V–James VII* (Edinburgh: Oliver and Boyd, 1971), 225. It was significant, however, that although some magistrates normally sat on each session, they never predominated, thereby threatening the church's independence: see the perceptive remarks in J. Kirk, *Patterns of Reform: Continuity and Change in the Reformation Kirk* (Edinburgh: T. and T. Clark, 1989), 273–275.

[19]See S. J. Davies, "Law and Order in Stirlingshire, 1638–1747" (Ph.D. diss., University of Saint Andrews, 1983), chap. 4. It is worth noting that the baron courts had also supported ecclesiastical jurisdiction before the Reformation. In 1529, for example, all tenants of the barony of Alloway were ordered to accept any censures imposed by the church within forty days, and anyone condemned by the church for adultery was automatically to lose his land: see M. H. B. Sanderson, *Scottish Rural Society in the Sixteenth Century* (Edinburgh: John Donald, 1982), 12. Statutes against adultery had also been passed by the Scots Parliament—for example in 1551—but the sanctions stopped at outlawry: see the important discussion in J. Wormald, "'Princes' and the Regions in the Scottish Reformation," in *Church, Politics and Society: Scotland 1408–1929*, ed. N. A. T. MacDougall (Edinburgh: John Donald, 1983), 65–84, esp. at 82 n. 4.

Sin and the Calvinists

And the secular courts returned the compliment: with very few exceptions, town magistrates, sheriffs, and holders of heritable jurisdictions went out of their way to support the decisions and laws of the church courts. In the Baron Court of Stitchill, in 1660, for example:

> The said Barroun, takeing to his serious consideratioun how great a necessity Church Discypline of this Paroch has of the assistance and concurrence of the Civil Magistrat and helpe of his authority . . . thairfor the said Barroun heirby judicially decernes and ordaines his ordnar officer of the Barroun [Court] to put in execution all Acts and Sentences of the Kirke Sessioun again[st] all persouns whomsoever within this Barrouny and poynd for all penalty and fines to be imposed be them, and take the extract of the Kirke Session their Act for his warrand.[20]

But there was a price to be paid for this apparently perfect union of church and state: the Kirk had to accept that it was sometimes inadvisable to follow the Book of Discipline's injunction to proceed against "all estates within this Realm" with equal energy. Although in 1573 the General Assembly of the church still insisted that "great men offending in sick crymes as deserve sackcloth should receive the samein as weill as the poor," and although the records of several courts include examples of the successful discipline of local notables, it did not always happen. After all, town magistrates and local landowners often possessed rights of patronage over the parish church and were sometimes impropriators of its tithes: their influence over the minister (and perhaps over some elders) could not be ignored. Their sins might accordingly be either tacitly condoned or else privately settled. Thus in 1585 the provost of Elgin (an elder) confessed himself guilty of the sin of fornication, but was spared public penance in return for the cost of glazing a window in the church; while in Fife, somewhat later, although Lord Lindores was widely "noted for his whoredom"

---

[20]SRO CH2/983/1, p. 1: minutes of the parishes of Cromdale, Inverallen, and Advie, December 14, 1702; G. and C. B. Gunn, eds., *Records of the Baron Court of Stitchill, 1655–1807*, Scottish History Society, vol. 50 (Edinburgh, 1905), 21: declaration of November 26, 1660— that is, directly after the Restoration of Charles II. For further examples, and some excellent general remarks, see B. P. Lenman, "The Limits of Godly Discipline in the Early Modern Period, with Particular Reference to England and Scotland," in *Religion and Society in Early Modern Europe 1500–1800*, ed. K. von Greyerz (London: Allen and Unwin, 1984), 124–145.

and the laird of Kemback "was said by some to be a great whoremaster," their respective sessions chose not to inquire more closely into the matter.[21]

In fact, it has been suggested, these "tactical concessions" may have "strengthened rather than weakened the system of Godly Discipline by making it more palatable to the ruling class."[22] Just how essential secular support really was, whatever concessions it cost, emerged unmistakably in the 1650s when, during the occupation of Scotland by the army of the English Commonwealth, the civil authorities briefly withdrew their backing for ecclesiastical censure. In January 1652 all existing courts and jurisdictions in Scotland were abolished by decree of the conquerors and, in the subsequent judicial settlement, there was no place for either baron courts or church tribunals. In the summer of the following year, a session of the General Assembly was forcibly terminated by English troops and the ministers silenced and sent home. The significance of these events was not lost on contemporaries. In November 1653, for example, the kirk session of Aberdeen was openly insulted by a servant of the Catholic laird of Pitfodels:

> [Alexander Gordon] being demandit whairfoir he did not compeir sooner, he anserit: If it haid not bein to hold in the offiris paines, he had not compeirit now, nor at all. And, being demandit if he did acknowledge us to be ane judicatorie, he anserit: Unles we was authorized be the Comon wealth. And, being demandit again if he wes of our profession [sc. was he a Calvinist], he anserit: He came not to give ane acquittance. And all the whole tyme he carried himselff uncivillie and upbraidlinglie, thanking God that the tymes were not as formerlie.[23]

---

[21]Examples from Mitchison and Leneman, *Sexuality and Social Control*, 74 (with more cases from a later period at 224–228); and di Folco, "Discipline and Welfare," 171. Counter-examples in which the great are made to submit to discipline are noted in Kirk, *Patterns of Reform*, 275–276; and K. M. Brown, "In Search of the Godly Magistrate in Reformation Scotland," *Journal of Ecclesiastical History* 40 (1989): 553–581, at 566–571.

[22]See the perceptive remarks of Lenman, "The Limits of Godly Discipline," 135f.

[23]J. Stuart, ed., *Selections from the Records of the Kirk-Session, Presbytery and Synod of Aberdeen*, Spalding Club, vol. 15 (Aberdeen, 1846), 121. Mr. Gordon was sent to the presbytery and was there excommunicated for papism and disobedience.

Such behavior was only possible as long as the civil authorities in Scotland offered no support for church discipline. Even before the Restoration, this policy was reversed and, from 1660 onwards, church courts everywhere in the kingdom could once more rely on the full support of statute, sheriff, bailie, and baron in enforcing their will.[24]

* * *

Most of the examples above are taken from the system in its heyday. They illustrate generalities that could be backed up by thousands of other cases in published and manuscript form which are almost identical in nature.[25] But how did it all begin? At what point did the new church courts, created after the Reformation, gain general acceptance; and when, precisely, did they first enter their symbiotic relationship with the established secular jurisdictions? The answer to this problem is not easy to provide, for the survival of the records of the church of Scotland is extremely uneven. In 1905, it was computed that documents from 16 synods, 84 presbyteries, and 1,324 parishes of Scotland then survived. But many of these sources began only in the eighteenth century, and some of those extant in 1905— including some of the earliest—have since disappeared.[26] In 1980, the survival of pre-1700 church records was as shown in Table 1.[27]

The parish of Saint Andrews in the later sixteenth century offers a unique glimpse of the process by which "godly discipline" was first estab-

---

[24]On these policy changes see L. M. Smith, "Scotland and Cromwell," chap. 9; and idem, "Sackcloth for the Sinner or Punishment for the Crime? Church and Secular Courts in Cromwellian Scotland," in *New Perspectives on the Politics and Culture of Early Modern Scotland*, ed. J. Dwyer, R. A. Mason, and A. Murdoch (Edinburgh: John Donald, 1982), 116–132.

[25]For three admirable studies of the working of the kirk in its prime, see D. Henderson, *The Scottish Ruling Elder* (London: John Clarke, 1935), esp. 100–145; W. R. Foster, *The Church before the Covenants 1596-1638* (Edinburgh: Scottish Academic Press, 1972), chaps. 4 and 5; and, above all, W. H. Makey, *The Church and the Covenant, 1638-1651* (Edinburgh: John Donald, 1978).

[26]T. Burns, *Church Property: The Benefice Lectures* (Edinburgh: G. A. Morton, 1905), 1–65, and 193–268 (a list of church records then extant).

[27]Calculated from P. Rayner, B. Lenman, and G. Parker, *Handlist of Records for the Study of Crime in Early Modern Scotland (to 1747)*, List and Index Society, Special Series, vol. 16 (London, 1982), 158–259. These totals include only volumes deposited in the Scottish Record Office or in Register House before 1980. It was then thought that about 130 more kirk session records dating from before 1750 were extant in private hands. Most church records have since been moved from Edinburgh to regional archives, making it extremely difficult to update these figures.

Table 1: Survival of Scottish church records, 1560–1700

Period	Kirk Session minutes surviving (in whole or in part)	Presbytery minutes surviving (in whole or in part)
1560–1575	2	0
1575–1600	23	11
1601–1625	70	23
1626–1650	202	45
1651–1675	352	62
1676–1700	527	82

lished in Scotland for three reasons. First, because its kirk session register commences before any other and continues unbroken up to 1600. Second, because many of the events therein recorded are described in detail in the *Diary* kept by one of its ministers, James Melville, during the 1580s and 1590s.[28] And third, because:

> Saint Andrews was in a unique position, and its peculiar advantages allowed it to offer an example to the rest of Scotland. It was small enough to be amenable to tight control, and sufficiently distant from the court and centre of government to be able to manage its own affairs without undue external interference. Its tradition as the ecclesiastical capital made it important enough to attract attention, while its university added the gravity of learning to what was being accomplished.

It offered, as the kirk session itself claimed, "the face of ane perfyt reformed kyrk."[29]

---

[28]David Hay Fleming's edition of the Register (hereafter cited as *Register*: see full citation in note 3) omitted only some of the coarser exchanges between various sinners and the session. They were indicated by dots (. . .) Volume 1covers the years 1559–82 and Volume 2 covers 1582–1600. The original register for 1559–1600, filling some three hundred folios, is still conserved at Holy Trinity Church in Saint Andrews. The session records for 1600–38 are incomplete, but five volumes cover the period 1638–1706 in some 1,600 folios: H. M. Register House, Edinburgh, OPR 453/5–9. A parallel to Melville's diary also exists for part of the later period: see T. McCrie, ed., *The Life of Mr. Robert Blair, Minister of St. Andrews, containing his Autobiography*, Wodrow Society, vol. 13 (Edinburgh, 1848).

The register of the kirk session began in October 1559, and the session itself had probably been active for some time before that—perhaps since soon after the town's "Reformation Day" on Sunday, June 11, 1559, when the people of the town literally awoke "in a town full of Catholic churches and went to bed that night with a Protestant burgh and a Reformed parish church."[30] But the early folios of the register contain a strange mixture of administrative, disciplinary, and "consistorial" business (the latter comprising matrimonial, testamentary, and other matters previously heard by the Archbishop's "commissary court"). There were two reasons for this, both of them associated with the presence in Saint Andrews of one of the "superintendents" created on the orders of the General Assembly after 1560 to "visit and plant kirks" in the dioceses of Scotland. John Winram, formerly sub-prior of the Augustinian house at Saint Andrews and vicar-general of the archdiocese, was elected superintendent for Fife and Perthshire in April 1561, and for the next eleven years he (assisted by the town's kirk session) handled 124 cases arising from his visits to parishes outside the burgh. All were entered in the session register, normally after the local cases.[31] Furthermore, Winram was at first also charged with "consistorial" business. Although in 1560 Parliament abolished all papal authority in Scotland, papally appointed bishops were permitted to continue their jurisdiction over matrimonial and other consistorial business, acting in their own names. Since some bishops did not subscribe to the Calvinist Confession of Faith this situation was plainly unsatisfactory, and gradually the "superintendents" took over the work. This situation only changed with the creation of separate commissary courts, first at Edinburgh in 1564 (for Lothian and for appeals from elsewhere) and shortly afterwards at Saint Andrews.[32]

---

[29]Quotations from the excellent article of Jane Dawson, "'The face of ane perfyt reformed kyrk': St. Andrews and the Early Scottish Reformation," in *Humanism and Reform: The Church in Europe, England and Scotland, 1400-1640: Essays in Honour of James K. Cameron*, ed. J. Kirk, Studies in Church History, subsidia 8 (Oxford: Basil Blackwell, 1991), 413–435, at 427; and *Register*, 1:198.

[30]The events of "Reformation Day"—quite a contrast to the Reformation process in other countries, which could take years—are discussed in Dawson, "'Ane perfyt reformed kyrk,'" 415.

[31]On the work of the Superintendent's Court in Saint Andrews see Dawson, "'Ane perfyt reformed kyrk,'" 431–433, and *Register*, 1:xxvii–xxxv, for details. Superintendent Winram led an interesting life: a pillar of the Catholic church right up to 1558, when he witnessed the burning of Walter Milne for heresy, he switched sides fast enough to help draft the Scots Confession and the Book of Discipline in 1560, and took advantage of the new order to marry in 1562 at the age of 70. He died in 1582. On the work of the superintendents, see the definitive essay of J. Kirk, "The Superintendent: Myth and Reality," in *Patterns of Reform*, ed. Kirk, 154–231 (on Winram's career see 176–179).

The intermingling of consistorial, disciplinary, and what later became presbytery matters in the same record renders the analysis of purely kirk session business before 1573 difficult, though not impossible. To be sure, until the fall of Mary Queen of Scots in June 1567 not all Scots were subject to discipline, for attending Catholic worship that stopped short of the Mass was no crime; and Gordon Donaldson has suggested that two alternative churches coexisted in the kingdom between 1560 and 1567.[33] But Saint Andrews was unusual. On the one hand, the Reformed party in the town was unusually strong, for the provost, magistrates, and burgh council, along with over three hundred leading citizens, had signed the Protestant "Band" in July 1559; on the other, the Catholics were disheartened and disoriented, with even Archbishop James Hamilton ambivalent towards the new order. It was therefore possible for the Saint Andrews Kirk Session to deal sternly from the start with sexual offenders (in 1562 adulterers were handed over to the "bailies present to be civile correctit and punisht according to the order resavit in this citie"), to demand a public recantation from those suspected of favoring Rome (and to imprison or banish those who refused), and to excommunicate those who declined to accept its authority.[34] A campaign to enforce proper observance of the Sabbath began in spring 1568. There were also other efforts to enforce Reformation doctrine that went unrecorded in the Register. For example, James Melville recalled seeing, as a student in 1571–72, "a

[32]For details on the commissary courts before, during, and after the Reformation, see G. Donaldson, "The Church Courts," in *An Introduction to Scottish Legal History*, Stair Society, vol. 20 (Edinburgh, 1958), 363–373. On page 366 there is an interesting analysis of the business handled by the commissary courts of Scotland in the first half of the sixteenth century:appeals from lower courts made up around one-third and, of the rest, about one-third concerned wills, one-quarter broken contracts, and one-fifth church property. The role of sex and slander cases, which became the staple of church courts after the Reformation, was negligible before 1560. In England, however, over 80 percent of the cases heard by the London Consistory Court between 1470 and 1516 concerned either sex or slander: see R. Wunderli, *London Church Courts and Society on the Eve of the Reformation* (Cambridge: Medieval Academy of America, 1981), 81.

[33]G. Donaldson, *The Scottish Reformation* (Cambridge: Cambridge University Press, 1960), chap. 3. John Carswell, a local laird, was both superintendent of Argyll and apostolic bishop of the Isles: see Kirk, *Patterns of Reform*, chap. 7. For the hesitant installation of the Reformation in other towns of the kingdom, see I. B. Cowan, *The Scottish Reformation: Church and Society in Sixteenth-Century Scotland* (New York: St. Martin's Press, 1982), chap. 8; M. Lynch, *Edinburgh and the Reformation* (Edinburgh: John Donald, 1981); idem, "From Privy Kirk to Burgh Church: An Alternative View of the Process of Protestantisation," in MacDougall, *Church, Politics and Society*, chap 5; and A. White, "The Impact of the Reformation on a Burgh Community: The Case of Aberdeen," in *The Early Modern Town in Scotland*, ed. M. Lynch (London: Croom Helm, 1987), chap. 4.

[34]Details from Dawson, "Ane perfyt reformed kyrk," 427–430. The first cases in the register (both from 1559) concerned adultery; the first case of fornication was punished in May 1560.

witche in St. Andros, aginst the quhilk Mr. Knox delt from pulpit, sche being set upe at a pillar befor him." Shortly afterwards he watched her burn to death. At the same time "Mr. Knox" also delivered a series of blistering sermons in the town church, execrating sin and commanding virtue, during which he "was lyk to ding [=smash] that pulpit in blads, and flie out of it." But the Register is silent about all this.[35]

The situation only changed after 1572. On the national scene, the government at last provided the Reformed church with access to some of the wealth of the former establishment (by the Convention of Leith, January 1572), and deprived of office all clerics who refused to accept the Confession of Faith (January 1573). Furthermore, the end of the civil war in the spring of 1573 ushered in a "time of repose which God has granted us after our long troubles."[36] In Saint Andrews itself, Winram resigned as superintendent in 1572 and left the minister and elders free to pursue local control single-mindedly. Shortly afterwards the session ordained that where a servant was fined for some moral lapse, his or her master should be responsible for payment; and henceforth there was less willingness to commute the normal penalties, imposed specifically to shame the transgressor, for money.[37]

So the "great work of discipline" in Saint Andrews really began only in 1573. That year the register commenced—significantly—with an injunction that all members of the session who missed a meeting should be fined "wythout exceptioun of personis and forgeving to ony man," followed by a supplication to the magistrates that they would "execut the actis and ordinances" of the session concerning fornicators, adulterers, Sabbath-breakers, and "thame that ar warnit to compeir . . . and comperis not."[38] It must have proved effective because by 1600 some 1,721 parishioners had "compeired" before the session, an average of over 60 per year.[39] The pattern of their offenses, however, is not what one might

[35]*Register*, 1:294ff. (for sabbath-breach); *Diary of James Melville*, 46 (on the witch) and 26 (on Knox's need to be virtually carried up into the pulpit, where he reached his full oratorical powers only after about half an hour).

[36]See Donaldson, *Scottish Reformation*, 171, 176, 183.

[37]*Register*, 1:377–378. The fine was to be half the hiring fee agreed between master and servant; since servants made up the largest single category of sexual offenders, this measure was of considerable importance. The General Assembly of the church ordained in 1573 that no minister "may dispence with the extremitie of sack-cloth prescryvit be the acts of the generall discipline, for any pecuniall sowme" (quoted *Register*, 1:lii). See also p. 168, above.

[38]*Register*, 1:373–374.

[39]Calculated from *Register*, 373–943. Annual totals are given in the appendix, pp. 193–196, below. Although where possible information on punishments is given in the text, many entries in the Register fail to state the penalty imposed so that quantification is impossible.

expect of an ecclesiastical court. Nor does it resemble the duties set out in the instructions issued to the elders of the urban parish of Stirling in 1600, which have been hailed as "typical":

> To tak attendence to the maneris of the pepill . . . ; to attend quhat straingearis resortis to the toun, and to quhat effect; . . . [and to search for] any Jesuitis or seminarie Priestis . . . within this toun.[40]

For it is clear that in Saint Andrews "the maneris of the pepill" occupied the lion's share of all attention, while the movement of "straingearis" and papists scarcely received any. And Saint Andrews was by no means unique: the few other Scottish parishes with surviving records from this period show almost exactly the same pattern. So do later ones, such as the disciplinary records of the Stirlingshire parish of Saint Ninians displayed in Table 2, for example.[41] The same applies to several Calvinist communities outside Scotland. Thus the Consistory of Amsterdam between 1578 and 1600 heard 403 cases, an average of 30 per year, of which 335 (83 percent) involved moral offenses. At Emden, in northwest Germany, precisely 80 percent of the 114 disciplinary cases tried by the Consistory between 1596 and 1600 concerned morals; while at Nîmes in the south of France, where a kirk session (*consistoire*) began work in 1561 and handled over 180 cases annually, four-fifths of all recorded business also concerned morals. It was the same in other Calvinist communities in France and Switzerland, probably including Geneva, where between 1559 and 1569, the *consistoire*

Table 2: Kirk Session Cases in Saint Ninians parish 1653–1719

Offense	Number of cases	Percent
Sexual cases	307	57
Disorderly conduct	162	30
Enforcement/Authority	46	9
Other	20	4
Total	535	100

[40]Quoted in Foster, *Church before the Covenants*, 72.

[41]Based on the tables in S. J. Davies, "Law and Order in Stirlingshire," chap. 4. See also Mary Black Verschuur, "Enforcing the Discipline of the Kirk: Mr. Patrick Galloway's Early Years as Minister of Perth," in *Later Calvinism: International Perspectives*, ed. W. Fred Graham, Sixteenth Century Essays and Studies, vol. 22 (Kirksville: Sixteenth Century Journal Publishers, 1994), 215–236. However, although sexual misconduct seemed as rife in sixteenth century Perth as elsewhere, Dr. Black omitted it totally, on the curious ground that it has received so much noteriety elsewhere (218).

disciplined some five hundred persons a year—representing perhaps one adult in fifteen.[42]

Discipline did not take up all the session's time at Saint Andrews, however. Between 1573 and 1600 the minister and elders also transacted 361 items of administrative business, such as arranging for church repairs and the purchase of equipment, for the parish Communion service (including an advance examination of the fitness of all church members to participate), and for catechism classes. And the 1,721 whose "disciplinary" offenses are analyzed in Figure 1 and Table 3 include those who applied for poor relief (thirty-five cases, almost all after 1597); for the baptism of illegitimate children or orphans (twenty-one cases); and for the enforcement of marriage vows about which one partner had had second thoughts (sixteen cases recorded—including one ingenious citizen in 1584 who successfully argued that "he nevir maid promis of mareage . . . bot onlie promittit to hir ane kow").[43] Finally, six cases of infanticide and eight of manslaughter also made a brief appearance before going on to the civil courts. All these items appear in the column labeled "other" in Table 3. Few testimonials given to (or required from) God-fearing "straingearis" are recorded (thirty-four cases); and fewer still of suspected religious deviance, whether involving witches (eight) or Catholics (seven). As in seventeenth-century Saint Ninians—and most other parishes of the kingdom that

---

[42]See H. Roodenburg, *Onder censuur: De kerkelijke tucht in de gereformeerde gemeente van Amsterdam 1578-1700* (Hilversum: Verloren, 1990), 137 (although note that further minor infractions may have been dealt with by the elders locally and recorded in the—missing—*wijkboekjes*: 142-144); H. Schilling, "Sündenzucht und frühneuzeitliche Sozialdisziplinierung: Die Calvinistiche Presbyteriale Kirchenzucht in Emden vom 16. bis 19. Jahrhundert," in *Stände und Gesellschaft im alten Reich*, ed. G. Schmidt (Stuttgart: Franz Steiner Verlag, 1989), 265-302; and R. A. Mentzer, "*Disciplina nervus ecclesiae*: The Calvinist Reform of Morals at Nîmes," *The Sixteenth Century Journal* 18 (1987):89-115. There are further (somewhat fragmentary) data on southern French, Rhineland, and Swiss Calvinist church courts in J. Estèbe and B. Vogler, "La genèse d'une société protestante: Étude comparée de quelques registres consistoriaux languedociens et palatins vers 1600," *Annales: Économies, sociétés, civilisations* 31 (1976):362-88; and J. R. Watt, "The Reception of the Reformation at Valangin, Switzerland, 1547-1588," *The Sixteenth Century Journal* 20 (1989):89-104. A detailed analysis of the copious surviving records of the Geneva Consistory is currently under way: see R. M. Kingdon, "Calvin and the Establishment of Consistory Discipline in Geneva," *Nederlands archief voor kerkgeschiedenis* 70 (1990):158-72. In the meantime, see the "guesstimate" of Monter, "The Consistory of Geneva," 484; and the general remarks of H. Höpfl, *The Christian Polity of John Calvin* (Cambridge: Cambridge University Press, 1982), 90-96, 115-121, 188-206.

[43]*Register*, 1:392-94. John Chaeplan *contra* Jonet Lawsoun, May 19 and June 9, 1584.

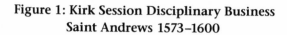

Figure 1: Kirk Session Disciplinary Business
Saint Andrews 1573–1600

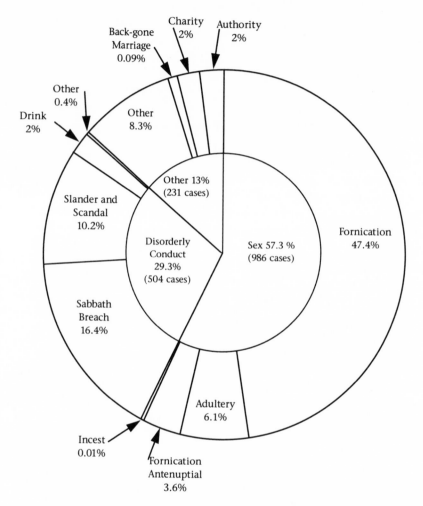

Table 3: Kirk Session cases in Saint Andrews parish 1573–1600

Offense	Number of offenders	Percent
Sexual cases	986	57
Disorderly conduct	504	30
Enforcement/Authority	38	2
Other	193	11
Total	1721	100

have been studied—everything else paled before the apparent obsession of Scots Calvinists with sex.[44]

Most of the 986 sexual offenders hauled before the session were charged with fornication (sexual intercourse between two single persons)—813 persons—or "fornication antenuptial" (intercourse between two persons whose marriage banns had been called but who had not yet been)—63 persons. Adultery (105 offenders) and incest (5 offenders) were relatively rare, and bestiality and sodomy do not appear at all. Given that the entire adult population of the parish was probably under two thousand, and that around 32 offenders were prosecuted for sexual misconduct annually, the chances that a young person would appear before the session at some point were relatively high.[45]

Almost all the fornicators arrived before the session in much the same way: a single woman was denounced by a neighbor or by an elder, either for having given birth or for being about to do so.

> [August 10, 1580] comperit Beteraige Bredfute and confessit and granted sche was deliverit off ane maiden bairne to James Wemis
>
> [August 31, 1580] comperit Agnes Angous and confessit and granted hir to be wyth chylde to Jhone Buge younger, and submitted hir to the discipline off the kirk; and siclyk confessit this to be the thrid tyme she committed fornication.[46]

The session almost always picked on the woman first, because the accusation was so easy to prove: either a girl was pregnant and single or she was not. As the elders of Killearn in Stirlingshire somewhat smugly observed of a pregnant spinster in 1733: "It is obvious that she has sinned, be the father who it will."[47]

---

[44]Generalization based on the survey conducted by Rayner, Lenman, and Parker for the *Handlist* (see note 27 above).

[45]It might be supposed that the presence of numerous university students in the town would have affected the picture; but this does not appear to have been the case, for all university persons were subject to the discipline of their own officers and their own parish of Saint Leonards. Students therefore figured rarely among those tried by the kirk session of Saint Andrews.

[46]*Register*, 1:449.

[47]Quoted by S. J. Davies, "The Courts and the Scottish Legal System, 1600–1747: The Case of Stirlingshire," in *Crime and the Law*, 120–154, at 125. In the 1,951 fornication cases recorded in various parishes of Stirlingshire between 1637 and 1747 only twenty-six women were not pregnant: see Davies, "Law and Order in Stirlingshire," 83.

It was far less easy to establish the father's identity. Some girls refused to tell, although usually everyone knew with whom they had been seen at the relevant time. Others named a man who denied the charge, and in such cases the man was allowed to take an oath of innocence before the whole congregation during time of service. Normally he was allowed a week or so to peruse the oath, with its fearsome penalties for perjury:

> Whereas I have been delated for fornication with X, I hereupon swear by the terrible and dreadful name of God the searcher of the secrets of all hearts, that I did never know the said X by having carnal dealings with her. And if this day I swear falsely, I do here before God's people in this congregation renounce my interest in Christ and my right to everlasting happiness in the life to come.

This was usually enough to break the resistance of all but the totally innocent or the totally corrupt—and the Kirk had no intention of allowing the latter to escape blameless. If a blatantly guilty man still seemed prepared to acquit himself on oath, the session could and did refuse him permission to do so, leaving him neither convicted nor acquitted but, as the phrase went, "lying under scandal." This, in effect, meant that he could not go to church, could not leave his parish, and could not find work or receive poor relief. He also risked a summons to the local secular court for disturbing the peace.[48]

One of the few alternatives to pregnancy as proof that sexual misconduct had taken place was the discovery of a couple *in flagrante delicto*. In 1589, for example, James Meldrum delated his own wife for adultery with Nicholl Broun. The two parties named appeared before the session "quha denyit the bill *simpliciter*" despite the fact that witnesses had found Mr. Broun hidden "eftir ten houris at evin, hid secretele in James Meldrumis hous in this citee, behind ane bed heid." The pair was therefore convicted, and condemned to appear in sackcloth before the congregation on Sunday in respect of their adultery, and before the magistrates "for the great sklander gevin by thame" in denying the charge.[49] Less spectacular behavior could also draw unexpected attention to forbidden liaisons: a

---

[48]The text of the oath was standard: see an example in Davies, "The Courts," 124 n. 13. In a survey of Scottish kirk session records from the 1760s, 72 percent of the men named as father by pregnant women owned up within a month: see Mitchison and Leneman, *Sexuality and Social Control*, 75.

[49]*Register*, 2:656.

couple marching purposefully into the countryside at dusk might be followed and spied on; the moans of a couple who had left their bed too near
an open window could attract the attention of bystanders; a careless boast
of sexual prowess might be reported to the elders for further investigation.[50] But even these cases lacked that element of incontrovertible proof
that pregnancy provided, and in the seventeenth century, the charge
might have to be reduced from fornication to "scandalous carriage." But
the Saint Andrews records scarcely mention this offense: under rigorous
questioning, almost all of those accused eventually broke down and confessed.

The Kirk disposed of a formidable arsenal of penalties against sexual
offenders. Those guilty of lesser misdemeanors might receive a "rebuke"
in private from the session; those whose lapse was greater, but fell short of
sexual intercourse, might be rebuked from the pulpit during church service. Parties to grosser offenses, however, were each sentenced to pay a
fine into the "poor box" and to appear in public on successive Sundays
seated on the church's "stool of repentance" (see p. 158). In most parishes
this was a high, four-legged, backless chair, rather like a modern bar stool,
sometimes cleverly constructed so that it would topple over if the sinner
failed to sit bolt upright; but elsewhere it was attached to a scaffold with
several settings—the higher the setting, the worse the offense. "The stool,"
wrote an English visitor in 1635, "is a public and eminent seat erected
about two yards from the ground... where the whole congregation may
take notice" of the offenders. In some churches, he added incredulously,
the stool was capable of holding "six or eight persons." At Tyninghame,
near Edinburgh, erecting a "stool" cost eight pounds for the woodwork
and one pound for the stone base: it was clearly a structure of substance.[51]

---

[50]See, for an example, *Register*, 2:523: case of Christene Mwir, March 18, 1584, "quha
grantis that sche, the xvij day of Marche instant [sc. the night before!], in the nicht, past out
with the South Gait Port of this citee, and thair committit the filthy crime of adultrie with
James Neilsoun." The record notes a previous adultery with Andrew, earl of Rothes, which
produced a bastard child. The case was therefore referred to the presbytery. For numerous
similar examples, see Mitchison and Leneman, *Sexuality and Social Control*, chap. 6; and G.
R. Quaife, *Wanton Wenches and Wayward Wives: Peasants and Illicit Sex in Early Seventeenth
Century England* (London: Croom Helm, 1979), 48–56.

[51]Sir William Brereton, *Travels in Holland, the United Provinces, England, Scotland and
Ireland*, Chetham Society, vol. 1 (London, 1844), 107; A. I. Ritchie, *Churches of St. Baldred:
Auldhame, Whitekirk, Tyninghame, Prestonkirk* (Edinburgh, 1880), 86. Ritchie, ibid., indicates
that the Aberdeen "stool" was certainly capable of seating seven at a time—women and men
at different times, of course. The Saint Andrews stool, still kept in the Town Church, was
somewhat more modest.

The usual penalty for fornication included three appearances on the stool on successive Sundays. If the sinner relapsed and fornicated again, six appearances were called for, and those who carried on in this way—charmingly referred to as "trilapses," "quadrilapses," and so on—were required to sit on the stool, clothed in sackcloth, on an indefinite number of occasions. While in public view, in this ungainly posture, the offenders endured a lengthy rebuke by the minister, after which they begged forgiveness of those they had wronged (often by shaking hands) and of the congregation at large. In addition they were fined. In Saint Andrews, until 1593, two Scots pounds was normally the price of a case of fornication, double for a relapse, and so on, each party paying the same penalty. Adultery, which led to appearances on the stool for up to nine months, and often a civil punishment, involved a fine of up to one hundred pounds. These sums were large: average wages in Scotland at this time were less than one pound a week, and the normal weekly collection in rural parishes might be counted in shillings rather than pounds. A few fornications and the occasional adultery were therefore good news for the church treasurer, and indeed for those of the poor who were dependent on alms from the session. Conversely, the financial hardship caused by the fines, especially to servants (who constituted the largest single category of sexual offender) was considerable, especially on top of the cost of raising the child.

But there were also other penalties. The illegitimate children of suspected sinners were often refused baptism until both parents submitted to discipline. Those who showed no contrition, or lacked the money for their fine—a total of at least 114 persons in the period studied—were imprisoned in the church steeple and received only bread and water for up to three weeks before being allowed to crave the church's forgiveness. Twelve more sinners were judged by the ministers and elders to be beyond redemption and suffered summary banishment. For example, Jonet Tod, "ane common harlot . . . nocht worthie of Christian society," was expelled from the burgh in 1598. The session also ordered a further eight persons whose offense was aggravated to stand in the "jougs" at the Market Cross, pinioned for an hour or more while passersby scorned or pelted them. Thus in December 1593, of three women condemned to be "jokit" for two hours, one had fornicated with the same person a second time; one had fornicated while on poor relief ("being ane that ressavit the puir folkis

almous"); and the third had fornicated with several persons ("with Adam
Duche . . . and certane utheris filthelie, as wes delatit to the session").[52]
Adulterers might be put through the full range of available penalties. Thus
in December 1594 James Keingzo was "jokit, cartit, and that throw the
haill streitis of the town," before being taken outside the burgh walls
where "the haill scolaris [= all the university students] and utheris, ane
great multitude of pepill" cast "rottin eggis, filth and glar [mud] at him."
Then he was "at last dowkit [ducked] ower the heid diveris tymes" in the
wintry sea, and subsequently condemned to sit in sackcloth "on the hichest degre of the penitent stuill" until "the kirk be satisfeit." After that, the
magistrates took over and banished him.[53]

The only other offenders who regularly appeared on the stool of
repentance were those found guilty of slander or insulting behavior. In a
society where people lived at close quarters, their every action surveyed by
countless others, public reputation mattered far more than it does today.
To allow an insult to pass unchallenged was, in effect, to admit that it was
true. Accusations of misconduct were therefore always taken seriously, not
least by the church, which encouraged parishioners to take their slanders
to court for fear that otherwise they might settle the matter with fists or
worse.[54]

The course of slander cases was as predictable as the sexual hearings.
They normally began when a parishioner handed in a complaint that he or
she had been maligned by another at a specified time and place. The party
named was then called, and both persons involved were required to put
down a deposit of two pounds—a precaution intended to discourage idle
or malicious actions, for the party who lost the case also lost the deposit.
At this point either the slander was withdrawn and an apology publicly
made or else evidence was produced to justify it. Witnesses were called to
speak of the character and reputation of someone accused of theft, witchcraft, or some other crime, so that in effect, a slander case became a com-
mittal hearing on the crime mentioned in the slander. Many of the

---

[52]*Register*, 2:850 and 766. "Jokin" seems to have been a penalty found especially suitable
for women. At Tyninghame, a second set of jougs was erected by the magistrates at the church
door, on the special request of the minister, because "there war sae many railers in the toun,
especiallie women, and that they troublit the session sae aft." See Ritchie, *Churches of St. Baldred*, 88.

[53]*Register*, 2:793, and similar cases in March 1595 (794) and August 1596 (819).

[54]It was the same elsewhere: see (for England) J. A. Sharpe, *Defamation and Sexual Slander in Early Modern England: The Church Courts at York*, Borthwick Papers, vol. 58 (York,
1980); (for France) Mentzer, "*Disciplina nervus ecclesiae*"; and (for the Netherlands) Roodenburg, *Onder censuur*, 321–382.

witchcraft cases heard by the secular courts of early modern Scotland began with an insult which was unsuccessfully challenged in a church court and ended with a public burning for which church and state shared responsibility and costs.[55]

Other forms of slander or insulting behavior, if proved, were likewise punished severely—although they stopped short of the death sentence. In 1579, John Scot was ordered "in presens off the congregatioun off this citee, to sitt down upone his kneis, confes his offence maed againis the said Jonett [his wife, whom he had falsely accused of adultery] and pronunce this wordis, haldand his awin tung in his hand: 'fals tung, thow leid.'" In 1594, a young man found to have threatened his father was condemned to "compeir in sek claith, beir heddit, and beir futtit, upon the hichest degre of the penitent stuill, with ane hammer in the ane hand and ane stane in the uther hand, as tua instrumentis quhairwith he menassit his father, within ane papir writin in great letteris about his heid thir wordis: 'BEHALD THE ONNATURALL SONE PUNISIT FOR PUTTING HAND IN HIS FATHER AND DISHONORING OF GOD IN HIM.'" After that he was, on successive days, to ask forgiveness of his father and of the church congregation; to stand in the jougs two hours; to be carted through the streets while his offense was proclaimed; and to receive solemn warning that "If he evir offend aganis his father or mother heireftir, in word or deid, that member of his body quhairby he offendis salbe cuttit of from him, be it tung, hand or futt."[56]

This was—and was meant to be—an exemplary sentence, to be carried out "without mercy, in exampill to utheris to abstein fra the lyke." The penalty for many non-sexual offenders was merely a fine and a rebuke. Most frequent in this category was "sabbath breach," a sin committed by doing almost anything on a Sunday except going to church. People were fined for "sleeping in the meadows in time of sermon," for selling or drinking ale on Sundays "except it be for the satisfying of nature," as well as for traveling, arguing, or beating their wives (or servants) on the Lord's

---

[55]See, for example, the detailed examination of Agnes Meluill (daughter of an elder and reader of the kirk in Anstruther) in July 1588: *Register*, 2:620–623. She was convicted (ibid., 799–800.) For a successful defense against a charge of witchcraft in 1587, see Kirk, *Stirling Presbytery Records*, 247, 249. On church and state sharing the cost of "justice," see Ritchie, *Churches of St. Baldred*, 105: the bill for burning two witches on the sands at Kirkcaldy in 1633 was shared between the town (which paid seventeen pounds for ten loads of coal, some tar and tows, and the executioner) and the kirk session (which paid seventeen pounds for the other expenses).

[56]*Register*, 1:441: case of September 24, 1579, and 2:785–86: case of April 17, 1594.

Day. But the commonest offense was working on Sundays: farmers struggling to harvest their crops while good weather lasted, like lax-fishers throwing their nets into the Tay whenever the salmon were running, found themselves summoned to the session and fined if they had done it on the Sabbath.[57] In 1574 it was ordained that every Sunday a magistrate, an elder, and two deacons should patrol Saint Andrews at time of service, seeking out sinners and sluggards; and by 1600 they had brought 286 persons (249 of them men) before the session for sabbath breach.[58]

* * *

The offenses dealt with by the kirk session were thus mostly cut-and-dried: a pregnant spinster, a scandal uttered before witnesses, a man found sleeping outside during a church service, or staggering round the streets "beastlie drunk." There was no problem of proof, no point in denying guilt. And with the local laird or the bailies sitting on the session, there was little chance of escaping justice and no advantage in challenging the authority of the court. Almost all of those summoned came, confessed, made whatever amends were required of them, and were reconciled to the party they had injured and to the congregation at large. And yet reluctance to "submit to discipline" was understandably great. To avoid humiliation, some sat on the stool of repentance with their face covered; others carried swords and pistols.[59] Others tried to avoid coming at all: there were thirty-eight cases of "resistance to authority," ranging from arguments (usually by local landowners) over whether the session's writ extended to a given

[57]Cameron, "Godly Nurture," 274–275, and Leah Leneman, "Prophaning the Lord's Day: Sabbath Breach in Early Modern Scotland," *History* 74 (1989):217–231, give a fine selection of offenses. Some sabbath-breakers earned severe punishment, however: at least fifty-one Saint Andrews offenders were condemned to the stool of repentance and six were also imprisoned, while seven were delivered for punishment to the magistrates.

[58]The same preponderance of male offenders in this category has been found in other records, suggesting that, in this respect, perhaps women were more disposed to respect the church's commands and to fulfill its requirements than men. This phenomenon has been observed in other societies—see S. H. Brandes, *Migration, Kinship and Community: Tradition and Transition in a Spanish Village* (New York: Academic Press, 1975), chap. 8; and K. V. Thomas, "Women and the Civil War Sects," in *Crisis in Europe 1560–1660,* ed. T. S. Aston (London: Routledge and Kegan Paul, 1965), chap. 13—but not, so far as I am aware, for Scotland.

[59]Stuart, *Selections from the Records of the Kirk-Session of Aberdeen,* 62–63 (1608) and 116 (1651) about covered faces; *Register,* 2:806 (1595: "na persoun sall cum to the stuill of repentance armit with sowrd nor gun"—nor indeed to the session). See also K. M. Brown, *Bloodfeud in Scotland, 1573–1625: Violence, Justice and Politics in an Early Modern Society* (Edinburgh: John Donald, 1986), 185f.

area, to violent words exchanged between session and accused.[60] A hard core of parishioners seems to have refused to accept the standards set by the session, and appeared several times. Thus eighty-one persons appeared twice or more between 1573 and 1600 for fornication (one person managed six appearances and another five), and seven persons appeared twice for adultery. One person even came three times. But by the time the Register closed, "repeaters" such as these were virtually a thing of the past, and scarcely any cases remained outstanding in which those delated would not appear. In the whole period under study, resort was made to the ultimate sanction of excommunication only five times.[61] It seemed as if, in Saint Andrews at least, "all estates" had indeed become subject to discipline.

This changed situation of the 1590s deserves some further attention. It would be wrong to suppose that the fluctuations in annual totals shown in the appendix (pages 193–196 below) resulted solely from variations in the number of offenses committed—that the relative absence of sexual offenses in the last decade of the century necessarily indicates a reduction of illicit liaisons. On the contrary, it may have reflected a new fear among the congregation, following the great plague of 1585–86, that God was not to be scorned. But equally it may have stemmed from the undoubted changes in the priorities and activities of the ministers and the members of the session.[62]

---

[60]*Register*, 2:556–57 (James Lermonth, heir to the barony of Balcomie, alleged that he did not live in the parish of Saint Andrews in April 1585; it was one of his many appearances for various forms of sexual misconduct. See also pp. 168–169 above); and ibid., 2:547–49 (Jhone Cambell's "dispytful and opprobrius wordis" to the session in December 1584). Note also the similar tensions and abuse in Auchtermuchty, somewhat later, recorded by di Folco, "Discipline and Welfare," 176–177.

[61]Two for contempt and one each for homicide, adultery, and sabbath breach. It is true that twenty-eight more offenders were threatened with the ban but (in its own inimitable words) the session was "nocht willing to be suddane to fulminat excommunication aganis ony person, if thai culd be brocht utherwyis to repentance and humiliatioun." (*Register*, 2:671: May 1590). It stood in stark contrast to the three hundred excommunications and more issued annually by the consistory of Geneva in the 1560s (Monter, "The Consistory," 484.)

[62]See Gatrell, Lenman, and Parker, *Crime and the Law*, 4, 49–75, and 190–237, on the methodological problems posed by "labeling" and by "panic prosecutions" in the historical study of crime. David Underdown has located a similar phenomenon at Dorchester in the early seventeenth century: following a great natural catastrophe—a devastating fire in 1613—some of the same laymen who had previously resisted the work of their Puritan minister suddenly became pliant and pious. See D. Underdown *Fire from Heaven: Life in an English Town in the Seventeenth Century* (New Haven: Yale University Press, 1992).

In the first place, the clergy became less complaisant. The record of Robert Hamilton, an early Reformer in the town and minister until his death in 1581, did not impress James Melville, who returned to Fife in 1580 to serve in an adjacent parish. "Efter the first zeall of the Reformation, in Mr. Knox and Mr. Guidmans dayes," he wrote in his *Diary*, "the cauldnes of Mr. Robert Hamiltones ministerie, and [the] ignorance and negligence of tham that sould haiff teatched theologie" caused great backsliding and disorder. "Yea it was evin a pitie to sie that ignorance and profannes that was amangs tham." But worse was to come: after Hamilton's death there was a hiatus, so that for more than three years there was no resident incumbent at all. James Melville and his uncle Andrew, a Geneva-trained minister and the principal of the "New College" (sc. Saint Mary's), therefore decided to help out by preaching at the town church and by stiffening the backbone of the session. The upsurge of business recorded in the Register in 1582–84 (see pages 193–196 below) is clearly a reflection of their efforts. But before long there was another reflection: some of their parishioners decided to drive the Melvilles out. For a "grait space," wrote James, "ther was na thing bot affixing of plackarts upon the Collage yett [= gate], bosting with batoning, burning and chaffing out of the town." James Melville confessed that he was afraid, but his uncle Andrew was made of sterner stuff. He immediately assumed the offensive and accused the town magistrates of deliberately keeping the town church vacant, so that they could spend its revenues themselves on "the goff, archerie, guid cheir etc."; and in his sermons he excoriated all who opposed him. From the pulpit one day he told James Lermonth of Balcomie, a somewhat dissolute member of a prominent local family who was identified as the author of one of the placards that threatened "batoning," that he would be punished for his lechery by having no legitimate offspring, and for his threats by being one day beaten to death himself. (Both prophesies, we are assured, eventually came true.) On another occasion, one of Melville's tirades from the pulpit caused the town provost to "ryse out of his seatt in the middes of the sermont, and with sum muttering of words to go to the dure out throw the middes of the peiple."[63]

Yet in the end Andrew Melville emerged victorious. The provost, "convicted in his conscience" by a visit to the local presbytery, "maid publict satisfaction be acknawlaging of his offence, and craving God and the

---

[63]*Diary of James Melvill*, 89–90. Calvin had also faced a determined group of opponents among the magistrates of Geneva in 1552–53, but they were vanquished: see E. W. Monter, *Calvin's Geneva* (New York: John Wiley, 1967), 82–88.

congregation forgiffnes"; and the town council then agreed to the appointment of a new minister. Although plague struck the town with unusual severity in 1585–86, during which time (according to the Register) "all gude ordour cessit in this citee," it merely served as a prelude to a new moral crusade in the town. The campaign began with the decision, in October 1586, "that ane generall delatioun be takin throch the haill town of the offendaris of Goddis Law" and was pressed home with rigor and determination by both ministers and elders for over a decade.[64]

Robert Bruce, minister from 1589, was (according to James Melville) "maist confortable to the guid and godlie, and maist ferfull to the enemies. . . . The godlie, for his puissant and maist moving doctrine, lovit him; the worldlings for his parentage and place reverenced him; and the enemies for bathe stude in aw of him."[65] David Black, who came in 1590 as a second parish minister, was eloquent enough to stop even the king in his tracks. The doubling of the permanent resident clergy and the existence of a presbytery of course played an important part in implementing godly rule, but the session itself increased both the number of its meetings and the size of its membership.[66] Although there were, in all, 812 meetings of the various sessions of Saint Andrews between 1573 and 1600, almost half of them took place in the 1590s. Moreover, in 1593, the fourteen elders were increased to thirty-nine, and the quarters of the parish from four to twelve. (see Table 4)[67]

The explosion of disciplinary business during the 1590s (see page 188) was naturally related both to the institution of new ministers and to the increased strength of the session; but perhaps of more importance was the presence among the elders of Andrew Melville, now rector of the university and (in the words of R. G. Cant) "the figure around whom the whole life of the city and university and most of that of Scotland revolved." He appeared on the session for the first time in January 1591, and was reelected four times until October 1597.[68]

---

[64]*Diary of James Melvill*, 90; *Register*, 2:559 n. 4, 576.

[65]*Diary of James Melvill*, 182.

[66]The role of the Saint Andrews presbytery in the process will become clear when the first volume of its minutes, which runs (with gaps) from 1586 to 1605, is published by Mark Smith. In the meantime, the extracts included in Hay Fleming's edition of the Register must suffice.

[67]*Register*, 2:760–761. From 1599 there were nineteen quarters with one elder and one deacon each (904).

[68]R. G. Cant, *The University of St. Andrews: A Short History* (2d ed., Edinburgh: Scottish Academic Press, 1970), 52; *Register*, 2:694–695, 760–761, 788–792, 801–804. Two of these Melvillian sessions continued in office for two years apiece.

Table 4: Activity of the Saint Andrews Kirk Session

Session	Meetings	Session	Meetings
1573–74	27	1586–87	41
1574–75	20	1587–88	24
1575–76	14	1588–89	37
1576–77	18	1589–91*	49
1577–78	12	1591–93*	83
1578–79	23	1593–94	35
1579–81*	28	1594–95	17
1581–82	36	1595–97*	42
1582–83	36	1597–98	52
1583–84	45	1598–99	62
1584–85	31	1599–1600	23
1585–86	11		
* = session serving for two years			

During the Melville years, "profanation of the Lord's day" was rigorously punished: of the 286 sabbath-breakers hauled before the session between 1573 and 1600, no less than 181 (63 percent) appeared after 1594. Likewise, of the 175 cases of slander and scandal, 131 (75 percent) came before the court during the last decade, and all but 4 of the 35 cases of drunkenness and riot came after 1594. "Swearing, blasphemy and cursing," which diminished according to the Register, were in fact dealt with after October 1596 in a different way. The session empowered each elder and deacon to impose a summary fine on all who "sueriis, banis or takis Godis name in vane" in their hearing. Those who refused to pay on the spot could have their goods impounded, and those who offered opposition could be imprisoned. The new vigilantes were issued with a special purse in which to collect the fines, and from time to time the proceeds were paid over to the church treasurer.[69]

Sexual offenders were also dealt with differently under the new regime. Savage and exemplary penalties in 1593–94 for adultery and fornication have already been noted (pages 181–182 above). They did not stand alone. After 1593, all fornicators were required to pay punitive fines: the full rigor of the 1567 Statute was now to be enforced—forty pounds for the

[69]Ibid., 2:821; see also 929, 942, 943.

first offense, or eight days in prison, and double for a relapse.[70] The records show that this penalty was exacted at first; but then something remarkable happened. Fornication in Saint Andrews seems to have ceased! Although twenty-eight cases were investigated in 1594 (which was itself a drop from the fifty to sixty annual cases of the pre-Melvillian era), there was only one each in 1595 and 1596. Adultery, too, almost disappeared from the Register between 1594 and 1597.

There are four possible explanations for this striking development. The first is that, with the penalties increased to such draconian levels, neighbors were reluctant to delate, or elders to prosecute, persons who were manifestly unable to pay such heavy fines.[71] But this ignores the fact that most fornication cases began with the birth of an illegitimate child, which was exceedingly difficult to conceal. Furthermore, "concealing sin" was itself also liable to a heavy fine.[72] The second possibility is that spinsters who suspected they were pregnant might leave the parish in good time, in order to avoid fine and humiliation. But this, too, is rendered improbable by the common practice of kirk sessions in sending back unmarried mothers to the parish where their "sin" had been committed.[73] Third, it is conceivable that Melville and his fellow elders suddenly relented in response to popular hostility to their policies. Certainly in the summer of 1592 there was a "maist dangerus uproar and tumult of the peiple of St. Andros" against Melville following the accidental shooting of a local man in Butts Wynd by a college student practicing archery. The "wicked, malitius misrewlars of the town" [sc. the magistrates] seized the opportunity to attack one of Melville's power bases—the University—ringing the town alarm bell and inciting the assembled multitude to break down the outer door of the college. A mob got as far as the main rooms, calling for fire, before the tumult was stilled. But the opposition endured.

[70]Ibid., 2:767.

[71]Similar considerations clearly operated in eighteenth-century England with regard to the game laws, after poaching became a capital offense: see D. Hay et al., *Albion's Fatal Tree: Crime and Society in Eighteenth-Century England* (London: Allen Lane, 1975), and E. P. Thompson, *Whigs and Hunters: The Origin of the Black Act* (London: Allen Lane, 1975).

[72]The Register records five persons fined two pounds and two persons sent to the stool of repentance for concealing sins committed by others. (The punishment accorded to seven others is unknown.)

[73]See some English examples of "girls in trouble" fleeing from the hostile parish in which they lived in K. E. Wrightson, "The Nadir of English Illegitimacy in the Seventeenth Century," in *Bastardy in its Comparative History,* ed. P. Laslett, K. Oosterveen, and R. M. Smith (Cambridge: Harvard University Press, 1980), 176–191. There was at least one good reason for firmness: unless the father of a bastard could be found, the parish might become responsible for its upkeep.

In 1597, one of Melville's most devoted followers was deliberately slain by a group of opponents as he walked in the country.[74] But had these unpleasant events led the session to reduce its vigor, the effect would have been visible in all areas of its disciplinary work; instead of which, although sexual cases dramatically diminished, other categories (as we have seen) soared.

So the only remaining explanation for the relative absence of sexual offenses in these years, improbable though it may seem, is that fornication, adultery, and the rest had become too dangerous a risk in Saint Andrews, and that a genuine "reformation of manners" took place in the burgh.[75] There was certainly a change in the case of Sabbath observance because, in the summer of 1600, the session proudly noted that "the peopill convenis sua frequentlie to preaching that the kirk may nocht convenientlie containe thame," and the university chapel had to be opened as an overflow church for the town.[76]

By then, however, the Melvillian period in Saint Andrews was over. In 1596 and 1597 the extreme presbyterian party was defeated in the General Assembly; while David Black, having called the king's mother a whore and Elizabeth Tudor an atheist, was deprived of his ministry, Andrew Melville was dismissed as rector of the university and removed from the kirk session. Their work, however, was not undone. The same General Assembly in 1596 ordered a session to be created in every parish of the kingdom, with order to "strik nocht onlie upon gros sinnes, as hurdome, blodshed etc., bot upon all sinnes repugnant to the Word of God, as blasphemie of Gods nam, swearing in vean, banning, profaning the sabathe, disobedience to parents, idle unrewlie annes [=ones] without calling, drunkards, and sic

---

[74]*Diary of James Melvill*, 206.

[75]It is a remarkable fact that bastardy seems to have reached a peak in other countries of western Europe at precisely this time: D. Levine and K. E. Wrightson, "The Social Context of Illegitimacy in Early Modern England," in *Bastardy and its Comparative History*, ed. Laslett, Oosterveen, and Smith, 158–175 (for England), and M. del C. González Muñoz, *La población de Talavera, siglos XVI-XX* (Toledo: Diputación Provincial, 1974), 109 (for Spain) both found an "explosion of illegitimacy" in the 1590s. It is difficult to be absolutely sure what happened in Saint Andrews at this time because there is no usable register of births.

[76]*Register*, 2:925–926. See also Leneman, "Prophaning the Lord's Day." There is some debate about the likelihood of short-run "reformations of manners" in early modern times, however. Contrast D. Levine and K. E. Wrightson, *Poverty and Piety in an English Village: Terling 1525-1700* (New York: Academic Press, 1979), who clearly found something of the sort in the Essex parish that they studied (as did David Underdown at Dorchester: note 62 above), with M. J. Ingram, "Religion, Communities and Moral Discipline in Sixteenth and Seventeenth-Century England: Case Studies," in von Greyerz, *Religion and Society*, 177–193, who looked carefully for parallels in other parishes but failed to locate any.

lyk. . . ." It seems a perfect description of the recent work of the Saint Andrews kirk session, and now it was "to be an universall rewll throuchout the realme." James Melville noted it all in his journal with deep satisfaction.[77]

And, except during the Cromwellian occupation of the 1650s, the ecclesiastical tribunals of Scotland remained supreme until the mid-eighteenth century when first a serious schism in the church (the "Great Secession"), then spectacular improvements in transport, and finally industrial growth began to erode traditional society and its values.[78] Meanwhile, the work of the church courts was seconded by the provision of sound Christian dogma and doctrine over almost all the kingdom via schools, universities, sermons, and catechisms. So, through a combination of education and discipline, most Scots came to accept that intercourse would take place only between married partners (and the practice of handfasting, whereby parties cohabited as soon as they were betrothed, entirely died out); that insults should be swallowed rather than expressed; that one should be sober in food, drink, and apparel; and that everyone should go to church on Sunday.

Needless to say, Scotland was not alone in its attempts to inculcate godly discipline and inward piety. Almost every state in Europe possessed some sort of Inquisition to enforce Christian standards of behavior as well as Christian articles of belief: the "bawdy courts" of England, the *consistoire* in Geneva, the church courts of Lutheran Germany, Denmark and Sweden, the Holy Office in Italy and Spain.[79] But where Scotland excelled them all was in the intensity of control exercised by her church courts. The Calvinist congregation of Amsterdam in the later seventeenth century probably approached fifty thousand, but the city's consistory handled less than fifty cases annually; even the tribunals of the Spanish Inquisition,

---

[77]See *Diary of James Melvill*, 231, and Donaldson, *Scottish Reformation*, 222.

[78]See the pertinent remarks of Mitchison and Leneman, *Sexuality and Social Control*, chap. 2, on the decline in "discipline" in the mid-eighteenth century, balancing extrinsic changes in the economy and the intellectual environment against a softening in the attitudes of church leaders towards the necessity for discipline. Some "softening" certainly seems to have happened in the Calvinist city of Emden at the same time: see the tantalizing remarks of H. Schilling, "'History of Crime'or 'History of Sin'? Some Reflections on the Social History of Early Modern Church Discipline," in *Politics and Society in Reformation Europe*, ed. E. Kouri and T. Scott (New York: St. Martin's Press, 1987), 289–310, at 299.

[79]For Sweden, see J. Sundin, "Control, Punishment and Reconciliation: A Case Study of Parish Justice in Sweden before 1850," in *Tradition and Transition: Studies in Microdemography and Social Change*, ed. A. Brändström and J. Sundin (Umeå: Demographic Data Base, 1981), 9–65; for Denmark, see T. Dahlerup, "Sin, Crime, Punishment and Absolution: The

each monitoring the actions of up to half a million people, only resolved twenty or thirty cases a year.[80] Yet most Scottish kirk sessions, although they seldom held authority over more than three thousand parishioners, dealt with far more.

Thanks to this intensity, godly discipline had a further unexpected but highly significant influence on the long-term development of Scotland. In Saint Andrews, the session in the 1590s helped to turn a sort of "Montaillou-sur-mer" into a strict, restrained, and eminent university town. But this achievement was not unique. By the end of the seventeenth century there were well over five hundred kirk sessions active in Scotland, from the Borders to the Northern Isles, all administering the same swift justice, all run by local professionals, and all applying more or less the same standards. The importance of this achievement, in a country of such strong regional and local identities, can hardly be overstated: church building in early modern Scotland far outstripped state building. It played a crucial part in grooming the kingdom for its future role as a major industrial power. By accustoming the workforce to social discipline, and by stressing the value of order, restraint, and hard work, the Reformed Kirk unwittingly became the handmaiden of nascent capitalism. It may have tamed Scotland for another, higher, purpose; but Scotlan d was tamed all the same.[81]

Disciplinary System of the Danish Church in the Reformation Century," in Grane and Horby, *Die dänische Reformation*, 277–288; for Germany, see W. J. Wright, *Capitalism, the State and the Lutheran Reformation in Sixteenth-Century Hesse* (Athens: Ohio University Press, 1988), chap. 6; L. J. Abray, *The People's Reformation: Magistrates, Clergy and Commons in Strasbourg, 1500–1598* (Ithaca: Cornell University Press, 1985), chap. 8; Schilling, "Reformierte Kirchenzucht"; L. Roper, *The Holy Household: Women and Morals in Reformation Augsburg* (2d. ed., Oxford: Oxford University Press, 1991); and the sources cited in the notes to idem, "History of Crime."

[80]For Amsterdam, see Roodenburg, *Onder censuur*, 72, 137. For the Inquisition, see sources cited in G. Henningsen, J. Tedeschi, and C. Amiel, eds., *The Inquisition in Early Modern Europe: Studies on Sources and Methods* (Dekalb: Northern Illinois University Press, 1986), 121f.; and G. Parker, "Some Recent Work on the Inquisition in Spain and Italy," *Journal of Modern History* 54 (1982): 519–532. The increased attention paid by the Spanish Inquisition to fornication (which made up 33 percent of the business handled by the Toledo Tribunal in the later sixteenth century) is noted and explained by J. P. Dedieu, "L'Hérésie salvatrice: La pédagogie inquisitoriale en Nouvelle Castille au 16e siècle," in *Les frontières religieuses en Europe du 15e au 17e siècle*, ed. R. Sauzet (Paris: J. Vrin. 1992), 79–87.

[81]The crucial importance of "fundamental discipline," involving both secular and ecclesiastical institutions, in preparing Europe for rapid social and economic change was first highlighted by Gerhard Oestreich. See his studies, posthumously published in *Strukturprobleme der Neuzeit* (Berlin: Duncker und Humblot, 1980) and *Neostoicism and the Early Modern State* (Cambridge: Cambridge University Press, 1982). See also the interesting remarks of Schilling, "History of Crime," 293ff., and of V. A. C. Gatrell in Gatrell, Lenman, and Parker, *Crime and the Law*, 300.

The Disciplinary Work of Saint Andrews Kirk Session, 1573–1600

I. Sexual Offenses

	Fornication		Antenuptial		Adultery		Incest	
	M	F	M	F	M	F	M	F
1573	10	10	2	2	2	2	1	1
1574	2	3	1	2	5	4	0	0
1575	6	5	2	2	1	0	0	0
1576	3	4	0	0	0	0	0	0
1577	6	5	1	2	2	2	0	0
1578	2	7	0	0	0	0	0	0
1579	5	10	1	1	1	2	0	0
1580	15	18	0	1	0	2	0	0
1581	6	5	0	0	3	2	0	0
1582	12	12	4	4	1	0	0	0
1583	20	23	0	0	1	0	1	0
1584	40	41	2	3	5	4	0	0
1585	10	13	2	3	1	1	0	0
1586	18	23	1	1	0	1	1	1
1587	29	33	2	2	6	4	0	0
1588	20	20	2	2	1	1	0	0
1589	31	30	1	1	2	1	0	0
1590	33	38	1	2	4	4	0	0
1591	23	26	0	0	2	3	0	0
1592	11	14	1	0	3	2	0	0
1593	26	28	1	1	2	2	0	0
1594	12	16	0	0	1	1	0	0
1595	1	0	0	0	1	1	0	0
1596	1	0	1	1	0	1	0	0
1597	4	1	0	1	1	1	0	0

I. Sexual Offenses

	Fornication		Antenuptial		Adultery		Incest	
1598	14	16	0	0	2	2	0	0
1599	16	11	2	2	6	6	0	0
1600	13	12	2	1	1	2	0	0
Total	389	424	29	34	54	51	3	2
Total	813		63		105		5	

II. Disorderly Conduct

	Sabbath breach		Slander/scandal		Drink/riot		Other	
	M	F	M	F	M	F	M	F
1573	5	0	1	1	0	0	0	0
1574	27	0	0	1	1	0	0	0
1575	2	0	3	1	1	0	0	0
1576	20	2	1	2	0	0	0	0
1577	0	1	1	1	0	0	1	0
1578	0	0	0	0	2	0	0	0
1579	0	0	1	2	0	0	2	0
1580	0	0	1	1	0	0	0	0
1581	0	0	2	1	0	0	0	0
1582	23	0	2	0	0	0	0	0
1583	5	0	0	3	0	0	0	0
1584	0	0	2	1	0	0	0	0
1585	0	0	0	0	0	0	0	0
1586	0	0	1	1	0	0	0	0
1587	0	0	1	2	0	0	0	0
1588	0	0	2	0	0	0	0	0
1589	0	0	0	0	0	0	0	0
1590	5	0	3	6	0	0	0	0
1591	8	0	1	5	0	0	1	0
1592	1	0	1	1	0	0	0	0
1593	6	0	2	0	0	0	0	0
1594	38	5	8	0	10	0	0	0
1595	11	3	11	2	0	0	0	0
1596	13	1	6	2	6	0	0	0
1597	12	8	5	7	0	1	1	0
1598	18	3	18	7	10	0	0	0
1599	34	12	28	9	1	0	2	0
1600	21	2	17	1	3	0	1	0
Total	249	37	118	57	34	1	8	0
Total	286		175		35		8	

III. Other Business

	Other		Poor Relief/ Charity		Marriage		Resistance to Authority	
	M	F	M	F	M	F	M	F
1573	3	3	0	1	1	0	3	2
1574	10	1	0	0	0	0	1	0
1575	5	0	0	0	0	0	4	0
1576	2	2	0	0	0	0	0	1
1577	6	4	0	0	1	0	0	0
1578	0	2	0	0	1	0	0	0
1579	1	0	0	0	0	0	0	0
1580	1	0	0	0	0	0	0	0
1581	1	1	0	0	1	0	0	2
1582	3	4	0	0	0	0	2	0
1583	8	1	0	0	0	1	0	0
1584	0	4	0	0	1	0	0	0
1585	0	2	1	0	2	0	0	0
1586	1	4	0	0	0	0	1	0
1587	9	5	0	0	1	0	1	0
1588	2	3	1	0	0	0	0	0
1589	2	2	0	0	2	0	0	0
1590	3	1	0	0	0	2	0	0
1591	1	2	0	0	0	0	2	0
1592	3	3	0	0	0	1	0	0
1593	5	4	0	0	0	0	0	0
1594	2	0	0	0	0	0	2	0
1595	3	3	0	0	0	2	4	2
1596	0	1	0	0	0	0	4	1
1597	2	0	3	1	0	0	0	0
1598	4	2	1	0	0	0	2	0
1599	6	1	11	5	0	1	0	0
1600	3	1	6	5	0	0	1	0
Total	86	56	23	12	10	7	27	8
Total	142		35		17		35	

IV. Annual Total of All Items of BusinessTransacted

	Administrative	Disciplinary
1573	11	55
1574	12	60
1575	5	32
1576	5	37
1577	5	42
1578	2	14
1579	4	26
1580	1	39
1581	8	24
1582	13	68
1583	15	65
1584	20	103
1585	4	35
1586	12	51
1587	14	85
1588	10	54
1589	17	72
1590	11	102
1591	9	73
1592	2	41
1593	11	78
1594	10	93
1595	6	44
1596	14	38
1597	45	49
1598	50	103
1599	19	145
1600	26	92
Total	361	1720

This paper grew out of a study of crime in early modern Scotland funded by the British Academy and the (then) Social Science Research Council. It was originally prepared for a workshop on the History of Crime organized by Jan Sundin and held at Stockholm in 1983. I should like to thank in the first instance the other members of the workshop— Bruce Lenman, Ken Lockridge, Birgit Petersen, Heinz Schilling, Marja Taussi Sjöberg, Jan Sundin, and Martin Vejbrink—for their invaluable comments. I am also most grateful to Nancy Wood for research assistance. In 1988 the paper was published in L. Leneman, ed., *Perspectives in Scottish Social History: Essays in Honour of Rosalind Mitchison* (Aberdeen: Aberdeen University Press, 1988), and I am grateful to both the editor and the publisher for permission to reproduce it again here. In both preparing and revising the paper I acknowledge with gratitude the assistance of James K. Cameron, Jane Dawson, Leah Leneman, Rosalind Mitchison, R. N. Smart, and David Underdown. Finally, I learned much from the students of Saint Andrews University to whom I taught Scottish Reformation history, particularly James Pratt, who graduated in 1986 and was killed in a mountain accident the next year. I dedicate this paper to his memory.

About the Contributors

Philippe Chareyre is *maître de conférence* at the University of Pau.

Michael Graham is a member of the History Department at Coker College.

Robert M. Kingdon is Hilldale Professor, University of Wisconsin, Madison.

Raymond A. Mentzer is Professor of History at Montana State University.

Geoffrey Parker is Robert A. Lovett Professor of Military and Naval History, Yale University.

Heinz Schilling is Professor of History at the Humboldt University, Berlin.

Index

Mental illness, 4, 10
Meyrueis, 101–125 *passim*
Monifieth, 137–152 *passim*
Montauban, 100–126 *passim*
Moral order, 66–67, 111–112, 161
Morals, reformation of, 191–192
Musical instruments, 89

N

Nîmes, 63–96, 100–126 *passim*, 175

O

Oath of innocence, 179
Offices, ecclesiastical, 116
Order. *See* Moral order
Ordinances, 22–23, 140

P

Pacification, social, 78–85
Paganism, 113
Parades, 94
Parents, 51–53, 69
Parliament, Scots, 166
Pastors, 28, 65
Patronage, 168–169
Peacemaking, 152–155
Penance, 121–123, 144–145, 147, 149, 150, 153, 156
Penitence, 109
Pietism, 38, 51–52, 56–58
Pilgrimages, 149–150
Playing cards, 3, 7
Plays, 91–93
Pont-de-Camarès, 101–122 *passim*
Popery. *See also* Apostasy; Catholicism, 108, 113–114, 124
Population, 137
Pregnancy, 178
Presbyteries. *See also* Consistories; Kirk sessions
definition of, 17
discipline by, 42
establishment of, 132, 134
and family life, 39–44
functions of, 134

Presbyteries (*continued*)
registers of, 17
responsibilities of, 29, 33
Prostitution, 74–75
Public order, 78
Pulpit, 70
Punishments, 76, 183

Q

Quarrels, 79–80
consequences of, 105–107, 112
penalties for, 153–154
in Scotland, 152–153
Quirinus, 39–40

R

Rebellion, 108, 114
Reconciliation, 7–8
by the consistory, 83–85
of marriage partners, 13
through communion, 118
Recordkeeping, 97–98
Referrals, 163–164
"Reformation Day," 172
Reformation of morals, 191–192
Registers, 17, 131–133
Regulation
business, 80
of the Christian community, 99
of marriage, 20–21, 28–29
Religious dissent, 145–147
Religious instruction, 144
Remarriage, 1–2, 11
Repentance, 5, 121–123
Rights, judicial, 120–121
Roman civil law, 6
Rothiemay, 152
Royal legislation, 96

S

Sabbath
breach of, 142, 183–184, 190
enforcment of, 173
preservation of, 139–143
violation of, 140–143

Colophon

Design and typesetting by Gwen Blotevogel
Cover and title page by Teresa Wheeler

Text and display set in Stone Serif and Stone Informal,
designed by Sumner Stone

Printed and bound by Edwards Brothers, Ann Arbor, Michigan
Distributed by Sixteenth Century Journal Publishers

Acknowledgments

Woodcuts were made available
through the generosity of
James and Devon Gray Booksellers
35 Charles Street
Winthrop, MA 02152

ISBN 0-940474-34-4